Joseph Hume:
The People's M. P.

Joseph Hume. Courtesy of the National Library of Scotland.

JOSEPH HUME: THE PEOPLE'S M.P.

Ronald K. Huch
and
Paul R. Ziegler

American Philosophical Society
Independence Square Philadelphia
1985

MEMOIRS OF THE
AMERICAN PHILOSOPHICAL SOCIETY
Held at Philadelphia
For Promoting Useful Knowledge
Volume 163

Printed in the United States of America by
Science Press, Ephrata, Pennsylvania

Library of Congress Catalog Card Number 83-73276
International Standard Book Number 0-87169-163-9
US ISSN 0065-9738

CONTENTS

PREFACE

"He is the modern Prynne, who defies all reprint comment or review," so wrote a fellow Scotsman about Joseph Hume.[1] We have learned, all too readily, the wisdom in that judgment. We suspect that others have learned it too, for surely we are not the first to think about writing a biography of Hume. When he died in 1855 Hume's contemporaries assumed he would be remembered as one of the most important politicians of his time.

Hume was a champion of free-trade principles and radical reform. He was in the forefront of nearly every major reform endeavour in the first half of the nineteenth century; and, though he never held office, his name was a household word in England for over thirty years. He rose to popularity on the basis of his attack on government spending, and he remained a favorite of "the people" because he seemed unencumbered by personal avarice. Like most other free traders, Hume believed that no government could be satisfactory until it recognized the full measure of citizen freedom, whether that involved economic liberty, civil liberty, or religious liberty. It is sometimes difficult for those of us imbued with twentieth century liberal ideas to grasp that the early nineteenth century free-trade radicals were the most determined protectors of constitutional freedoms. They helped to convince Englishmen that there was hope the government could be changed by a properly motivated Parliament.

There are many frustrations awaiting those who write about Joseph Hume. His personal life largely remains a mystery, because his private papers were destroyed by fire. The lack of Hume papers also creates problems in dealing with his parliamentary career, the main topic of our book. We have had to go through many manuscript collections of those who were close to Hume in order to put his life together. The most useful of these collections were the papers of Francis Place, John Cam Hobhouse, and Richard Cobden.

Hume was entangled in so many of the great and small issues that came and went during his thirty-seven years in Parliament that we were forced to make some very arbitrary decisions on what to include. Some interesting and important matters are given short shrift, and we hope for understanding from those readers who might wish we had emphasized other aspects of Hume's life. We also found organization to be a problem, primarily because there is so much room for repetition in recounting Hume's career. We eventually decided that an old fashioned chronological approach resolved this problem better than any other scheme.

We wish to acknowledge the support and encouragement we received from Professors Maurice R. O'Connell and Ross J. S. Hoffman of Fordham University, and from Professors J. F. Maclear and Richard A. Morris of the Duluth Campus of the University of Minnesota. The work was pushed along by many other historians in England and America who took time to discuss Hume with each of us. We also wish to acknowledge the support given to us by Assumption College, Worcester, Massachusetts,

[1] *The Scotsman,* 24 February 1855.

and by the Graduate School of the University of Minnesota which gave Mr. Huch two grants for research and a single quarter leave.

We are grateful to Sir Feargus Graham of Netherby for permission to use the Graham papers and to M. Russell Ellice of Invergarry for providing access to the Ellice Papers. The authors also gratefully acknowledge the valuable assistance of Margo Laskowski Michel, whose expertise with the semi-colon is unparalleled.

CHAPTER I.

FROM MONTROSE TO WESTMINSTER, 1777–1818

"I am a fool," proclaimed a grave Joseph Hume in the House of Commons on 28 July 1842, and one hundred of his colleagues shouted "Agreed! Agreed!" *The Times* reported that Hume's statement was "acknowledged truth." Still, the newspaper wondered what had come over this old Scottish radical that he should now see himself as others saw him. Was he drunk; did he wish to make up for some "tiresome manhood" by trying to give the members a little merriment? "Madness they say is allied with great wit, else we should suspect insanity," opined the paper. It seemed to *The Times* more likely that "Hume's present conception of his mission (as the phrase is now used) is to become the 'jackpudding' of the House."[1]

By 1842, Hume was accustomed to this sort of ridicule. It had been a part of his life since the early 1820s. No aspect of Joseph Hume had escaped the rapier-like pens of his political foes. They had made fun of the fact that he was short and had virtually no neck; they had written much about his curious transposition of common phrases, so that "wear and tear" came out "tear and wear"; and they had accused him of ill-gotten wealth and of being primarily interested in emulating the manner of life reserved for the aristocracy.

Most of the time, Hume accepted personal and political criticism with equanimity. There was not much bitterness in "Old Joe," and it is likely that he thought being the "radicals' martyr" was an indication of his importance. The vicious comments about him made in such conservative publications as *John Bull, Blackwood's Edinburgh Magazine,* and *The Courier* were signs that he had influence, and that he was an opponent to be taken seriously. "They [the Tories] show their teeth through the medium of a sneer," wrote one liberal observer, "and while they denounce him as a most dangerous plotter, they declare him to be a fool too notorious to be dreaded."[2]

It is fair to say at the outset that no one ever worked harder at being a member of Parliament than did Joseph Hume. He was usually the first to arrive in the chamber and the last to leave. David Ricardo once wrote, "that in persevering exertions, Mr. Hume had never been surpassed by any former or present member."[3] In her *Biographical Sketches,* Harriet Martineau called Hume "the plodder of Parliament."[4] Anyone who has had occasion to read the *Parliamentary Debates* between 1819 and 1855

[1]*The Times,* August 1, 1842; *John Bull,* 30 July 1842.

[2][*John*] *Saunders' Portraits and Memoirs of Eminent Living Political Reformers....* (London, 1840):61. See also James Grant, *Random Recollections of the House of Commons, From the Year 1830 to the Close of 1835* (Philadelphia, 1836): 261–67.

[3]Peter Sraffa, ed., *The Works and Correspondence of David Ricardo* (Cambridge, 1952), 5:471.

[4]Harriet Martineau, *Biographical Sketches, 1852–1868* (London, 1870):306.

will surely know that Hume spoke more often, on more subjects, and at greater length, than any other member in the Commons.

From the point of view of most (though not all) radicals and liberals, Hume's role in advancing the cause of reform was significant. When he died in February 1855, the liberal *Morning Advertiser* wrote that

it may be questioned whether any man not in office accomplished as much good as Mr. Hume . . . his memory will be regarded with the most profound veneration; nor will that veneration be confined to the present generation, it will also be felt by our posterity.[5]

The *Morning Chronicle* wrote simply that Hume's "greatest merit was his usefulness," and the *Daily News* contended that "old Joe's" value to reform came from his "private worth, his unswerving integrity, unselfishness, gentleness and consideration for others. . . ."[6] Such praise did not come strictly from liberals and radicals. Sir Robert Peel once called Hume "one of the most useful members to sit in the House of Commons";[7] and *The Times,* which had so often belabored his weaknesses, decided that Hume was "a ceaseless labourer for the public good."[8] Every obituary writer assumed that Hume would be one of the politicians most remembered from the nineteenth century.

Joseph Hume's origins were not the sort that usually produce men of wealth and fame. He was born at Ferryden, near Montrose, in January 1777, the first son of parents who found hard work the only solution for poverty. His father, James Hume, had advanced through various stages from an ordinary fisherman to master of a small vessel trading from Montrose. By the time Joseph was born, the family enjoyed the moderate comfort of a lower-middle class living.

Little is known of Joseph's first decade of life, but friends noted that he and his father spent much time together on the boat that provided their income. Joseph assisted in whatever way a young boy could at the oar and at the helm. There was precious little time for these "cooperative" efforts, for James Hume died in 1786. Since Joseph was just nine years old, his mother became the dominant influence in his life.

In later years Hume praised his mother for maintaining the family's modest status after his father's death. He claimed that by observing her business talents he had learned all the essential rules of economics. The small crockery shop she started in Montrose in 1787 provided enough profits that Hume was able to gain the sound education his father had wished for him. His mother impressed on Joseph the value of persistence and the necessity for prudence. It was necessary to account for every penny, thus attention to detail could never be exaggerated. There is a temptation, not readily resisted, to see these circumstances as the antecedents of Hume's lifelong devotion to the accumulation of money. The gaining and keeping of

[5]22 February 1855.
[6]*Morning Chronicle,* 22 February 1855; *Daily News,* 22 February 1855.
[7]*Morning Advertiser,* 22 February 1855.
[8]22 February 1855.

money were major concerns for Hume in his personal life and in his public life. He thought government should be as frugal as a private citizen.

The success of his mother's shop made it possible for Hume to attend Montrose Academy, easily the best school in his region. Early and late little Joseph toiled in the attic of his mother's house—a plain, but substantial and comfortably furnished old residence in the northern part of Montrose. Hume became a star pupil in Latin (a specialty in the academy) and in arithmetic. His closest friend in the academy was a young man destined to become a leading spokesman for political economy, James Mill. Mill was four years older than Joseph, but the two boys shared several interests. Both were serious about their schoolwork and both enjoyed outdoor activities. They were physically strong young men, but Hume, short and stout, usually had the edge on his older and leaner companion. Walking from Montrose to Aberdeen was a frequent adventure, with an occasional diversion to climb the Castle Rock of Dunnottar at Stonehaven.[9] In these strenuous undertakings there were inklings of Hume's enduring capacity for physical exertion that astounded his political colleagues in later years.

Hume did so well at the academy that in 1790, at age thirteen, his mother decided to prepare him for a career in medicine. He was apprenticed to a certain Dr. John Bale, whose ability had made him something of a "provincial celebrity."[10] Hume remained under Bale's tutelage for three years. His primary responsibility during that time was to compound prescriptions for his famous mentor. In 1793 Hume entered the University of Edinburgh where he concentrated on studying anatomy, midwifery, and chemistry. He went on to assist the controversial Scottish physician, John Bell, in carrying out anatomical dissection.[11]

While it is widely recorded that Hume joined the College of Surgeons at Edinburgh in 1796, there is no evidence to substantiate the claim. He did gain admittance to the less prestigious London College of Surgeons in 1797. It was also in 1797 that Hume, through the influence of David Scott (M.P. for Forfar) became a physician in the marine service of the East India Company. Scott helped Hume because his family (the Scotts of Dunninald) had a political interest in Montrose and the Humes had regularly supported that interest.[12] Hume's first tour of duty required him to spend nearly eighteen months in India. During this time, he found that medicine did not fascinate him as much as the operations of the East India Company. He was not yet ready, however, to cast aside the opportunities that medicine opened to him.

[9]Alexander Bain, *James Mill: A Biography* (New York, 1882):7; *The Aberdeen Free Press*, 23 February 1855; *The Scotsman*, 24 February 1855; *The Times*, 22 February 1855; *Edinburgh Courant*, 24 February 1855; *Montrose Standard and Angus and Mearns Register*, 23 February 1855.

[10]*The Scotsman*, 14 August 1824.

[11]*The Times*, 22 February 1855; F. Platt, "The English Parliamentary Radicals—Their Collective Character, Their Failure to Find a Leader: A Study in the Psycho-Sociological Sources of Radical Behavior, 1833–1841" (unpublished Ph.D. dissertation, Washington University, 1969): 322–39.

[12]*The Scotsman*, 24 February 1855.

In November 1799 the company made Hume a full assistant-surgeon. On his second voyage Hume found himself assigned to the *Houghton*, properly described as the "ancient ark" of the company's fleet. The tired old boat left for India on 12 November 1799, crammed with passengers from all backgrounds. Hume served as medical officer for the vessel, and he carried a number of letters of introduction which he expected would advance his career in Asia. It was a slow moving trip with stops at Madeira, the Cape of Good Hope, Columbo, Malabar, and Madras. Somewhere near the middle of the voyage the ship's purser died, and Hume promptly assumed his duties. Handling accounts was one activity that Hume relished. The *Houghton* finally limped into Calcutta on 20 June 1800. It had been an exhausting venture for Hume, but a highly successful one. He had made many new friends; some of whom were undoubtedly in a position to further his interests.[13]

In early July, Hume went to Bengal in the hope of obtaining a comfortable appointment. At first he complained that his letters of introduction did not "mean much" (including one written by the governor-general of India, Marquis Wellesley); but after a time he received a post in a small hospital. It was not what he had expected, and he made no effort to hide his disappointment. "It is as low a situation as they can give me," he wrote to one acquaintance. He was pleased about one thing. The position freed him from "any obligation to my friends."[14]

No one with Hume's ambition could remain satisfied with the income from a minor hospital appointment. It was now clear to him that he needed to combine business with medicine. He knew that whatever he achieved in India would depend in large measure on his ability to communicate in the local languages. Accordingly, he devoted an enormous amount of time to learning Hindustani during his first months of residence. It was time well spent, for his ability to talk directly with the native population proved to be the stepping stone to wealth.

During the Mahratta war (1802–1803) Hume accompanied Major-General Powell on his march from Allahabad into Bundelcund and served as the officer's interpreter. As the campaign progressed, so did Hume's responsibilities. By virtue of his facility with the local language, he assumed the duties of paymaster, postmaster, and commissary-general to the army of over twelve thousand men. In addition, he was the chief medical officer for six regiments.[15] He further enhanced his reputation for resourcefulness by discovering a method to dry damp gunpowder. He credited his training in chemistry for this success. As one writer explained, "so multifarious were his activities that only an unwearying frame, and an extraordinary capacity for business could have enabled any one person to perform [them]."[16] But

---

[13] *The Times*, 22 February 1855; *Edinburgh Courant*, 24 February 1855; *Montrose, Standard and Angus and Mearns Register*, 23 February 1855.

[14] Hume to O. Humphrey, 12 July 1800. The letter is in the National Library of Scotland (NLS), MS. 2521.

[15] *The Times*, 22 February 1855; *The Scotsman*, 24 February 1855.

[16] *Aberdeen Free Press*, 23 February 1855.

for Hume, labor was something to enjoy, especially if there were some rupees in it.

Each position held by Hume provided an excellent chance to increase his personal wealth. None offered more opportunity than his job as commissary-general. Hume did not hesitate to take full advantage of the circumstances. He agreed to become an agent for food and clothing interests who wanted to sell to Powell's army. Hume then entered into contracts to supply these necessities for the troops—contracts that were approved through the post he held. Not surprisingly, this arrangement made Hume a rich man. In later years, his political enemies would allude openly to this conflict of interest. There was, however, nothing illegal in the Scotsman's dealings, and most men were willing to attribute his success to diligence and shrewd business sense.

By 1808 Hume had amassed more than £40,000 and he seemed ready to return to England where he expected to have the benefit of social acceptance and political influence. These were, after all, the rightful rewards for substantial wealth. At least one historian thinks that Hume's overriding interest in these days, and perhaps throughout his life, was the desire to achieve status commensurate with that of the aristocracy.[17] "Status anxiety," then, motivated Joseph Hume. Only a well-developed psychological profile could determine the accuracy of this contention, and the details for such an analysis are simply not available. Whatever social considerations may have entered his mind, there is no question that Hume found the accumulation of money a worthwhile end in itself.

For some weeks after his return from India, Hume seemed at loose ends. He spent a listless autumn near Bath trying to decide what he ought to do next. His days consisted of rounds of "forenoon calls," and in the evening he usually went partying.[18] A man of such boundless energy could not abide the idle life for long. He had a definite interest in becoming a director of the East India Company. He thought the organization should be more efficient and he had several suggestions for improving operations. A directorship was scarcely a possibility for someone of Hume's limited connections, and he realistically suppressed this goal for the moment. It is also probable that Hume wished to sit in the House of Commons—a logical consideration for a man thirty-one years old, unmarried, with recently acquired wealth.

Whether it was to prepare for a political career, or simply to improve his knowledge of conditions in England, Hume began a tour of towns and cities in 1809. He visited every industrial center in England, Ireland, and Scotland. He intended to learn as much as possible about how laborers lived, and he hoped to gain information on the relationship between workers and factory managers. What he learned on these visits Hume later put to use when he debated issues involving workers' interests in the House of Commons.[19] There were two basic conclusions that Hume reached from

[17]Platt, "The English Parliamentary Radicals," 330.
[18]The Scotsman, 14 August 1824.
[19]Aberdeen Free Press, 23 February 1855; The Scotsman, 24 February 1855; The Times, 22 February 1855.

his investigations of working class conditions. First, he was convinced that employers had unacceptable power in dealing with complaints from labor. Secondly, he believed that some form of national education was the only hope for improving the existence of those who lived on the edge of poverty.

In 1810 and 1811, Hume continued his travels, but this time outside of England. He toured Spain, Portugal, Turkey, Greece, Egypt, Sicily, Malta, and Sardinia.[20] Such activity may have been an attempt to emulate the behavior of young aristocrats before they entered politics. It certainly provides circumstantial evidence for those who saw Hume consumed by a desire to identify with the nobility. Yet it seems more likely that Hume, with the freedom his wealth assured, simply wished to indulge his sense of adventure and his desire for useful information.

When his months of travel ended, Hume gave more thought to pursuing a political career. When Sir John Lowther Johnstone, M.P. for Weymouth and Melcombe-Regis in Dorsetshire, died in January 1812, Hume had his first chance for a seat in Parliament. The Duke of Cumberland "introduced" Hume to the constituency in return for a large sum of money. The amount was almost certainly in excess of £10,000. With Cumberland's help (the duke thoroughly enjoyed this opportunity for borough-mongering), Hume was returned. He had, in effect, bought his seat from Cumberland.[21]

In these days Hume claimed to be a Tory pledged to support the ministry of Spencer Perceval. But right from the start, the Scotsman disagreed with his Tory colleagues on a number of matters. The major source of his discontent with the ministers came from his devotion to the principles of free trade. Since his student days in Edinburgh, Hume had followed the writings of Adam Smith and the French physiocrats. He found the basic laissez-faire ideas of these economists most compatible with his own opinions on economics. His personal experiences from the time of his father's death through the first decade of the nineteenth century seemed to confirm the efficacy of free-trade precepts. Hume achieved financial success largely by his own resources; and it is easy to see why he thought individual effort the most important factor leading to economic prosperity.

Hume's advocacy of free-trade ideas came to the surface early in his parliamentary career. In July 1812 he opposed the Framework Knitters Bill which was intended to prevent frauds and other abuses in the framework knitting industry. The bill also contained clauses designed to stabilize prices and wages. The impetus for the bill came from the United Committee of Framework Knitters based in Nottingham. The committee came into existence after Parliament, responding to a serious instance of Luddism, made framework breaking a major crime. The committee hoped to show Parliament that reforms were necessary in the framework knitting business. Once a bill was written, the Nottingham committee undertook to

---

[20] *Liverpool Mercury,* 16 June 1826.
[21] *The Scotsman,* 24 February 1855; Roger Fulford, *Royal Dukes* (London, 1949): 212–13; T. H. B. Oldfield, *The Representative History of Great Britain and Ireland,* 3 (London, 1816): 376–86. Cumberland eventually came to "hate the sight" of Hume.

promote it with members of the House of Commons. The committee did its work well, but not well enough. The ministerial side gave unenthusiastic support to the measure; the free-traders opposed it as a violation of the precepts of Adam Smith. Finally, in late July 1812, a watered-down Framework Knitters Bill passed its third reading in the Commons.[22]

The bill passed after a long speech by one "ministerial" member opposed to the legislation. That member was Joseph Hume. He argued that the government had no justification for regulating manufacturers. He thought the principle behind regulation erroneous and "contrary to those axioms of sound policy which have been approved by the ablest political economists, and which have, by experience, been found most conducive to the increase and prosperity of trade." It was his view that only a few of the low quality manufacturers were guilty of fraud and that their reputation would soon bring them ruin. He would, however, agree to support a move to put "quality" labels on merchandise.[23]

Hume complained bitterly about a clause in the bill that established a fixed rate of wages masters must pay their artisans. "Viewing capitalists and artisans equally as traders," argued Hume, "I consider an uncontrolled competition as beneficial to both, and the strongest spur to ingenuity and industry." Hume did not defend manufacturers with this contention, for he went on to point out that owners would surely try to fix wages at the lowest possible rate. "All the laws connected with our manufacturing system," Hume concluded, "appear to be founded on the . . . principle that the capitalists and masters are the only part to be protected against combination and injustice, though the artisans or workmen have an equal right to be protected in their property or skill . . . they have an equal right to sell their labour and skill to the highest bidder as the masters have to get their work at the lowest rate."[24]

From Hume's perspective the issue at stake was not one of preventing abuse, but rather involved government limiting essential liberties. The Combination Laws had already served to restrict the freedom of workingmen, and this bill would only compound the violation of rights. Hume's speech did not excite his colleagues. He delivered it at the very end of deliberations on the measure when there was no chance to sway opinion. Moreover, it was late at night; there were few in attendance, and those who were there were anxious to vote. The speech did, however, contain the basic components of Hume's political economy. For the rest of his life he never appreciably deviated from the line of thought he expressed in the summer of 1812. As for the Framework Knitters Bill, whether for change of mind or lack of interest the government did not push it in the Lords and it was quickly defeated.

During July and August Hume continued to antagonize Tory leaders with his independence. He usually voted with the government; but there

---

[22]See E. P. Thompson, *The Making of the English Working Class* (London, 1961), 583–91.

[23]*Hansard*, first series, 23:1163–64.

[24]Ibid., 1165.

were times, as in the debate over the Framework Knitters Bill, when he seemed more comfortable with the opposition. He had especially angered the regulars when he sided with the radical Henry Brougham on the need to eliminate sinecures. Beyond this Hume had indicated support for radical interests when visiting his constituents in Weymouth.[25] When Lord Liverpool asked for a general election in September 1812, it was apparent that the Tories intended to dump the unpredictable Scotsman. The Duke of Cumberland, furious at the conduct of his protégé, decided to replace him.[26]

Hume did not gracefully surrender his seat. He promptly sued his patrons (Cumberland and two other trustees), claiming that he had, on their encouragement, paid heavily for his first election in Weymouth. He had been promised the seat for as long as he desired. The parties settled the suit out of court with Hume receiving a partial reimbursement from Cumberland. All of these developments temporarily soured Hume on politics and for the next six years he showed little interest in returning to Parliament. It is clear that this rather harsh exposure to the borough system had much to do with making him a leading proponent of parliamentary reform.

Records of Hume's life between 1812 and 1818 are scarce; but it is possible to trace some of his activities. Shortly after his disappointment in politics, Hume renewed his friendship with James Mill. Since Hume left Montrose Academy in 1790 they had apparently not met for over twenty years. Mill quite naturally saw in Hume someone with potential for defending the tenets of free trade. The two men had many animated discussions about the prospects for breaking down the system that perpetuated sinecures, protection, and wasteful spending.[27] In these discussions Hume told Mill that he had no wish to return to Parliament, but he did hope to become a director of the East India Company. Hume owned a large block of stock in the Company and he wanted the post so that he could push his laissez-faire views on the proprietors. He also thought he knew how to help the organization operate more efficiently. Eventually he persuaded Mill to approach a certain Presbyterian minister, the Reverend Dr. James Lindsay, who was known to have influence with several East India Company proprietors. Lindsay agreed that Hume would make a good director, but he balked at the prospect of canvassing the stockholders.[28] That was the end of Hume's hopes on this occasion.

Mill could not help Hume become an East India director, but he did help him form an association that would become a significant part of his life. Mill convinced Francis Place to take Hume into his confidence. Place first met Hume when they were introduced by Joseph Fox on 30 July 1813.[29]

[25] *The Scotsman,* 24 February 1855.

[26] Ibid.

[27] Hume to Francis Place, 17 March 1818, British Library (BL), Add. MS. 27823.

[28] Bain, *James Mill,* 120–21. On the East India Company see Brian Gardner, *The East India Company* (New York, 1971).

[29] BL, Add. MS. 27823.

Place's reaction was not favorable. He found the Scotsman "devoid of information, dull, and selfish. From the country he came from, India, and the way in which he commenced his public life here, I had no reliance on him for good service, and no grounds for placing confidence in his integrity." Mill insisted, however, that there was "much in him [Hume] that will grow with good nursing."[30] Place eventually was convinced of Hume's worth and they developed a rapport that lasted over thirty years.

Hume's first meeting with Place resulted from a concern each of them had for the educational system devised by Joseph Lancaster. The scheme promoted by Lancaster called for the creation of schools where children would teach other children. He had established such a school on a small scale in 1798, but Lancaster wanted to expand his effort. Ideally each Lancastrian school would contain one thousand children taught in teams of ten by a hundred slightly advanced students.

Lancaster's plan had the virtue of promising inexpensive education. He estimated that it would cost no more than five shillings per child annually. Such potential efficiency, coupled with the commendable industry of one group of students teaching another group of students, attracted the attention of free-traders. In addition, dissenters were pleased with Lancaster's schools because the religious studies did not support any one religion. Hume thought Lancaster's system might lead to a truly national plan of education and he became an active supporter in 1811.

At the time, Hume was not aware of the difficulties Lancaster had faced during the first decade of the nineteenth century. Lack of funds proved the most serious problem. In 1804, Lancaster's debts reached such proportions that he had to make an appeal for money to keep his one small school alive. Francis Place and others responded with monthly subscriptions, but Lancaster fell deeper into debt with each passing year. His friends were loyal, however, and they continued to bail him out. Joseph Fox, the Quaker dentist who introduced Hume to Place, once paid a large sum to save Lancaster from arrest. Clearly, Lancaster's mishandling of financial matters could not be allowed to continue. In order to preserve the educational experiment, Lancaster's supporters formed the Royal Lancastrian Association in 1810 to help him manage his affairs. The governing committee of the association included Place and Brougham. For a year or so the Lancastrian Association flourished and Lancaster opened many schools throughout the country. The progress was short-lived. Inevitably, Lancaster's independent personality and personal extravagance (some of which his detractors exaggerated) led him into conflict with his creditors and members of the governing committee.

These were the problems that brought Hume and Place together in July 1813. Their meeting was not accidental. It was arranged by the Duke of Kent, who asked Joseph Fox to see that Hume had every opportunity to discuss Lancaster's difficulties with Place. The duke was a long standing

[30]Graham Wallas, *The Life of Francis Place, 1771–1854* (reprint of 1918 edition, London, 1951):183.

patron and friend to Lancaster, and he wanted to put an end to the continuing financial uncertainty. He had known Hume since 1812,[31] and he had high respect for the Scotsman's business talent.[32]

On 31 July, Hume had a rather lengthy discussion with Place about Lancaster's future. This time Hume brought word that the Duke of Kent had decided to bring Lancaster, his creditors, and the governing committee of the Lancastrian Association[33] together to consider the prospects for getting out of the financial morass. The duke requested that Hume and Samuel Whitbread, a prominent radical politician, act as moderators at the gathering.[34] They were also to file a report on what they thought should be done in the future.

Lancaster did not appreciate the "interference" of Hume and Whitbread. He complained to Place that Hume should not be allowed to view the private papers of the association. Place replied that Lancaster's unwillingness to cooperate would not help his situation.[35] On 3 August, Hume informed Lancaster that they must arrange a meeting so that Lancaster could explain his differences with the governing committee.[36] Lancaster immediately wrote to Kensington Palace protesting that Hume and Whitbread were intolerable as moderators and ought to be removed. He was particularly critical of Hume. This brought a quick response from the duke. He made it clear that Whitbread was approved not only by himself but by the Dukes of Sussex and Bedford, and that Hume (though not a first choice) was selected as "a gentleman of tried and acknowledged talent in business, and one whose perseverance, impartiality, and justice cannot, upon any fair ground, be called into question. . . ."[37] The duke had no intention of retracting his choice, and the review of Lancaster's operations proceeded.

Hume undertook his responsibilities with characteristic verve. Over the next several weeks he gave "diligent and careful" attention to Lancaster's problems. He took such charge of the inquiry that Whitbread was completely overshadowed. "Mr. Hume went heartily into the business," wrote Place, "he was more at leisure than I was, and he gave a very large portion of his time to it."[38]

After two weeks of interviews and meetings, Hume told Lancaster what he had learned. "The measure of oppression which you complain of,"

[31]They apparently met just before Hume was returned for Weymouth.

[32]BL, Add. MS. 27823. See also Place to Lancaster, 1 August 1813, in Lancaster Papers housed at the American Antiquarian Society (AAS), Worcester, Massachusetts (hereafter cited as Lancaster Papers).

[33]The name was changed to British and Foreign School Society in November 1813.

[34]BL, Add. MS. 27823; Place to Lancaster, 1 August 1813, Lancaster Papers. Like Hume, Whitbread had a great interest in the education of the poor. In 1809 he became an advocate of Lancaster's monitorial system. See Dean Reginald Rapp, "Samuel Whitbread (1764–1815): A Social and Political Study" (unpublished Ph.D. dissertation, Johns Hopkins University, 1971):231–42.

[35]Place to Lancaster, 1 August 1813, Lancaster Papers.

[36]Hume to Lancaster, 13 August 1813, Lancaster Papers.

[37]Duke of Kent's secretary to Lancaster, 15 August 1813, Lancaster Papers.

[38]BL, Add. MS. 27823.

Hume wrote to Lancaster, "has been [brought on] by yourself and by the line of conduct which you have observed, completely at variance with the good sense of every one of your friends; *I have not been able to find any enemy to Joseph Lancaster except Joseph Lancaster himself.*" Hume hoped that "for once" Lancaster would doubt "the correctness of your own judgment" in acting against the advice of friends.[39] Following several more days of study, Hume decided that he and Place ought to take charge of Lancaster's interests. Hume had almost come to the conclusion that Lancaster should declare bankruptcy to satisfy some one hundred creditors. He warned Lancaster that writs were out against him and he must be circumspect about going away from his home.[40]

Hume made an effort to salvage what he could from the quagmire of Lancaster's debts. He planned a meeting of Lancaster's principal creditors on the evening of 2 September for "the purpose of considering the best measures for an adjustment of the present difficulties."[41] Lancaster objected to the scheme, but Hume insisted that "the only thing for us to do now is to meet the worst firmly."[42] The meeting at the Three Tuns Tavern resulted in the preparation of a long list of substantial debts. Even if Lancaster had been giving full cooperation to Hume it would have been nearly impossible to appease so many creditors. In fact, Lancaster showed no willingness to cooperate at all. After several more weeks of no progress, Hume determined that Lancaster had to be set aside. It was the only way to save the Lancastrian system.[43]

In November, at Hume's instigation, Place arranged for Lancaster to be pensioned off with the title of superintendent. At the same time, Hume recommended that the Royal Lancastrian Association become the British and Foreign School Society. He reasoned that this title would make the educational system appear broader in scope. The governing committee voted to make the change on 13 November, and it went into effect early in 1814.[44] In May 1814, the society announced a total separation from Lancaster. Whitbread explained that the society "must not suffer the man who had reared so noble a temple to destroy it."[45]

Hume remained an advocate of national education based on the Lancastrian system for many years, but unlike Mill and Place his interest in promoting the schools waned after the spring of 1814. He had grown weary of the unsavory debates on Lancaster's behavior, and he found it increasingly difficult to sit on the same committee with Joseph Fox. Fox seemed to think he had some special right to dominate all meetings of the governing

[39]Hume to Lancaster, 23 August 1813, Lancaster Papers.

[40]Hume to Lancaster, 28 August 1813, Lancaster Papers.

[41]Hume to Lancaster, 29 August 1813, Lancaster Papers.

[42]Ibid. See Hume circular of August 1813.

[43]Hume to Lancaster, 28 October and 29 October 1813, Lancaster Papers.

[44]See Wallas, *Francis Place*, 93–95; David Salmon, *Joseph Lancaster* (London, 1904), 49; Brian Simon, *Studies in the History of Education, 1789–1870* (London, 1960), 149; Rapp, "Samuel Whitbread," 242–43; Chester New, *The Life of Henry Brougham to 1830* (London, 1961), 198–227; Kevin McGarry, "Joseph Lancaster 1778–1838: A Bibliographical Account of his Life and System of Teaching," Ph.D. dissertation, University of London, 1966.

[45]Rapp, "Samuel Whitbread," 243.

committee. Hume eventually concluded that he could no longer attend discussions where "the committee was of no use except to register Mr. Fox's edicts."[46]

Not wishing to lose Hume's enthusiasm for the Lancastrian system, Place and Mill tried to encourage his participation in the West London Lancastrian Association. This association had been formed in 1813, and its objective was to create model Lancastrian schools in West London north of the Thames. The W.L.L.A. rented schools from the British and Foreign School Society. Hume seemed disinclined to do much more than attend a few meetings and help occasionally as an auditor. He approved of the W.L.L.A. motto "Schools for All," but he refused to become a subscriber despite the urgings of Place. Hume's reticence came from his uncertainty about the financial responsibility of the organization. He also doubted whether the governing board had sufficient dedication to the scheme. In time, Hume expected that a well-organized national plan for educating the poor would emerge from Parliament. After the fiasco with Lancaster, and the various committees formed to advance his monitorial system, Hume thought it might be wise to wait for that day.

While the Lancastrian schools were an important concern for Hume in 1813 and 1814, he had other things on his mind. One of those was a renewed determination to push his free-trade theories in the Court of Proprietors of the East India Company. In a speech before fellow proprietors on 13 January 1813, he argued against the "narrow minded and erroneous policy of monopoly held out and insisted upon in so bold and confident a manner by the ... Directors." He proposed a resolution favoring open trade and calling for an end to the Company's exclusive trading rights in the East. Hume contended that it would mean more overall trade for England if all English merchants could participate. England, he said, would become an "emporium of Eastern commodities." When it came to a vote, Hume was the only one to support his resolution.[47]

Hume's speech did not enhance his standing among the Company's shareholders. He had hoped to advance his continuing campaign to become a director of the company, but his advocacy of free trade made that unlikely. His chances were further reduced when he opposed granting an annual pension of £2000 for ten years to Lord Melville (first lord of the Admiralty). The pension was to compensate Melville for debts left to him by his father. The directors believed that Melville deserved the pension because his father had done a great deal for the East India Company while he served as president of the Board of Control from 1784 to 1793. Hume called the pension plan a "waste" and demanded to know "specifically, act by act and measure by measure," what Melville's father had contributed to the company's prosperity. He wondered how the directors could propose an annual subsidy for a minister of the Crown when they denied claims made

[46]Hume to Place, 23 November 1814, BL, Add. MS. 37949.

[47]Joseph Hume, *Speech on January 19, 1813 Delivered to an Adjourned General Court of Proprietors of East India Stock* (London, 1813).

by widows and orphans of those who were employed by the company.[48]
Whatever the merits of his presentation, Hume appeared once more as an
obstructionist to those who made company decisions. From time to time
over the next few years, Hume went before the stockholders to dispute
policies, promote the cause of free trade, or urge reform in the company's
procedures. His views were always in the minority. Some time later Hume
told Place, ruefully, that his experiences with the proprietors prepared him
well for his many years in the minority in the House of Commons.[49]

One positive development did result from Hume's attempt to "improve"
the East India Company. Joseph Burnley, a shareholder with four votes,
found the Scotsman a likable fellow and befriended him. Burnley did not
appreciate Hume's obvious desire for a directorship, but he did listen when
Hume tried to point to abuses in the Company's operations. Hume became
a frequent visitor at the Burnley estate in 1814 and 1815. During the
course of these visits Hume's attention was often distracted by Burnley's
daughter, Mary. A courtship developed and in 1815, at age thirty-eight,
Hume married this young woman. The marriage did not help Hume's
campaign to become a company director, but, as his enemies were quick to
point out in later years, it certainly increased his wealth. It was the sort of
connection, wrote one opponent of the Scotsman, that might be expected
from a man who put money above all else.[50]

For two years after his marriage, very little changed in Hume's life. He
remained a gadfly in the cause of free trade principles. In 1816 he became
one of the managers of the Panton Street Provident Institution for Savings.
This savings bank was established to assist the poor in managing their
money. In describing the institution, Hume said that servants, laborers, and
mechanics needed an opportunity to invest. Their money would be put into
government securities. The Provident Institution was the free-traders' ideal
of how to increase the prosperity of those persons on marginal incomes.[51]
For many years Hume remained an outspoken advocate of savings banks
and repeatedly urged the government to give them whatever support was
necessary.

Later in 1816, Hume published a pamphlet explaining a plan to put
English currency on the decimal principle. He encouraged the adoption of
such a system to lessen confusion in exchanging foreign currency, and also
to bring about a greater efficiency in all money transactions. In subsequent
years, it was generally agreed by Hume's contemporaries that few of his
ideas ever had more merit than this one.[52]

[48]*The Substance of a Speech of Joseph Hume at a General Court of Proprietors . . . on the
19th of June, 1814 Upon the Motion for Granting a Pension of £2000 per annum for Ten Years
to the Present Lord Melville* (London, 1841).
[49]Hume to Place, 14 August 1819, BL, Add. MS. 35145.
[50]John Wilson Croker to W. H. Ellis, 14 January 1816, Private Letter Book 5, 14–15,
Croker Papers, William L. Clements Library, Ann Arbor, Michigan.
[51]Joseph Hume, *The Provident Institution for Saving* (London, 1816).
[52]Joseph Hume, *Short Account of A Plan for the New Silver Coinage for Improving the
Currency of the Kingdom and Introducing the Decimal Principle Into All Money Transactions* (London, 1816).

Hume derived some satisfaction from his efforts on behalf of savings banks and the decimal system, but in 1817 he seemed without direction. There was not enough to occupy his time. This posed quite a problem for someone with his energy and ambition. Thwarted in his attempt to win a directorship of the East India Company, Hume began to think about returning to Parliament. Although he had not forgotten his unhappy experience in 1812, Hume's ego and forceful personality demanded a forum for his opinions on government and economy. He wanted to expose the "wasteful, corrupt, and oppressive" policies of the Liverpool administration. Hume had come to agree with James Mill's observation that the primary objective for free-traders was "the diffusion of great principles."[53]

The state of the country had something to do with Hume's rekindled interest in politics. Most politicians with radical inclinations (even those who had not experienced personal disappointment) took a hiatus between 1812 and the end of the Napoleonic War. Reform seemed a hopeless cause in Parliament while the fighting continued on the Continent. Hence, reformers tended to throw up their arms in discouragement. After Waterloo the situation changed. Domestic politics regained center stage. England's mammoth post-war problems and the government's inadequate response to them brought the radicals into the political fray again. By 1817 Hume was a part of the revitalized radical movement in England. In these circumstances he made no effort to hide his desire for another try in the House of Commons.

Early in 1818 Hume's friends encouraged him to stand for the Scottish border burghs.[54] This time, unlike 1812, Hume ran on his own terms. The free-trade radicals made "Economy, Retrenchment, and Reform" their slogan in 1818, and Hume intended that all three should become a reality. According to newspaper accounts, he promised his supporters that

his principles were as independent as his circumstances, that he should never sully the character which he had laboured to raise, by one act of mean subservience or apostasy, or by adding one more to the catalogue of injuries which the public had already a number too many, sustained at the hands of their official servants.[55]

The electorate in the border burghs was split between reformers and anti-reformers, but in 1818 the reformers had the edge and there was not much doubt that Hume would win. The general election was held in July, and initially the results heartened Liverpool's opponents. There were impressive gains, of which Hume's victory was one, and some even dared to think that the long Tory domination might soon come to an end. This proved to be overly optimistic, for the government majority was still substantial.

Hume's victory in the summer of 1818 marked the beginning of nearly thirty-six years in the House of Commons. His attitude in 1818 did not

[53]Hume to Place, 16 September 1819, BL, Add. MS. 35145.

[54]The burghs were Aberbrothock, Brechin, Aberdeen, Inverbervie, and Montrose.

[55]*Caledonian Mercury*, 16 July and 20 July 1818; *Edinburgh Evening Courant*, 14 July 1818.

differ much from what it had been in 1812. He still had the exaggerated confidence in himself that self-made men often display; that assuredness that enables them to pass judgment on almost any issue that catches their fancy. Hume commissioned himself to set things right in government, and he was one of the opposition members who believed the 1818 election results reflected the people's will for reform. He thus returned to the Commons full of fight and hope. He was anxious to take on the Tories; and, if need be, the "second-rate" Tories as well.[56]

Although he willingly cooperated with the Whigs when they stood against the government, Hume considered himself an independent. His perspective on politics and economics was an amalgam of his own views with those of James Mill, Jeremy Bentham, David Ricardo, and Francis Place.[57] Such opinions were rarely compatible with the political ambitions of either Tories or Whigs. Hume therefore took his seat at the beginning of the 1819 session as a member of the diverse radical faction. His thoughts on free trade, government corruption, and parliamentary reform were so "extreme" that moderates in the House of Commons thought them revolutionary. Hume's radicalism, like that of Mill, Bentham, and Place, had grown out of the late eighteenth-century rationalism that required parliamentary reform as a necessary first step to escaping the "corrupt system" that had evolved since the seventeenth century. Hume accepted the position taken by the London Corresponding Society in 1794 that a representative Parliament would lead to "liberties restored, the press free, the laws simplified, judges unbiased, juries independent . . . the public better served, and the necessaries of life more within the reach of the poor."[58] Place, a prominent member of the Corresponding Society, encouraged Hume at every opportunity to pursue this course in the House of Commons. Both understood that the way to gain support for parliamentary reform, at least outside of the Commons, was to reveal the current system to be wasteful and corrupt.

It was Place who reassured Hume that Mill and Bentham were pointing the way toward a vastly improved society. Hume never had much doubt on this score, but there were times when questions arose in his mind. He once wondered if a Benthamite could always accept the rule of the majority. "What will prevent the poor of a community (in majority) from demanding that the rich sacrifice property?" he asked Place on one occasion. He also wondered about the "greatest happiness principle," especially "if 29 want to roast and eat the 30th."[59] Place responded to these and other queries by reminding Hume that only "a rational society can practice utilitarianism."[60] The radicals could help to ensure a rational society by encouraging

[56]Henry Brougham's term for those Whigs who supported the government on crucial votes.

[57]Ricardo was sent to Parliament in February 1819 for the Irish pocket borough of Portarlington. See Barry Gordon, *Political Economy in Parliament, 1819–1823* (London, 1976).

[58]Quoted in Harold Silver, *English Education and the Radicals 1780–1823* (London, 1975), 12.

[59]Hume to Place, 19 October 1819, BL, Add. MS. 35145.

[60]Place to Hume, 25 October 1819, BL, Add. MS. 35145.

a plan of national education and by making certain that the populace received the proper information about the state of the country.

There was one other attribute of the "rational" society that Hume and Place hoped to see in England, and that was a reduction in the power and influence of the Church of England. Place did not hide the fact that he was an atheist, and Hume, while he did not deny his Anglican faith, could never muster much religious fervor. Religion had never meant a great deal in Hume's private life. For most early nineteenth-century Englishmen, however, religion was something to get excited about, and Hume aroused controversy by his insistence that all religions should be treated equally in Great Britain. He may not, strictly speaking, have believed this possible or desirable, but it was the impression he intended to give. This attitude, plus his association with Place, led to frequent charges by his political opponents that he was an atheist. In later years, these accusations, always stoutly refuted by Hume, may well have cost him political support.

In addition to his ideas on reform, Hume's personality placed him squarely in the radical camp. His deportment in the Commons would bring more wrath upon him than any belief he espoused. It was the combination of his free-trade radicalism, his unorthodox behavior, and his boundless vitality that made Hume a focus of public attention in the 1820s.

CHAPTER II.

"FROTHY AND VAPID" 1819–1823

Joseph Hume's "second" parliamentary career had lasted only slightly longer than two years when the Tory newspaper *John Bull* wrote about him: "He is such a profound dunce—a dull-headed ass, who plods night and day in order to discover the surest way of going wrong at last."[1] There were many in the House of Commons who shared *John Bull's* reaction to the Scotsman's efforts. These were members (mostly Tory but including quite a few in opposition) already tired of Hume's constant harping on the need for fiscal reform. They saw him as a bore and meddler who had no consideration for his colleagues.[2]

By the spring of 1821, Hume had risen to speak in the Commons well over two hundred times. Had he been an outstanding orator, it is doubtful he could have sustained the interest of the House day after day. Alas, he was, by agreement of friend and foe, an excruciatingly dull speaker. As one member complained, his speeches "were all facts unendowed with wit or jest."[3] Nothing fazed him. Neither the time of night nor the obvious inattention of the House slowed him in the least. The Commons had never seen such a talking machine. His speeches were too long, too repetitive, had virtually no eloquence, and contained an overabundance of statistics. Hume was convinced that strings of numbers somehow left no doubt about the correctness of his position. He imagined that the more detail he supplied the stronger his argument would appear. The reverse was true. Opponents seized upon the slightest error in his statistics and used it to "prove" his unreliability.

Hume's oratorical deficiencies at first caused government members to treat him with contempt rather than fear. He did not seem to be the sort of person who would pose a serious threat to the ministry. More than anything else he appeared to be the parliamentary mouthpiece for Francis Place, and it was generally thought that Place's inept ideas tallied well with Hume's inept mouth.[4] It soon became clear, however, that Hume was a more potent enemy than the Tories had thought. Hume's success, not his failure, prompted the verbal assault from *John Bull.*

Whatever his shortcomings in the House of Commons, Hume's dogged harassment of a government slow to admit the need for change won him popularity in the country. In the same year that *John Bull* and other conservative newspapers damned him for his "senseless" interference, the liberal *Morning Chronicle* praised him for "that industry that renders him so particularly valuable as a member of [Parliament]" and for having "laid open to the public gaze a few of the hidden springs of the political

---

[1]16 April 1821.

[2]John Carroll Amundson, "Joseph Hume and Financial Reform in England, 1819–1822," Ph.D. dissertation, University of Pittsburgh, 1933, 44.

[3]Ibid., 44–48.

[4]See R. K. Huch, "Francis Place and the Chartists: Promise and Disillusion," *Historian,* 45 (August, 1983), 63–83.

machine."[5] This is something the "respectable" opposition never could
have achieved.

When Hume re-entered Parliament in January 1819, the outlook for the
opposition was clouded. One of the uncertainties was the degree to which
the opponents of Liverpool could be organized. Since the death of Charles
James Fox in 1806, no one had emerged as an effective leader of all the
anti-Tory factions. The two men most frequently mentioned as opposition
leaders were George Ponsonby and George Tierney. Neither of these men
offered much in the way of political acumen. They were, for the most part,
perfect examples of the type of Whigs Brougham called "second-rate
Tories." The radicals had never trusted Ponsonby or Tierney, and
considered each as useless in offering tough opposition to the Tory
ministers.[6]

Between 1809 and 1818 the radicals had looked for guidance from a
variety of men who were able to articulate their interests. Samuel
Whitbread, Samuel Romilly, Lord Folkestone, and Brougham were among
those who were, from time to time, considered leaders by the parliamentary
radicals. In 1818, however, nearly all of the potential leaders were
eliminated for one reason or another. Whitbread and Romilly were dead.
Folkestone and Brougham, while still valuable to the cause, had gained
reputations for being unreliable—not in their ideas so much as in their
demeanor. Folkestone suffered from a liaison he had with the infamous
Mary Anne Clarke, and Brougham had caused a furor in 1816 by making
scurrilous charges against the prince regent.[7]

George Tierney, distrusted as he was by many radicals, seemed to
provide the one hope for strong leadership in 1819. It was leadership by
default, but if the opposition wished to make progress after the limited
gains in the 1818 election there had to be some organization. The
opponents of Liverpool had an abundance of issues to pursue. A united
front might work wonders. In July 1818 John William Ponsonby
(Viscount Duncannon) moved to solidify Tierney as the official chief of the
opposition. Duncannon worked diligently to get support from radicals. His
efforts met with some success, and he anticipated that the opposition in
1819 would prove better directed than it had at any time in the past
decade.[8]

For a few months early in 1819 it appeared that Duncannon's plan
might succeed. The discipline of the opposition surpassed anything in
memory, and the improvement did not go unnoticed by the government.
Castlereagh (Liverpool's foreign minister) observed that the opposition
members kept their "eyes front." Many of the radicals also were impressed.
Brougham and Sir Robert Wilson both expressed satisfaction that Tierney

[5]*Morning Chronicle*, 27 February 1821.

[6]Archibald Foord, *His Majesty's Opposition* (Oxford, 1964), 451–66; R. K. Huch, *The
Radical Lord Radnor: The Public Life of Viscount Folkestone, third Earl of Radnor,
1779–1869* (Minneapolis, 1977), 72–73.

[7]Sir Samuel Romilly, *Memoirs*, edited by his son (London, 1840), 3: 236; Huch, *Radnor*,
86–87.

[8]Foord, *His Majesty's Opposition*, 456.

had finally brought the opposition together.[9] The opponents of Liverpool appeared all the more formidable from the inability of the ministry's whip, Charles Arbuthnot, to keep the government's benches full. The administration lost several votes on minor issues in the Commons and refused to push other matters to a division.

In March and April opposition leaders expectantly prepared lists for a Whig cabinet. On 18 May, Tierney decided to force a showdown by moving for a committee on the state of the nation. The ministry, under direct threat from Tierney's motion, marshaled the government members and overwhelmed the opposition 357–178.[10] This defeat, coupled with a breakdown in Tierney's health over the next several months, brought an end to Whig hopes. Liverpool often complained that his administration was in peril, but whenever he needed a majority it was not much trouble to get one.

Hume had no direct connection with any parliamentary faction when he took his seat in January 1819. But anyone who associated with Ricardo, Mill, Place, and Bentham, as Hume did, was certain to become aligned with the radicals in the House of Commons.[11] These were the members who had tried for more than ten years to make governing as difficult as possible for Tory ministers. They had steadfastly contended that the ending of corruption and waste in government was by far the most important reform to be considered. Included in this element were such outspoken men as Thomas Creevey, H. G. Bennet, Sir Robert Wilson, Lord Archibald Hamilton, Folkestone, Lord Milton, and Viscount Althorp. They came from disparate backgrounds, had varying opinions on how far reform should go, and disagreed on the best long-range strategy to ensure reform. Yet, they did agree on two matters: first, Whigs were not trustworthy; second, it was necessary to keep pressure on the Tories.

Hume brought new life to this faction of radicals in the early 1820s by arousing public indignation through his charges that excessive government spending was at the heart of the country's economic sorrows. Hume did not need a Mary Anne Clarke to find a scandal; he saw impropriety enough in sinecures and unnecessary spending. Beginning in 1819, and continuing throughout the 1820s, Hume operated as the "watchdog of the British treasury." He carefully dissected every budget matter brought before the Commons. Whether for king, army, navy, admiralty, or for keeping Napoleon on St. Helena, Hume and his cohorts (mostly Creevey, Bennet, and Ricardo) never failed to argue that the planned appropriations exceeded reasonable expenditure. Hume acted from the conviction that government refusal to reduce appropriations would create public discontent. The people, he said, wanted their government ministers to stop "pulling down pillars of the Constitution in order to strengthen the Corinthian Capital."[12]

[9]Austin Mitchell, *The Whigs in Opposition* (Oxford, 1967), 34–35.
[10]Foord, *His Majesty's Opposition*, 457–58.
[11]*Hansard,* first series, 39: 275.
[12]Ibid., 589–91.

The radicals connected government spending with the rate of taxation, and the assumption was that when expenditure declined numerous taxes could be reduced or eliminated. This, in turn, would remove one of the major reasons for an unsteady economy. The radicals had support from agriculturists for their campaign against taxes. Between 1819 and 1822 agriculture suffered a depression in England. A huge harvest in the north in 1819 sent wheat prices plunging. The farmers thought that the government should lower or remove annoying taxes such as those imposed on malt and horses.[13]

Hume was pleased to have the support of agriculturists, whether great Whig landowners or country Tories, but he realized that their motives were strictly those of self-interest. They would not endorse sweeping economic reform. Hume could never count on the great Whig landowners to join his attacks on the ministry's appropriations.

One of Hume's favorite tactics was to cause as many divisions in the House of Commons as possible on budgetary matters.[14] Depending on the issue, and the lateness of the hour, his following varied from fifteen to seventy. He could usually depend on Creevey, Ricardo, and Bennet to stick out his long-winded battles, but most of his other supporters came and went according to the situation. Each time any portion of the army, navy, and ordnance estimates came before the Commons, Hume prolonged discussion far into the night before yielding to inevitable defeat. On one memorable occasion in March 1821, Hume and a few friends, through amendments and irrelevant motions, forced eleven divisions on the army estimates. At 4 A.M. new candles were brought into the House to permit the members to complete their business. J. C. Lambton, working closely with Hume, promptly moved that the new candles be excluded. After some absurd debate, the last division occurred at 5 A.M. and the Commons adjourned.[15]

Hume's stamina during these debates amazed his opponents and followers. He was looked upon as something of an "animated fixture." His seat in the old House (before the fire) was against one of the posts that supported the side gallery to the left of the Speaker's chair. Most members shifted their places from time to time, but every day Hume went to his regular fourteen inches of space. He was so regular that, according to James Grant, one Tory wag could not resist remarking, "there is Joseph always at his *post*."

In the 1820s just attending the House of Commons could prove to be a bit of a trial. It may not have been, as Grant described it, "the second edition of the Black Hole of Calcutta," but it was cold and dank in winter and quite often oppressively hot in summer. The ventilation was poor and the building so small that only about 400 of the 658 members could be seated comfortably.

[13]A. J. B. Hilton, *Corn, Cash, Commerce: The Economic Policies of the Tory Government, 1815–1830* (London, 1977), 137–138.

[14]*The Times* defended this as "vexatious for the ministers but necessary," 19 May 1821.

[15]*Hansard*, first series, 39: 861.

These "unhealthy" conditions seemed to make no impact on Hume. There were many theories about the wellspring of his endurance, one of which focused on his penchant for eating pears. Each day (when pears were in season) he stuffed his pockets full of the fruit and on more than one occasion it was all he ate for dinner. "Can it be," conjectured Grant, "that there are salubrious qualities in pears?" A more popular theory held that Hume's huge chest (it appeared larger than it was because of his squat body) accounted for his unusual vitality. Hume's physique attracted a good deal of notice from his contemporaries. Besides his ample chest, he had a short neck and a plump, round face set on a large head. His hair was dark brown and it was usually long and bushy. His overall appearance gave the impression of someone who had purpose and will.[16]

Hume spoke with strength and clarity when he rose from the shadow of his pillar, but he did not modulate his voice. Hence, there was a tendency for his listeners to lose interest very quickly. Everyone in the House knew when Hume planned a marathon address. On such occasions he carefully put his hat, always filled with notes, on the bench near the spot where he was sitting. As he rose to speak, he had one or more parliamentary papers rolled up and firmly grasped in his right hand. In emphasizing certain points, Hume would strike his left palm with the paper in his right hand, and when saying something he thought particularly dramatic, he would "stretch out his right arm to its full length and whirl the roll of paper with considerable force in the air."

Another habit Hume had while speaking was to indicate a desire to conclude long before he actually did. It was not until he glanced at his hat two or three times that members knew he intended to sit down.[17] While most of his colleagues flagged around 10 P.M., the Scotsman had just warmed to the task. In commenting on Hume's capacity for lengthy discussion, John Cam Hobhouse complained,

It almost destroyed us; we divided on every item of every estimate; we were glued to these seats. The evening sun went down upon us in this hostile array; and when he arose in the morning, he shone upon our undiminished ranks. If ever opposition despised hunger and thirst . . . for conscience sake, it was the opposition led by my honourable friend during those never-ending sessions.[18]

As difficult as these "never-ending sessions" were, they did produce some results. Hume gained considerable attention outside Parliament. From the summer of 1819, a large number of newspapers, most notably *The Scotsman* (Edinburgh), the *Morning Chronicle*, and *The Times,* gave ever-increasing coverage to his call for retrenchment. It was no secret that Hume persisted in his efforts more for the masses beyond the walls of Parliament than for the few who listened to him within. He appealed directly to the public whenever possible. In January 1820, he prepared and had published a list of sinecures that momentarily awakened public ire.

[16] James Grant, *Random Recollections of the House of Commons from the Year 1830 to the Close of 1835* . . . (Philadelphia, 1836), 266–68.
[17] Ibid., 268–70.
[18] Quoted in A. Aspinall, *Lord Brougham and the Whig Party* (Manchester, 1927), 122.

Hume continued these tactics during the general election in March 1820. Parliament had been dissolved following the death of George III in January. The elections were relatively quiet with the opposition forces managing to hold their own. In the Scottish burghs, however, the election did not go smoothly. A significant challenge was mounted against Hume by conservatives in Aberdeen and Berne. They brought in a wealthy Londoner, John Mitchell of Bond Street, to stand against Hume. Details of the election are scanty, but Hume appeared at many rallies urging the people in his district to demand reform. This strategy inflamed tempers on both sides to the point where a military unit had to be brought in to restore order. The election was determined on 13 March with Hume winning in Montrose, Arbroath, and Brechin, while his conservative opponent carried Aberdeen and Berne.[19] Hume had prevailed in a close contest. It was the last time he had to worry about maintaining his seat until 1830.

The new parliament began its work on 27 April. Hume seemed anxious to resume his battle against excess spending in government and in favor of radical reform. He hoped the malcontents could be encouraged to apply pressure on the ministers and on the moderate opposition. Hume understood that the Whigs did not feel comfortable with any attempt to stimulate public opinion on the issue of reform; but he thought their urge for power might bring them to take up some of the reform causes from a pragmatic, if not principled, motive.

The Whigs did not hesitate to exploit public discontent when it did not involve specific demands for reform. This was the case during the affair of Queen Caroline in 1820.[20] Hume and other radicals were more than willing to join forces with the Whigs, for it provided an excellent opportunity to embarrass the Tories. The temporarily united opposition defended the queen against a bill of pains and penalties brought by the ministers on behalf of George IV. The king planned to divorce the queen by proving her guilty of adultery. Henry Brougham was the architect of the queen's defense, and the subject became the primary concern of Parliament and the nation for many months. The radicals had attacked George IV unmercifully while he was the prince regent, and they now found perverse pleasure from the fact that Caroline had become a cause célèbre with a large portion of the population.

The ministers successfully pushed the Bill of Pains and Penalties through the House of Lords, but wisely decided not to pursue the matter in the Commons. Instead, Parliament was prorogued in the autumn of 1820 before debate on the bill began in earnest. This action saved the day for the ministry and frustrated the hopes of those who anticipated a smashing victory over Liverpool.

Hume had been vocal in his defense of the queen's innocence,[21] but it is hard to escape the conclusion that he did not really care very much about

[19]*Edinburgh Advertiser,* 17 March 1820; Mitchell, *Whigs in Opposition,* 140–41.

[20]Elie Halevy, *The Liberal Awakening 1815–1830,* trans. E. I. Watkin (New York, 1961), 84–104; J. E. Cookson, *Lord Liverpool's Administration, 1815–1822* (Edinburgh, 1975), 215–300.

[21]*Hansard,* second series, 3: 65–73.

her fate. He began to see that she distracted attention from more vital questions. He did not like to defer his retrenchment campaign. Early in 1821 he lost interest in her (particularly after she indicated a willingness to accept a £50,000 payoff from the government to give up her claims), and blamed the Whigs for giving her poor advice.[22] They were, he wrote to Place, "in general despicable as a party and quite unworthy of support from the people."[23]

After January 1821 it was widely acknowledged that Hume had taken over leadership of the radicals in the House of Commons. Moreover, through his instigation the radicals had taken the initiative in challenging the Tory government. While the Whigs equivocated following the Caroline debacle, Hume and his associates applied relentless pressure.[24] The *Liverpool Mercury*, in February 1821, declared that Hume's efforts led to a growing "demand for reform of the system" and in April, the *Morning Chronicle* wrote that the "people" must rely on such a "zealous, active, and honest representative" as Joseph Hume.[25] *The Times* reported on May 3 that the country would be "grateful to Mr. Hume" for "opening eyes." This extra-parliamentary following caused ministers to treat Hume with greater respect than they had in the past. The Scotsman's position was further enhanced by the opposition's successful, and nearly successful, attempts to repeal certain taxes Liverpool wished to preserve.

The malt tax and the agricultural horse tax were both challenged in March and April of 1821. Agricultural problems had worsened in 1820 and 1821, and this was reflected in numerous reform meetings held in January and February. The great farming interests continued to demand reduction of taxation as one method of alleviating distress. Whig and Tory gentlemen in Parliament were willing to vote against Liverpool's desire to maintain existing taxes. The country gentlemen and the radicals (each for different reasons) supported C. C. Western's motion to abolish the malt tax on 27 March. This combination provided sufficient strength for Western to carry the first reading. The ministers then threatened to resign (a tactic Liverpool employed with consummate skill) and the Tory gentlemen came back into line.[26] Western's proposal then failed its second reading. This became a pattern for the Tory farmers. They voted for tax reductions to nudge the administration, but they would not desert the prime minister on any crucial vote. The country gentlemen were quite willing to back Hume when he attacked high taxes, but they did not share his economic theories or political motives.[27] A. J. B. Hilton has called their actions an attempt to

---

[22]*The Journal of Mrs. Arbuthnot, 1820–1832*, ed. Francis Bamford and the duke of Wellington (London, 1950), 1: 67.

[23]Hume to Place, 20 December, BL, Add. MS. 35135.

[24]Hilton, "Economic Policy of the Tory Governments," 153.

[25]10 April, 1821; Amundson, "Joseph Hume," 56, 72–73.

[26]Mitchell, *Whigs in Opposition*, 160. For a brief resume of the economic ideas of leading free-trade radicals in the House of Commons, see Barry Gordon, *Political Economy in Parliament, 1819–1823* (London, 1977), 168–223, and his *Economic Doctrine and Tory Liberalism, 1824–1830* (London, 1979), 14–26.

[27]Hilton, "Economic Policy of the Tory Government," 153.

"blackmail ministers" into granting tax relief without delivering them a mortal wound.[28]

The great farmers did win some concessions from the ministers. The administration agreed to create a committee on agricultural distress, and it offered little opposition to a move to eliminate the agricultural horse tax.[29] The ministry did not make these concessions from any new attachment to free-trade principles, but rather from a sense of political reality. Appeasing the "blackmailers" from time to time, even if not absolutely necessary, was good politics. There was never an intent to depart from the government's "do-nothing" policy on economic misery. Key members of the ministry, William Huskisson, Nicholas Vansittart, and Liverpool himself, believed that sooner or later things would right themselves. Any attempt to take decisive action would create serious opposition and inflame passions. Doing nothing, or appeasing in selective instances, seemed the only reasonable course.[30] In its own way, this may have been the ultimate laissez-faire policy.

Whatever the government might have done in the spring of 1821, it is safe to conclude that Hume would have found it inadequate. As it was, he intensified his attack on "loose" spending. Hume received encouragement from David Ricardo. Ricardo had never thought that agricultural troubles were caused by high taxes.[31] He therefore supported Liverpool's stand against tax reductions. But Ricardo strongly favored retrenchment; and he did not hesitate to assist Hume when he confronted the administration on matters other than taxation. Such was the case on 27 June when Hume spoke for more than three hours on the grave condition of the country's economy. Hume and Ricardo had collected, arranged, and interpreted thousands of figures since the end of the war in 1815. They concluded that the national debt still grew by more than £115,000 each year. At the end of his marathon address, Hume moved for an investigation into the economy of the country. The Marquis of Tavistock, a Whig, seconded the motion. He did so primarily from the hope that a general inquiry would put an end to the radicals' insistence on scrutinizing every article of every budget.[32] In fact, Tavistock specifically criticized Hume for bringing "all these details of the estimates before the House," and he thought such proceedings to be "deviating widely from the common and ancient usage of Parliament." Tavistock concluded that he did not wish to see the House assume the functions of the executive.[33] As Austin Mitchell has aptly noted, the Whigs (for whom Tavistock spoke) did not like Hume's behavior; but they had nothing to offer in its stead.[34]

After much debate, Hume's motion lost 174 to 92. The 92 votes in favor

---

[28]Ibid., 152.

[29]The agricultural committee was chaired by Ricardo. This did not please the agriculturists since Ricardo did not place much importance on high taxes as a cause of agricultural problems.

[30]Hilton, "Economic Policy of the Tory Governments," 79–80.

[31]Ricardo to J. R. McCulloch, 8 February 1822, BL, Add. MS. 34545.

[32]Hansard, second series, 5: 1345–418.

[33]Ibid., 1417–18.

[34]Mitchell, Whigs in Opposition, 160–61.

were nearly twice Hume's usual support (except on questions of taxation), but he had hoped for more. He blamed his setback on the Whigs' lack of genuine concern and the fact that the session was drawing to a close.[35] Hume had no chance of getting support from farming interests or parliamentary waverers for his motion. Liverpool had made it clear that he considered this a critical vote; hence, his majority was never in doubt.

Although he lost in the Commons, Hume's performance established him as a primary spokesman for those most vaguely termed "the people." This term usually meant those outside of Parliament (without representation) who where were unhappy with the conditions of their life. The London newspapers played a big part in advancing the Scotsman's reputation in the summer of 1821. "The pettish retainers of office have snarled and carped at him with impotent malice," wrote *The Times,* "but he now overpowers them by the extent and accuracy of the intelligence he has gained. He drives into the very penetralia of corruption and lays open all its practices."[36] The *Morning Chronicle* similarly praised Hume for persevering against "extravagance and corruption."[37] The liberal press held Hume in considerable esteem for more than one reason. John Walter, publisher of *The Times,* was pleased that Hume had accused the government of denying official advertising to his paper for political reasons.[38] All London newspapers were grateful to Hume for providing large numbers of division lists for publication. This was the responsibility of the chief whip on each side of the House, but Hume supplemented the efforts of the opposition whip in the early 1820s. The publication of voting lists was part of Hume's plan to appeal to the malcontents outside of Parliament.[39]

Hume's standing among his radical associates in the Commons seemed as solid as his reputation with the radicals outside. In August, Sir Francis Burdett wrote to John Cam Hobhouse, "I am glad to hear you speak so [well] of Hume for I have formed a high opinion of him." Burdett hoped that the radicals could soon "break the chain that has been fastened link by link since the year 1688 . . . by the hand of corrupt Parliaments."[40] Burdett believed that the government's failure to react positively to the relentless pressure from Hume and his supporters was proof enough that the "system" was evil. Sir Francis completely agreed with the *Morning Chronicle's* biting assessment that "ministers respond to criticism by cutting allowances for storeroom cats from 6p to 3p and leaving sinecures go untouched."[41]

Despite this rather grim portrayal of government inaction, the ministers were preparing to do more than lower allowances for storeroom cats. It was not a startling departure from its "do-nothing" policy, but the administration did announce a reduction of 12,000 men and officers in the army.[42] In

[35]*Hansard,* second series, 5: 1440–42.
[36]27 June 1821.
[37]29 June 1821.
[38]A. Aspinall, *Politics and the Press, 1780–1850* (London, 1949), 130.
[39]Mitchell, *Whigs in Opposition,* 38.
[40]Burdett to Hobhouse, 24 August 1821, BL, Add. MS. 47222.
[41]5 July 1821.
[42]Amundson, "Joseph Hume," 99.

addition, the ministry quietly abandoned over 160 sinecures. Among those who lost pensions and sinecures were Charles Lamb and William Wordsworth. Lamb blamed his plight on "the foul enchanter," Joseph Hume.[43] Indeed, the view that Hume had brought about these economies prevailed among his friends and opponents.[44] Hume may have deserved some of the credit for the cutbacks (certainly for the fact they gained public notice), but it is possible that the Liverpool ministry would have made the reductions anyway. Whatever precipitated these reductions, the most that can be said for them is that they were not of much consequence. These minor retrenchments did, however, embolden Hume to think that his constant badgering of ministers might produce better results in the future.

Fighting the ministers in the Commons represented only a part of Hume's reform activities in 1821. He and other radicals frequently attended gatherings in the countryside to demand reform and retrenchment. The *Quarterly Review* put them in the category of revolutionaries: "speeches delivered in the present year at public meetings by Lord Folkstone, Hume and [H. G. Bennet] have been the same in doctrine, tendency, even language as those of Hunt—one calls for revolution and the others say it is inevitable."[45] Hume had no interest in revolution as the *Quarterly* used the term; but he did speak in favor of substantial political reform, including more frequent elections, expanded franchise, and the ballot. He further believed that serious efforts at retrenchment would not become a reality until there was reform of representation. At times Hume did get carried away by his dislike for the "system" as it operated under Liverpool. In September 1821 he wrote to John Cam Hobhouse that there existed in England a "system of terror, intimidation, and military government."[46]

At a meeting in his honor in Hereford, where he received a silver tankard and a hogshead of "prime Hereford cider," Hume urged the crowd to resume their ancient right of control over their representatives in Parliament. It seemed the only remedy for existing abuses in expenditure.[47] The idea that "the people" had had greater control over members of Parliament in earlier times was a popular one with many radical reformers. Radicals like Hume, Folkstone, Burdett, even Cobbett, justified their "extreme" views by contending that they amounted to nothing more than attempts to return to conditions that had obtained at some indefinite time in some indefinite way.[48] Hume's efforts at Hereford were promptly assailed by the anti-reformers. "Cider, we know, is a thin beverage," wrote *The Courier,*

[43]*The Works of Charles and Mary Lamb,* ed. E. V. Lucas, (London, 1905) 3: 563.
[44]*The Bury Post,* 24 October 1821.
[45]"The Opposition," *Quarterly Review,* 28 (1821): 214.
[46]Hume to Hobhouse, 16 September 1821, BL, Add. MS. 36549. The occasion for Hume's remarks was the dropping of Sir Robert Wilson from the Army list. Sir Robert (a radical) was removed because the government thought he had tried to incite a riot at the funeral of Queen Caroline. See J. E. Cookson, *Lord Liverpool's Administration, 1815–1822* (Edinburgh, 1975), 323–324.
[47]See account of Hereford meeting in *The Scotsman,* 22 December 1821. See also Peter Sraffa, ed., *The Works and Correspondence of David Ricardo,* 5 (Cambridge, 1952): 471–74.
[48]See Huch, *Radical Lord Radnor,* 3–16.

"and so are Mr. Hume's talents; [cider] is vapid if not swallowed immediately, and so are Mr. Hume's arguments."[49]

The conservatives rejected any suggestion that a connection existed between the poor economic conditions in the country and the need for reform of representation. But Hume continued to press this point. In addition, he never missed an opportunity to say that the government's response to "the people's" demand for reform was either to do nothing or to use oppressive measures to stop unrest. He cited the repeal of *habeas corpus* in 1817 and the passage of the Six Acts in 1819 to prove his contention. These were the arguments that *The Courier* called "frothy and vapid," but they made their impression on Hume's audience. There were lusty cheers everywhere the Scotsman appeared.

The success of these reform gatherings led Hume and his associates to assume that they had built considerable momentum by the end of 1821. They believed there was every reason to think that demand for reform, both within and without the walls of Parliament, would steadily increase in the months ahead. Their specific expectations were unclear—at least in the short run—but they had no doubt the general cause would advance. Hume was so sanguine that he predicted to Hobhouse that the Tories could not last another six months in the face of public pressure.

Hume continued to appear at various reform meetings during the early weeks of 1822. In February he told a gathering at Liverpool to seek reform in the House of Commons as an essential first step for any improvements in the system. "It is truly gratifying to me," said Hume, "to find that the line of public conduct I have adopted, from a conviction of its utility . . . has received such approbation."[50] The Scotsman obviously enjoyed his role as "spokesman" for "the people."

The Whigs were not enjoying Hume's prominence in the least. Since the spring of 1821 they had steadily lost initiative in the opposition. The brief unity of the opposition under Tierney in 1819 was long forgotten. The Whigs, who wanted power more than they wanted reform, were not anxious to lead the public to expect substantial changes. Tavistock, Lansdown, and Tierney might join the radicals when they thought there was a chance to beat the government, but never because they had a great appreciation for radical objectives.[51] In fact, while the hopes of the parliamentary radicals soared near the end of 1821, the Whig opposition approached the 1822 session quite dispirited. Brougham, sliding over from his close association with the radicals, tried to take a leadership position with the opposition but had little success. His one bright moment occurred when the opposition registered 108 votes on a motion to cut taxes. The radicals, with Hume taking the lead, heartily endorsed Brougham's

[49]Amundson, "Joseph Hume," 101.

[50]*Liverpool Mercury,* 22 February 1855.

[51]For a slightly different view, see Hilton, *Corn, Cash, Commerce,* 138–139.

[52]Lansdowne to Holland, 21 January 1822, BL, Add. MS. 51687.

[53]*Hansard,* second series, 6: 61.

[54]For a solid biography of Croker, see Myron F. Brightfield, *John Wilson Croker* (London, 1940).

motion. The size of the opposition vote again reflected the willingness of some Tories to support anti-taxation efforts. It could not be viewed as significant progress for the opponents of Liverpool, for on non-taxation questions the total vote against the government dropped by at least thirty-five.[52]

When the parliamentary session began in 1822, Hume knew that Brougham wanted to take the lead; but he was in no mood to defer to his colleague. Instead, Hume moved straight to the offensive himself. He began by announcing that the House would do a better job with five hundred tradesmen instead of nobles and gentlemen.[53] He then settled in to continue the tactics he had used since 1819. On 22 February, he attacked the navy estimates with his usual vigor, pointing out a myriad of inefficiencies. This time the government counterattacked with devastating effectiveness. It was a sign that the administration intended to take Hume more seriously than in the past. John Wilson Croker, secretary to the Admiralty and, Canning excepted, perhaps the Tories' best spokesman in the Commons, berated Hume for his misinformation about the navy.[54] Croker noted errors Hume had made in geography and in the use of statistics. Hume had, said Croker, "mistaken land for water" and "storehouses for ships." Since it was apparent that the ministry would have no trouble defeating Hume's motion for an investigation into the condition of the navy, Croker aimed his speech, as Hume had so often done in the past, beyond the two hundred or so in the Commons. The secretary of the Admiralty was incensed that Hume and H. G. Bennet (the Scotsman's chief lieutenant in the attack on the navy) had intimated that he was the owner or editor of *John Bull*. Croker had no connection with the paper.[55]

Croker wanted to make Hume appear foolish to his supporters. In that he failed, but the ministry's decisive defeat (144–54) of Hume's motion deflated the radical reformers.[56] There was no Whig support and the Tory waverers would have nothing to do with this sort of retrenchment. The excitement of the public gatherings had not carried over into the House of Commons. The hope of making some dent in the government's forces (a hope in which many radicals had indulged late in 1821) quickly dissipated. From expectations of an improved climate for reform, the radical opposition now faced the grim and continuing prospect of bearing Hume's long, dull speeches on some aspect or other of a boring budget without the slightest possibility of defeating the administration.[57]

Hume continued to dissect each part of the navy estimates until 18 March. Ricardo, Creevey, Folkestone, and a few others remained loyal, but most had no heart for his daily tirades. Moreover, Croker and his associates were relentless in exposing the slightest errors made by Hume. "Doctor Hume of Montrose is ... incorrigible," wrote the *Leeds Intelligencer* in late February, and there were not many who disagreed with the judgment.[58] Some weeks later Mrs. Arbuthnot observed that "Mr. Hume

---

[55]Brightfield, *Croker*, 50–55.
[56]*Hansard*, second series, 6: 61.
[57]Mitchell, *Whigs in Opposition*, 164; Amundson, "Joseph Hume," 123.
[58]28 February 1822.

has been detected and exposed in many false statements, and his own party are now beginning to turn against him as they are jealous of his popularity."[59] Much of this opinion was shared by John Cam Hobhouse. Hobhouse had praised Hume in August 1821; but on 22 March, 1822 he wrote, "Hume was detected in and owned an error he made in half pay [accounts]—there is a general feeling of uneasiness on all sides—respecting these details of Hume, and he daily produces less effect."[60]

Adding to the problems for the opposition (radical and moderate) was the improved strength of Liverpool's ministry. The ministry entered 1822 with a revenue surplus of five million pounds, and thus Liverpool could see no need to tremble over charges of inefficiency and wastefulness. This surplus put the administration in a position to reduce certain taxes to appease the complaints of country gentlemen. In addition to a better financial condition, there were cabinet changes that indicated a "new constructiveness and energy."[61] In January Robert Peel succeeded Viscount Sidmouth as home secretary and in February C. W. W. Wynn replaced C. B. Bathurst as president of the Board of Trade.[62] It is arguable whether Peel and Wynn were more "liberal" in their social, political, and economic ideas than Sidmouth and Bathurst; but they did give the ministry a greater vitality. Peel had a good grasp of problems in Ireland (he had served as Irish secretary from 1813–1819), and he was known to have specific reforms in mind.

The direct political advantage gained from the cabinet alterations is a matter of some uncertainty. Liverpool insisted that he made the changes strictly for political expediency. He thought Peel would improve the ministry's strength in the House of Commons. There seemed every reason to think that Peel and Canning (generally acknowledged the best speaker for the government) would overawe the opposition. But in this the prime minister miscalculated. Peel was so concerned with his work in the Home Office that he gave little help in the House. Canning, meanwhile, was angered by some of the ministerial changes and concern existed that he might bolt to the opposition. This was an unlikely prospect, but it is clear that Canning and Peel were not the dynamic duo Liverpool expected in 1822.

In his study of the Liverpool ministry, J. E. Cookson argues that the "real" political benefit of the new men in the government was that they "broadened the bottom of the administration." By expanding the base of support, so the argument runs, the prime minister absorbed the waverers who might pose a threat to the stability of the government. This left only the Whigs and radicals as potential allies against the administration. Since the Whigs were as afraid of the radicals' "republican" leanings as the Tories, they would not agree to such an alliance.[63] The problem with this reasoning is that the waverers would never have deserted the government

---

[59] *Journal of Mrs. Arbuthnot, 1820–1832*, 1: 153.
[60] 22 March 1822, BL, Add. MS. 56544.
[61] Hilton, *Corn, Cash, Commerce*, 165.
[62] Sidmouth remained in the cabinet without office until 1824.
[63] Cookson, *Lord Liverpool's Administration*, 338–39.

on a crucial vote anyway. The administration already had firm control in Parliament. Peel and Wynn were important to the cabinet because they did their work better than their predecessors, not because they increased the prime minister's support in the Commons.

The strength of the Liverpool ministry, politically and qualitatively, proved almost as discouraging for Hume as it did for his Whig and radical colleagues. The *Hansard* reporters recorded only twenty-eight speeches by the Scotsman between April and July. This was about one-third the total recorded in February and March. Although the reporters did not set down every address made by Hume (they resented his late night speech-making and sometimes left the House when he rose to speak), his exuberance had clearly ebbed since the opening of the session. But even a subdued Hume was twice as enthusiastic as most of his associates. He told Charles Arbuthnot (joint secretary of the Treasury) in June that he would allow no estimate to pass without "being badgered."[64] On 20 July he made a long presentation on the state of the economy. This effort was born of frustration rather than from any expectation of reviving the spirit of his followers. In the course of his remarks he condemned the government for failing to take steps to reduce spending, and castigated the landed families for letting the administration get away with such negligence. He concluded by offering thirty-eight resolutions on the economy, none of which gained any significant support.[65]

At the end of the 1822 session, Hume returned to Scotland for several weeks. There he received praise for his conduct in the House of Commons. Dinners were held in his honor in Aberdeen and Montrose, and local officials congratulated him for pushing the government toward becoming more accountable to public demands. Hume received credit for forcing ministers to give detailed reports of spending, and also with causing appropriations to be explained in a way "the people" could understand. The approbation heaped on him in Scotland pleased Hume, but it did not fool him into thinking his achievements had been of great moment.[66] He knew that major reform (not the small doses handed out by Peel)[67] was still some distance down the road. No free-trade radical could feel optimistic about the future until Parliament was substantially overhauled.[68] He had no illusions that the majority of the Whigs, whatever they might say in public, were anxious to carry out reform of representation. In fact, during his appearances in Scotland he "disavowed all connexion" with the Whigs.[69] They were not interested in taking the bold steps necessary to change the country.

Hume's first four years in Parliament had brought him wide-spread recognition. He was said to be one member of Parliament who put "the

[64]*Journal of Mrs. Arbuthnot, 1820–1832*, 1: 166; A. Aspinall, *Three Early Nineteenth Century Diaries* (London, 1952), 23n.
[65]*Morning Chronicle*, 22 July 1822.
[66]*The Scotsman*, 16 September 1822.
[67]See Norman Gash, *Mr. Secretary Peel* (Cambridge, Mass., 1961).
[68]*Liverpool Mercury*, 11 October 1822.
[69]Tierney to Lady Holland, October 6, 1822, BL, Add. MS. 51586.

people's" concerns above his own or those of his wealthy colleagues. He articulated in the Commons many of the anxieties expressed at county meetings throughout England. When things did not go well for Hume in the House (and they usually did not), he could always be assured of a warm greeting outside.

CHAPTER III.

"VOICE OF THE PEOPLE," 1823–1827

The fact that so little of Hume's correspondence has survived is especially troublesome in trying to explain his political activities from the end of 1822 until the collapse of the Liverpool government early in 1827. It would help to know more of his thoughts about himself and his family, more about the nature of his friendship with Place, Ricardo, and Mill, and more about what he thought he was accomplishing during these years. It would also be helpful to have a fuller account of Hume's reaction to the scandal that touched his life in 1826.

Much that happened between 1824 and 1826 ought to have given Hume satisfaction. The Liverpool administration made sporadic attempts at retrenchment; and, thanks to a realistic concern to protect its majority in the House of Commons, showed an inclination to follow policies that encouraged freer trade, if not Free Trade.[1] The government's policies seemed to complement a much livelier economy in 1823. The repeal of the Combination Laws—a major objective for Hume—was achieved with ministerial support in 1824. Beyond this the ministry showed a more enlightened attitude toward difficulties in Ireland (though there were notable exceptions), and a willingness to relax some of England's Draconian legal codes. Moreover, Hume must have appreciated how Liverpool's cabinet improved after 1821. Peel joined it as home secretary in January 1822, Canning became foreign secretary in September 1822, Frederick Robinson replaced Vansittart (a man Hume considered incompetent) as chancellor of the Exchequer in January 1823, and William Huskisson entered the cabinet as president of the Board of Trade in October 1823. All of these individuals were of quite high calibre and gave promise of continuing the "liberal" policies that increased the popularity of the Tory regime.

In the long run, however, Hume found little reason to rejoice in any of the aforementioned developments. The "minor reforms" (as the radicals referred to them) carried out by the ministers were strictly ameliorative from Hume's perspective, and the substantive reforms could not begin until Parliament reformed itself. It was thought by the radicals in 1822 that parliamentary reform was not far from reality; but the improved economic conditions in 1823, the ministry's new vitality, and the government's successful effort to frighten moderates by holding out the spectre of democracy and republicanism, dashed this expectation. The reform meetings of 1821–1822, in which Hume was so prominent, were not duplicated until 1830.

In 1825, Lord Lansdowne wrote, "the prosperity of the country has driven [parliamentary] reform almost out of the heads of the reformers."[2]

---

[1] Barry Gordon, *Economic Doctrine*, 14–21; Cookson, *Lord Liverpool's Administration*, 300–301.

[2] Quoted in Mitchell, *Whigs in Opposition*, 182.

For Whigs like Lansdowne this may have been true, but parliamentary reform was still very much in Hume's head. Although often disillusioned, and nearly always in the minority, Hume continued to spar with ministers on a regular basis. He did this while Whigs, Tories, and even some radical colleagues, castigated him for any number of sins. He was charged with intemperance, with delaying the business of the House, and with encouraging rebellion. These were old accusations to be sure, but their accumulated effect eventually reduced Hume's stature in Parliament to that of a stubborn obstructionist.

The conservative press constantly and viciously ridiculed Hume in the mid-1820s. *John Bull* had the most success in making Hume appear dull-witted. It pointed out his odd, and one suspects attention-getting, penchant for creating words on the spot. Such examples as "fustifigation," "congloberation," and "collification" were, said *John Bull*, "Hume words" which he made up as needed.[3] The paper did not fail to mention the time Hume, in discussing certain allegations made by Canning against radical reformers, concluded his remarks by stating: "I am sorry to say that the Right Honourable Gentleman opposite is one of the greatest allegators that ever sat in this House."[4] The occasions when Hume's comments, wittingly or unwittingly, provided the House with a light moment were not frequent enough. There was more than a little truth in the government's sarcastic claim in 1827 that "Hume's influence is unquestionably on the increase, for when he rises the other members prepare to go home."[5]

That the Scotsman persevered in the face of this continuing onslaught of abuse amazed his contemporaries.[6] They concluded that personal attacks could not faze him. Somehow, he seemed impervious to all rebukes. Only in rare instances did Hume acknowledge any aspersions on his character or intelligence. The explanation for this is that Hume decided the Tories were going to bombard him no matter what he did or said and there was little use in rebuttal. Then, too, he saw in the attention he gained in the Tory press an opportunity to further disseminate his views on reform. What Hume may not have known, or what he may have put out of his mind, is that many in opposition agreed with the Tories (for different reasons) on the value of his conduct in the Commons. As we shall discuss, this was especially true after 1825. Hobhouse, Folkestone, Milton, et al., generally kept their thoughts among themselves, but it is clear that they saw Hume as a nuisance to the cause of reform. While they found him a most personable companion apart from parliamentary business, they complained to each other that he could never keep his mouth shut and that he lacked sufficient discretion.

Outside of Parliament, Hume's popularity did not diminish between 1823 and 1827. He remained the most visible spokesman for reform in the lower House. He earned the continuing respect and admiration of those

[3] *John Bull*, 13 March 1826.
[4] Ibid.
[5] *The Courier*, 27 February 1827.
[6] *Morning Chronicle*, 10 May 1826.

who thought themselves forgotten by the "system." Hume's appeal to this
large segment of the population stayed constant, and was not influenced to
any great extent by economic ups and downs.

As he had from 1819 through 1822, Hume dissected every budget bill
that came before the House. He precipitated more than one-half of all
divisions on economic matters between 1823 and 1830.[7] In his *Political
Register,* William Cobbett generously applauded the Scotsman's determination to "force retrenchment." Such publicity from Cobbett is one reason
for Hume's popularity among non-parliamentary radicals. He also won
praise for his stand on questions relating to Ireland. Hume gave support to
Daniel O'Connell's Catholic Association and strongly opposed any attempt
to pass legislation outlawing the association. At the same time, Hume
bitterly criticized the Orange Societies in Ireland. He saw them as nothing
more than organizations determined to intimidate the Catholic majority.
He blamed the tactics of the Orangemen for creating violent disturbances,
the same charge that ministers had made against O'Connell's association.

Hume also condemned the activities of the established Church and never
failed to insist, in each session after 1822, that the Protestant power should
be reduced in Ireland. Invariably, he pointed to the evils of non-residency,
and to the excessive numbers of archbishops and bishops. On numerous
occasions he moved for a select committee to study the Anglican Church in
Ireland with an eye toward preparing the way for reform.[8] Although his
motion always failed, the radical press carried stirring accounts of his
struggle against oppression in Ireland.

The reform issue that occupied most of Hume's time from 1823 through
1825 was the attempt to repeal the Combination Laws. It was an
undertaking that made Hume a hero with the industrial workers. In the
midst of repeated setbacks in the Commons, the ultimate elimination of the
Combination Laws must stand as a major triumph for Hume and the
free-trade radicals. Yet, this success did not prove to be a "victory" in the
conventional sense, for repeal had the active (if not enthusiastic) support of
several members of the administration, including William Huskisson.
Moreover, the repeal measure moved through Parliament with scarcely
any notice, and the *Hansard* reporter made no mention of it at all on the
day of its final approval.

The laws forbidding combinations (unions) came into existence rather
piecemeal during the course of the eighteenth century. They were directed
against journeymen tradesmen who, in the interest of protecting their
livelihood, tried to form combinations. In 1799 Parliament passed a general
law which forbade "unlawful combinations of workmen."[9] The legislation

---

[7]Mitchell, *Whigs in Opposition,* 182.

[8]See *Hansard,* second series, 8: 367–90.

[9]See Sidney and Beatrice Webb, *The History of Trade Unionism* (London, 1894), chap. 3;
Wallas, *Francis Place,* 197; S. Maccoby, *English Radicalism, 1786–1832* (London, 1855),
514–17; R. G. Kirby and A. E. Musson, *The Voice of the People: John Doherty, 1798–1854*
(Manchester, 1975), 13–14.

could not prevent unions from starting, particularly under the guise of a benefit society, but it did enable a master to punish selected workers for their union activity. If an unemployed tradesman, for example, refused work offered by an employer, he was liable to be imprisoned or impressed into the army or navy.[10]

Hume's interest in the Combination Laws came from his opinion that they placed restrictions on the free market for labor and gave an unfair advantage to masters. Employers could "combine" to keep wages low without penalty, but tradesmen had no way to upgrade conditions of labor without harassment. Workers were rarely given a fair hearing by local magistrates. Hume did not oppose the Combination Laws because he supported unions; quite the contrary, he thought repealing the laws would obviate the need for such organizations. He had the mistaken idea that masters and workers could handle their differences calmly and reasonably once the threat of punishment was removed. He shared with Francis Place the view that the Combination Laws held down wages, degraded workers, and caused unnecessary friction.[11]

In the House of Commons, Hume took charge of the repeal effort. It was widely believed at the time, and by most historians ever since, that Place directed the activities of his Scottish friend from outside the walls of Parliament. Place did not shy from taking credit for bringing about repeal. He claimed to have created pressure to abolish the laws among workmen and to have charted each step by Hume in the Commons. Place gave no thanks whatever to workingmen's leaders for repeal agitation, and praised Hume only to the extent that he followed his (Place's) instructions.[12] Graham Wallas was so convinced by Place's account of the matter that he was moved to write "the repeal of the Combination Laws in 1821–25 was the most striking piece of work that Place carried through single-handed."[13] This is a substantial exaggeration, yet there is no gainsaying the influence Place brought to bear in preparing the way for repeal.

Although he had opposed the Combination Laws since before 1800, Place began to attack the anti-union measures in earnest in 1814. He wrote articles (for whatever newspapers would publish them) on why the laws should be abolished. Over the years he had collected voluminous evidence on the injustices created by the legislation.[14] In 1816 William Cobbett lent his support to the early stages of the repeal campaign. Although he broke with the free-traders over the new Poor Law in 1834, Cobbett's views and those of the free-trade radicals nearly always coincided before that time.[15]

[10]Kirby and Musson, *John Doherty*, 33.
[11]Wallas, *Francis Place*, 199–200. See discussion in E. P. Thompson, *Making of the English Working Class* (London, 1961), 566–69.
[12]Kirby and Musson, *John Doherty*, 34. See Barry Gordon, *Economic Doctrine and Tory Liberalism* (Macmillan, 1979), 26–38. Also Frank W. Fetter, "The Rise and Decline of Ricardian Economics," *History of Political Economy*, 17(1969): 67–84.
[13]Wallas, *Francis Place*, 197.
[14]See BL, Add. MSS. 27799–806.
[15]Kirby and Musson, *John Doherty*, 34. Unlike Place and Hume, Cobbett looked forward to the successful creation of workers' combinations.

Cobbett and Place took advantage of every dispute between workmen and masters to push their point of view.[16]

The cause received a further boost in 1818 when J. Wade, a woolcomber, began a publication called the *Gorgon*. According to Place, he and Bentham helped to finance the weekly paper. With Place supplying the information, Wade wrote about the virtues of free trade and why it was necessary to repeal the Combination Laws. The *Gorgon* no doubt had some impact on members of Parliament and might well have influenced Hume to become more active in the cause.[17] On 22 June 1819 Hume presented a petition against the laws from tradesmen and mechanics in London and Westminster. He also said that he would shortly introduce a repeal measure.[18]

Based on letters which he wrote to Hobhouse and Thomas Hodgskin, Place apparently hoped that repeal might occur as early as 1820. He expected that a select committee to study the Combination Laws would be established in 1819 and a bill would be introduced soon after. "The repeal of the Combination Laws," he wrote to Hobhouse in August 1819, "would make thousands of reformers among the master tradesmen and manufacturers."[19] He promised to keep the pressure on to assure that the achievement of this goal would not be delayed.

Place proved to be overly optimistic on the timing of repeal. With Parliament strained on the issues relating to the Peterloo tragedy, the Six Acts, the Caroline affair, and general unrest, the Combination Laws did not seem so important. The enthusiasm in the radical camp at the end of 1821, created in no small way by the public response to Hume's retrenchment campaign, brought a renewed interest in the Combination Laws. By this time, Hume had become as determined an opponent of the laws as Place. Indeed, Hume put a much greater emphasis than did Place on the repeal of all restrictions against the emigration of artisans and on the abolition of all laws limiting the exportation of machinery. Whereas Place wanted to focus primarily, if not excusively, on the anti-union laws, Hume saw all of these matters as interconnected. He wanted workers to be free to sell their labor to the highest bidder wherever work existed. The Combination Laws and the laws against the emigration of artisans to the Continent prevented this free market exchange. The laws restricting exportation of machinery were detrimental to the economic freedom of both manufacturers and workers. Hume's broader view of the situation may be, in part, attributed to the influence of David Ricardo. Hume and Ricardo had cooperated in the Commons since 1819, and the former seldom gave a speech on economic matters without consulting the latter.[20]

[16]Kirby and Musson, *John Doherty*, 34.

[17]See Wallas, *Francis Place*, 205; Kirby and Musson, *John Doherty*, 34–35.

[18]See discussion in M. Dorothy George, "The Combination Laws," *Economic History Review*, 6 (1936): 172–78 and M. Dorothy George, "The Combination Laws Reconsidered," *Supplement to Economic Journal* (May, 1927), 214–28.

[19]Place to Hobhouse, 16 August 1819 and Place to Hodgskin, 8 September 1819, BL, Add. MS. 27798. Also quoted in Wallas, *Francis Place*, 205–6.

[20]Hume to Place, 10 September 1819, BL, Add. MS. 27798.

Hume showed some inclination to bring forward a repeal bill during the 1822 session, but circumstances were not favorable. He needed more time to marshal support. Towards the end of the 1822 session, Hume told Place that many in opposition were prepared to agree to an investigation into the Combination Laws; and, most promising, several members of Liverpool's administration, including Huskisson, were willing to accept the appointment of a select committee.[21] Huskisson's flexibility on the Combination Laws had little to do with any concern for the well-being of the workingmen, and less to do with any interest in free-trade theory. Huskisson's primary motivation was to prevent the Combination Laws from developing into a workers' *cause célèbre*.[22]

With Huskisson's tacit approval, and with the rising demand on the outside, it seemed the 1823 session would provide the perfect time to proceed with repeal. But the assault by Place, Hume, and Huskisson on the Combination Laws was outflanked by Peter Moore, a member from Coventry. On 3 March 1823 Moore surprised the better known opponents of the Combination Laws by moving for leave to bring in a bill to "amend" all such laws. The sweeping nature of Moore's proposal, and the fact that it preceded any consideration through committee, brought heavy criticism from the ministers.[23] When Moore saw that he had no chance to carry repeal, he agreed to delay discussion of his bill until the next session of Parliament. In the interim he and his friends would make an attempt to unite workers behind his measure.[24]

Hume did not appear distressed by Moore's effort, but Place clearly thought that the member from Coventry had trespassed on his territory. He wrote to Hume, "the bill is drawn with much ability, but under direction of a person who knows little about laws." Place further provided a list of his objections to Moore's proposal, and recommended that in future debate on the Combination Laws Hume ought not to mention it at all.[25] Moore's bill irritated Place because it was not based on the principles of political economy. The bill was actually inspired by Gravener Henson, a workingmen's leader in Nottingham, who had no use for political economists, and who wanted to see unions proliferate after the Combination Laws were repealed.

In the House of Commons, Hume intended to blunt Moore's effort by moving for a committee to study the Combination Laws as early as possible in the 1824 session. Even before Parliament met for the first time on 3 February, discussion of the Combination Laws had reached a peak of excitement. Most of the reason for this is traceable to the growing assertion of workers' displeasure. This unhappiness developed, for the most part, independent of Place's urgings. Men like Henson and John Doherty had a much greater impact on the workingmen. Place also had little to do with

---

[21]BL, Add. MS. 27798.
[22]See discussion of this point in chapt. 2, above.
[23]*Hansard*, second series, 8; 366.
[24]See Wallas, *Francis Place*, 208; Kirby and Musson, *John Doherty*, 35.
[25]Place to Hume, 3 May 1823, BL, Add. MS. 27800.

arousing demand for repeal in the House of Commons. He did submit articles to the *Black Dwarf* and he did provide much of the information for a comprehensive essay on the subject by J. R. McCulloch in the *Edinburgh Review,* but the influence of such writings seems unimportant. The fact that workers were restive, and that many of them blamed the Combination Laws for their misery, persuaded more politicians to back repeal than any well-reasoned essay. From the ministerial side there was a prevailing view that the Combination Laws were not worth a major fight.

Although support for repeal obviously was on the upswing, all was not smooth sailing in 1824. Huskisson favored action to assuage the workers, but he hoped to avoid controversy over Moore's 1823 bill. Huskisson therefore asked Hume to drop plans for a committee to study the Combination Laws, and to move instead for a committee to study the related issues of emigration of artisans and exportation of machinery. Hume assented to this arrangement because he feared that discussion of Moore's proposal could create a division in any committee established to study the Combination Laws. Moore's attitude toward political economy would be certain to alienate many members who supported repeal.[26]

This change of plans greatly distressed Place. On 5 February, he sent out a circular encouraging workers' societies to petition Parliament demanding that all restrictive legislation be abolished.[27] Almost simultaneously he learned of Hume's compromise with Huskisson. He immediately set out to convince Hume that he should not delay consideration of the Combination Laws. In this instance, it appears that Place had a decisive influence. In a letter to Hume, which Place wanted shown to Huskisson, he explained that Moore would continue to fight for his bill no matter what sort of committee the House created. He recommended full consideration of the Combination Laws and the inclusion of Moore on the committee. "Moore is not a man to be put aside," wrote Place, "and the only way to put him down is to let him talk his nonsense in the committee, where being outvoted he will be less [troublesome] in the House."[28]

In another letter to Hume, not intended for Huskisson to see, Place reminded his friend how much he had done to "prepare people to expect your motion [for a committee to study repeal] and many thousands do expect it."[29] He then mentioned all of the workers he had visited and all the circulars he had sent. He feared that if Hume did not act, Moore would take advantage of the petitions he (Place) had instigated.[30]

Over the next several days Hume did reconsider, and after discussion with Huskisson, he decided to follow Place's recommendation. Hume brought the matter before the Commons on 12 February in a speech that must be put among his best. He paid tribute to David Ricardo for helping to crystallize his ideas on the Combination Laws, and noted that before his

[26]Place to Hobhouse, 21 January 1824, BL, Add. MS. 27798.
[27]Kirby and Musson, *John Doherty,* 35.
[28]Place to Hume, 7 February 1824, quoted in Wallas, *Francis Place,* 209.
[29]Ibid., 211.
[30]Ibid.

death in September 1823, Ricardo had planned to work with him to achieve repeal in the Commons. Mention of Ricardo was a wise, as well as heartfelt, gesture on Hume's part. Except perhaps for the ultra-Tories, nearly all members in the House agreed that Ricardo had made great contributions to debates on economic matters. Those who did not like his free-trade theories nevertheless had found him a man of humility and integrity.[31] In addition to his comments on Ricardo, Hume did not let pass a chance to praise ministers who had "shown a disposition to simplify complicated laws and to repeal others that were venerable but ancient."[32]

Hume then went on to explain that he wished to propose a select committee to study emigration of artisans, exportation of machinery, and the Combination Laws. He thought the House ought to repeal every law that shackled free movement of labor. Why should a skilled worker be denied a basic right? As was required of free-traders in discussing such issues, Hume referred to Adam Smith in defense of his position. After Hume moved to create a committee, Huskisson rose to endorse the motion.[33] Huskisson made it clear, however, that he would leave open how his opinion might develop on the merits of the case. The House then approved Hume's proposal and he named his committee. It was weighted in favor of a free-trade philosophy. Among the members appointed were Hobhouse, Thomas Acland, Frankland Lewis, and H. G. Bennet. Peter Moore and Huskisson were included, but their participation was expected to be minimal. Hume asked for advice from any others who might wish to give opinions to the committee.[34]

In his position as chairman, Hume immediately assumed control of the Select Committee on Artisans and Machinery. The committee heard evidence from masters, workers, and other interested persons. Francis Place was one of the first to testify. He explained how he had helped to form combinations in the past twenty years for journeymen tailors, plumbers, and carpenters. It was necessary to create unions to increase wages and to provide some protection from masters who had combined to suppress the reasonable demands of their workers. The employers, Place stressed, were never prosecuted for such illegal activity. A combination of workingmen was the only way, said Place, to make the strike a useful weapon. He predicted that the elimination of the Combination Laws would not have a significant effect on journeymen's wages, but he thought there would be greater harmony in industry.[35]

After his appearance as a witness, Place asked to serve as Hume's assistant, but other members of the committee objected that they did not wish to be "dictated to."[36] They had accepted the long-held, erroneous

---

[31]See Gordon, *Political Economy in Parliament*, 12–13.

[32]*Hansard*, second series, 10: 141–46.

[33]Ibid.

[34]Ibid., 150–51. Moore, still disgruntled over the reaction to his motion in 1823, did not attend the meetings.

[35]"First Report From the Select Committee on Artisans and Machinery," *British Sessional Papers* (House of Commons, 1824), 44–47.

[36]Wallas, *Francis Place*, 212.

opinion, that Hume was Place's mouthpiece in the House of Commons. It is safe to assume that Hume did not want Place to attend the committee's sessions. The Scotsman thought his knowledge of the subject every bit as thorough as Place's. Place could still be of help to Hume, but away from the committee room.

Place assisted Hume by interviewing as many witnesses as possible before they testified. He discovered that most of the potential witnesses had no interest in advancing the cause of free trade. They were concerned with getting higher wages. Furthermore, they were reluctant to support any bill sponsored by the free-trade radicals. Place had to convince them that Hume's committee offered them their only chance to get the Combination Laws repealed. After Place spoke with each witness, he prepared briefs for Hume to use during the appearance of the individual before the committee. The briefs contained questions Hume should ask and responses he should expect. Place also attached documents to substantiate the testimony or to enable Hume to field objections. Just how helpful this was is questionable. Place thought his information crucial to Hume's success, but in light of Hume's well-established understanding of the arguments on both sides, and given the fact that his committee already seemed predisposed to recommend repeal, it seems that once again Place claimed too much for himself.[37] Moreover some witnesses were so obviously coached by Place that there may have been a backlash effect with committee members. The one great service that Place did for Hume was to make an index (from minutes given to him by Hume) of each day's proceedings.[38]

The committee was greatly interested in learning about the organization of workingmen's clubs, the dues paid, and the specific reasons for the existence of each association. Hatters, plumbers, shipwrights, cotton spinners, and carpenters all appeared to discuss their particular concerns. Some attention was given to the relationship between apprentices and journeymen and whether the one group supported the other.[39] One of the most impressive witnesses was Gravener Henson, the Nottingham leader, who testified that many English workers on the Continent would return if wages were decent.[40]

The committee also heard evidence from such free-trade theoreticians as Thomas Malthus and J. R. McCulloch. Their presence clearly established the bias of the committee. Hume asked them very general questions and they were allowed to discuss their ideas at length. Both men gave strong reasons for removing all laws that limited the rights of labor. Malthus urged that England permit the exportation of machinery since it was impossible to keep new technology secret anyway. Neither Malthus nor McCulloch advocated unions and both agreed that the motivation for

[37]See Kirby and Musson, *John Doherty*, 34–37.
[38]23 February 1824, BL, Add. MS. 27801.
[39]"Fourth Report of Select Committee on Artisans and Machinery," *British Sessional Papers* (House of Commons, 23 March, 1824), 191–206.
[40]"Fifth Report of Select Committee on Artisans and Machinery," *British Sessional Papers* (House of Commons, 15 April 1824), 554–56.

forming such organizations would disappear when the Combination Laws were removed.[41]

When all the evidence had been heard, Hume made a bold move that hastened the end of the Combination Laws. He decided to by-pass the wrangling over minor points that usually accompanied the preparation of final committee reports. Instead of writing a full-fledged report, he proposed that the committee approve short resolutions for presentation in the House of Commons. The committee accepted this idea without significant complaint. Considering the long-winded dissertations Hume frequently gave in the Commons, the brevity and clarity of the statements he brought before the committee are nothing short of remarkable. They were quickly approved. On 3 May 1824 Hume read them to the House as the Sixth Report of the Select Committee on Artisans and Machinery. The committee had concluded that the Combination Laws should be repealed, that laws regarding disputes between masters and workers should be consolidated and amended, and that laws preventing artisans from seeking work abroad should be removed.[42] Hume then introduced bills to accomplish these three objectives. The legislation was written by Hume and a barrister who had been approved by the attorney-general. In his account of these events, Place contends that he altered the printed bills before they were distributed in the House.[43] He may well have done so, but whatever changes were made were surely not significant.

Less than two weeks after Hume presented the committee's resolutions, the bills quietly passed their third reading. The *Hansard* reporter took no notice of the event. Only *The Times* complained about the progress of repeal in the Commons. On Saturday, 5 June, it urged members to "proceed with caution." The paper questioned whether the select committee understood and properly interpreted the evidence it heard. *The Times* saw repeal as an invitation for workers to organize unions, and, subsequently, to strike. The reaction of masters, argued the paper, would be to raise prices to compensate for lost income. Hume was furious when he read *The Times'* article. "It is important," he wrote to Place, "that the observations in the *Times* respecting our Combination Laws should be noticed in the [*Morning*] *Chronicle* of Monday, if possible—For which purpose I hope you will prevail on the editor. . . ."[44] On Monday, 7 June, the *Morning Chronicle* did take notice of *The Times'* article and defended the committee's work as Hume had hoped. This episode was a minor one, but it indicates how carefully Hume protected the committee's recommendations.

The dispatch with which the bills progressed still amazes, but it certainly indicated a widespread acceptance of repeal (albeit for diverse reasons)

---

[41]See *The Times,* 5 June 1824; John and Barbara Hammond, *The Town Labourer* (London, 1967, reprint), 137; "Sixth Report of Committee on Artisans and Machinery," *British Sessional Papers* (House of Commons, 10 May 1824), 592–601.

[42]*Hansard,* second series, 11: 811–14.

[43]Wallas, *Francis Place,* 215–16.

[44]Hume to Place, 6 June 1824, BL, Add. MS. 27801.

among the members. This need not detract from the skill displayed by
Hume in guiding the legislation through the House. Whenever he thought
a chance for success existed, Hume could combine his proclivity for hard
work with efficiency. It was when he knew there was no chance for success,
as in the debates over the estimates, that he tended to go on forever without
much apparent purpose. If we can believe Place's memoir (far from a
certainty!), he was the one who told Hume to avoid making speeches on the
Combination Laws while the committee deliberated, and he was the one
who asked for the short resolutions rather than a lengthy final report. In
accepting Place's counsel on this matter (if that is what he did), Hume
showed that he recognized repeal of the Combination Laws was not a
hopeless endeavour, but one likely to end in triumph. His customary
harassing tactics had no purpose in these circumstances.

After the repeal legislation passed the House of Commons, it still had to
get through the Lords. Hume did not hesitate to impress upon the peers the
need to confirm the action taken in the Commons. He told Lord Lansdowne
not to allow anything to "dissuade" him from backing the repeal
measures.[45] He then wrote to Place:

I send you a letter from Lord Lansdowne and a copy of my answer to him. I have
also written to Lord Rosslyn to the same purport, and wish you to press through
McIntosh and Brougham the support of Lords Lauderdale, Ackland, etc. You
should send the several deputies [workers] now in town to the several Lords who
take a part, and to the Lord Chancellor, Lord Liverpool, to request their support for
the bills. I have written to Mr. Huskisson to get the support of Lord Liverpool, who
is still uncertain. A canvass for the bills must be made to ensure success.[46]

The efforts of Hume, Place, and Huskisson, however effective they may
have been, were probably unnecessary. The bills passed more quickly in
the Lords than they had in the Commons. So quietly had the bills become
law that, in July, a magistrate in Lancashire sentenced several cotton
weavers for behavior that was no longer punishable.[47]

While the bills did not gain much publicity in London or provincial
newspapers, workers were aware of the effort made by Hume in Parliament. He earned praise for his "diligence and ability" and for his "rare
talents and indefatigable exertion."[48] The workers assumed that Hume had
intended to make it easier for them to pressure employers into higher
wages. How little they understood what motivated free-trade radicals.
Hume expected unions to disappear after repeal, and he experienced
considerable anxiety when this did not occur.

In 1824 employment was high, trade was increasing, and prices were
rising. These circumstances encouraged workers to participate openly in
union activity and to strike for improved wages.[49] In Manchester alone,
shoemakers, dyers, spinners, calico printers and foundry workers struck

[45]Hume to Lansdowne (copy) 9 June 1824, BL, Add. MS. 27801.
[46]Hume to Place, 9 June 1824, BL, Add. MS. 27801.
[47]Hammond, *Town Labourer,* 137.
[48]See clippings in BL, Add. MS. 27801.
[49]Kirby and Musson, *John Doherty,* 36.

between July and December. The situation was similar in other parts of the country. By the end of the year employers clamored for a reimposition of the Combination Laws. Hume and Place were properly shaken by the workers' aggressiveness. In the autumn of 1824 they wrote letters to many labor leaders and numerous provincial newspapers asking that workers refrain from strikes and any violent conduct.[50] In one letter, dated 27 December, Hume asked for copies of all correspondence between workers and masters in anticipation of a challenge to the repeal legislation. He expressed particular concern over "secret unions" in Stockport, Dublin, Dumbarton, and Renfrewshire. He hoped that operatives would act in a "manner more moderate and prudent."[51]

The workingmen's militancy did not sufficiently abate, however, and on 29 March 1825, Huskisson brought the matter before the House of Commons. He admitted that he had not attended many of the meetings held by Hume's committee, but he felt compelled to discuss the consequences of "Hume's Act" to repeal the Combination Laws. There had been reports of violence on the part of workmen against employers. He did not wish to blame all workers for the conduct of a few, but he thought a new select committee on the Combination Laws was needed. The Commons swiftly gave its assent to a committee to investigate the conduct of workmen.[52]

Place wrote that Hume "was astonished" by Huskisson's speech. He attributed this to Hume's "too good opinion" of Huskisson who, according to Place, made a practice of deception.[53] Huskisson planned to appoint a committee of individuals who were not quite so sympathetic to the repeal legislation of 1824. There was no way, however, that he could avoid placing Hume on the committee. His role in the original committee and his popularity with the workers dictated that he should be included.

Although their position was not nearly as advantageous as it had been in 1824, Hume and Place did not vary their strategy. The committee's deliberations were delayed two weeks because of the Easter holidays, and Place used that time to muster his forces. He sent letters and circulars persuading tradesmen to send delegates to the committee to protest any attempt to reverse the action taken in 1824. Trades committees were formed in many areas to organize opposition. Place opened his house to workers' delegates and he and Hume did all they could to prepare these men to testify before the committee. When the committee began its session,[54] Huskisson did his best to present the case for the employers. Those who testified on behalf of masters and owners were reimbursed for time as well as expenses. It was only with the greatest difficulty that the workers' delegates were permitted to give evidence. They were not to be reimbursed for lost wages. Despite his own reservations about what had happened since July 1824, Hume defended the workers with his usual vigor; and, as he had done in 1824, he kept Place informed on the

[50]See BL, Add. MS. 27801.
[51]*The Scotsman,* 12 January 1825.
[52]*Hansard,* second series, 12: 1288–314.
[53]Wallas, *Francis Place,* 223–26.
[54]Thomas Wallace served as chairman.

committee's activities. Together they were able to blunt the strategy of Huskisson and his allies, and to force the committee to consider the difficult position of the journeymen. The fear of a widespread rebellion of workers was prominent in this committee of middle-class interests. Hume tried to impress upon the members that any attempt to reverse the decision made in 1824 would certainly encourage greater militancy. This argument had a salutary effect on the committee.

The bill drafted following the committee's hearings did not provide for the reinstatement of the Combination Laws. It did impose penalties for using "intimidation," "obstruction," or "molestation" to coerce employers. The measure led to heated debate in Parliament, with Hume providing most of the heat. Supporters of the bill contended it only differed from Hume's act in that it made it easier for a magistrate to detain someone accused of violent behavior. Hume countered by noting that masters had never proven charges of violence against workmen.[55] But the bill passed both Houses of Parliament and received royal approval on 5 July.[56]

Place declared that the 1825 bill represented a victory for Hume and himself. He based this claim on the fact that the Combination Laws were not revived. In general, organized workers saw the measure as a "serious setback," and trade union leader John Doherty tried desperately to defeat the legislation right to the end. As it developed, neither Place nor Doherty interpreted the consequences of the bill correctly. With its new penalties it was not quite the success for free-traders that Place imagined, but, contrary to the fears of Doherty, it did not prevent the advance of unions.[57]

Hume's view of the 1825 bill was somewhere between that of Place and Doherty. He did not like the new penalties, yet he was pleased that the restrictive laws were not restored. His efforts to protect the repeal of the Combination Laws had not hurt his popularity among workingmen throughout England. Except for certain working class leaders, Doherty among them, there was an understandable tendency to forget Hume's free-trade theories. Perhaps it was obvious that whatever principles were behind Hume's conduct, he showed genuine concern for the well-being of workingmen. There was much less support among workers for Place. Since he preferred to move in the shadows, he was never completely trusted. Doherty and Henson had no use for him at all.

Hume spent most of the autumn of 1825 touring in Scotland and in some of the manufacturing centers in England. He enjoyed this annual orgy of adulation from his constituents and from those who now spoke of him as the "voice of the people."[58] These visits renewed his spirits and helped to affirm in his mind that he carried on a necessary struggle against the anti-reformers. It also convinced him, wrongly of course, that the free-trade philosophy he espoused had support from the workingmen.

---

[55]*Hansard*, second series, 13: 1404. See "Report of Select Committee on Conduct of Workmen," *British Sessional Papers* (House of Commons, 6 June 1825), 515–21.

[56]Kirby and Musson, *John Doherty*, 37–38; Hammond, *The Town Labourer*, 140–142.

[57]Kirby and Musson, *John Doherty*, 38–39.

[58]*The Scotsman*, 21 July 1825.

Although the Combination Laws were Hume's immediate interest in 1824 and 1825, he still had time to decry the lack of initiative on parliamentary reform, Corn Law repeal, and numerous other matters pertaining to religious and civil liberties. From time to time he would bring these questions to the attention of the House in a general way. There was one matter (apart from those already mentioned) raised by Hume in 1824 and 1825 that caused quite a few waves in the Commons. He wanted to remove from committee any member who had an interest in a private bill being discussed by that committee. The "above stairs" committees were a disgrace, said Hume, because M.P.s with something to gain from a private bill did nothing but "canvass and influence" others. He pointed out that since these men were not permitted to vote when their bill came before the full House, they should not participate in committee. When there were objections, he agreed to settle for a committee to study the situation.[59] Nothing came of this, but some months later Hume moved that "no member shall vote [in committee] for or against any question in which he has a direct pecuniary interest." The motion was readily defeated with most arguing that it was unenforceable.[60]

In comparison with other matters, Hume did not consider the private bill issue of much importance. It does show, however, his inordinate concern (even among free-trade radicals) to have the House of Commons operate as openly and as free from self-serving interests as possible. The problem of secrecy in government was one that Hume attacked regularly in his career. He objected to any attempt to deceive the public by withholding information or providing misleading data. Hume knew that his righteous indignation at such practices would be unappreciated in the House, but it would solidify his reputation for integrity among his followers outside. How much greater, then, was the humiliation for Hume when he, the virtuous example, came under grave suspicion of scandal before the end of 1826.

When the 1826 parliamentary session began in February, Hume returned to the issues that had occupied most of his time between 1819 and 1823. He demanded a reduction in the navy and army estimates. He thought there were too many seamen and that, in peacetime, the number ought to be cut to a bare minimum.[61] As for the army, he thought it could do without a large appropriation for the Royal Military College.[62] Between 2 February and 27 April he spoke at least ninety times, and some of his speeches probably went unrecorded. In this blitz of words, Hume did make several suggestions that were worthy of serious consideration. He recommended that the ministers stop the practice of having each department—army, navy, etc.—request money from the government. Instead, he thought the administration should start with a specific sum and dole it out to the various agencies.[63] Hume also made a strong point when he advocated

---

[59] *Hansard*, second series, 11: 910–18.
[60] *Hansard*, second series, 12: 973–74.
[61] *Hansard*, second series, 14: 520–23.
[62] Ibid., 1119ff.
[63] Ibid., 521–23.

saving £25,000 by not granting funds to the Society for Promoting the Education of the Poor in Ireland. He rightly argued that the Society educated just one-half as many persons as it claimed, and did not have proper regard for the concerns of Roman Catholics.[64] In all of these matters Hume's complaints and suggestions were unheeded. The House was usually empty during his speeches; and when he pressed for a division, he could count on no more than thirty to forty votes.

The prospects for the opposition could scarcely have been worse than they were in the spring of 1826. With Hume carrying the battle, the Whigs might just as well have stopped attending altogether. "Opposition as a party is quite extinct," wrote Tierney to Holland, "and my only object now [is] to support that branch of the administration whose opinion comes the nearest to my own."[65] There was a general feeling of futility that pervaded the Whigs and a few radicals as well. Criticism of Hume's tactics began to appear in the radical press. No other than William Cobbett, who usually gave support to Hume, observed that while he (Hume) was "incessantly" at work to reduce public spending he had not been responsible "for one farthing" reduction. Cobbett allowed that Hume ought to have "the thanks of the whole nation for his good wishes, for his real desire to do the country good," but, in fact, he was "doing it [the country] no good at all." Moreover, concluded Cobbett, Hume exposed himself "to the open hostility of one party, and the secret hostility of the other."[66]

Cobbett's criticism, as might be expected, had no effect on changing Hume's behavior any more than criticism from Whigs and Tories. In April Hume continued his barrage. He argued for an end to all taxes on navigation. He reminded ministers that Ricardo had said that "under the freest competition British shipping would keep its ground against all rivals."[67] When there was little response to his lecture on shipping, Hume moved right ahead to another issue. He presented a petition calling for an official end to prosecution for religious beliefs. He thought it said something for an "enlightened age" when persons were still subject to imprisonment for up to five years for "thinking as they pleased on speculative [assumptions]."[68] He was pleased that Peel had never encouraged such prosecutions, but he thought it best to get rid of any law that punished individuals for religious convictions. Hume's presentation in this instance gave added fuel to those who already considered him an atheist. The "charge" that he had no religion (used by Tories whenever they had an opportunity) caused Hume political embarrassment more than once. Hume was probably not an atheist (if he was he did not admit it), yet his attitudes on religion were casual. He read the Bible and did not hesitate to quote from it when the occasion seemed appropriate, but he thought the scriptures were open to many interpretations. He had little use for organized Christianity. Although he claimed to be an Anglican, he

[64]*Hansard*, second series, 15: 81ff.
[65]Tierney to Holland, 10 March 1826, BL, Add. MS. 51584.
[66]*Political Register*, 25 March 1826.
[67]*Hansard*, second series, 15: 274.
[68]Ibid., 275–76.

remained an enemy to the power of the Church of England throughout his years in the House of Commons. This anti-established Church position, as well as an interest in the fullest measure of religious liberty, was shared by nearly all the free-trade radicals in Parliament.

Near the end of April, Hume began to show some irritation at having so little support in the opposition. At one point he said that "if the opposition would do their duty great results might be expected." This comment aroused anger (no doubt what Hume intended) from the opposition benches. Hume's old acquaintance, John Cam Hobhouse, responded to his barb. Hobhouse, one of Hume's loyal associates in the early 1820s, had grown disillusioned with the prospects for worthwhile opposition. When he rose to speak on 27 April, ostensibly on the question of parliamentary reform, he first noted that Hume "by some strange accident" was not in his place. Hobhouse then asked rhetorically "what does Hume mean by the opposition doing its duty?" He then answered the question. "I suppose," said Hobhouse, "he means coming down in force night after night, and voting upon every disputed question." Hobhouse thought this would result in having the ministerial members attend as well. The majorities and the minorities would increase, but the proportion would remain the same. He hoped that Hume henceforth would refrain from saying the opposition did not do its duty, for such a comment "creates illusion in the public that it [the opposition] can do something."[69] Hobhouse's argument did not silence Hume, although it did vividly describe the dilemma of the opposition in 1826. Aside from Hume, virtually no one, Whig or radical, saw any use in expending energy in the House of Commons. Hume continued to make his daily speeches; but there were few who heard much of what he said, and fewer still who stayed to vote on the issues he raised. The House had not been so poorly attended since the 1808 session when, for nearly the same reasons, the opposition had no life.

For Hume, the situation was to grow worse, much worse, within the next several months. He suffered a personal humiliation and an embarrassment that might have ended his popularity with the people. Whatever accusations Hume's enemies had made in the past, no one had ever seriously impugned his integrity. There had been talk about shady dealings during his days in India, and rather malicious intimations about his marriage to the daughter of Joseph Burnley, but this sort of behind the scenes gossip was common in parliamentary circles. Furthermore, Hume had encouraged the notion that he was above suspicion by demanding openness in government spending, the end of speculation, the elimination of sinecures, and righteous conduct from ministers. Nevertheless, in the autumn of 1826 Hume found scandal on his own doorstep. More surprising still, his indiscretion involved financial gain for himself. The proud defender of the public against the government's greedy hand had fallen victim to avarice. The affair that brought Hume such pain was known as the Greek Loan Scandal.

The background to Hume's involvement in the Greek Loan scheme is

[69]Ibid., 691–93.

easily traced. In March 1823 a Greek committee was formed in London to encourage England to assist the Greeks in their fight for national independence. In addition to Hume, the committee included such free-trade radicals as Hobhouse, Bentham, H. G. Bennet, Alexander Baring, and John Bowring. Some Whigs, including Edward Ellice (a friend to Hume who often slipped into the radical camp) and John Russell, also were members. Hume, Hobhouse, Ellice, and Bowring were the committee's most active participants.

The committee's immediate goal in 1823 was to raise as much money as possible through the sale of bonds. Right from the start Hume evinced some anxiety over the way in which the collected funds were being handled. He worried that the bonds might not be worth as much as the subscribers had paid. In October 1823, Hobhouse tried to reassure him by writing, "you will find matters not quite as bad as you at present suspect—It will be advisable I think to take the committee books at once into your own keeping to prevent interpretations. . . ."[70] The correspondence does not identify Hume's specific concerns, and, though tantalizing for the biographer, there is not enough evidence to speculate on why Hobhouse advised Hume to take the committee books into his "own keeping."

Whatever doubts Hume may have had about the sale of scrip, plans proceeded to arrange a loan for the Greek national government. The loan was to come from funds garnered through the sale of the bonds. In February 1824, the committee met several times with agents of the Greek government, Andreas Lureottis and Jean Orlando.[71] The amount of the loan was to be something over £800,000.[72] The money would be used by the Greeks to purchase various types of ocean-going vessels. The agreement included the proviso that all money sent from England to Greece had to be sanctioned by three members of the committee. Hume was one of the members selected for this role because he was considered to be exceptionally cautious on money matters. He did not betray his reputation. As it developed, Hume became a major stumbling block to getting the money to Greece.

Shortly after the arrangements for the loan were complete, Hume began to have doubts about Lureottis and Orlando. The Greek government refused to make any guarantees about how the money would be used. In August 1824, Hume questioned the entire project. He explained to Ellice that he felt a duty to "attend to the interest of subscribers as well as those of Greece. . . ."[73] His concern for the buyers of the Greek bonds came at just the time Hobhouse prepared to leave for Greece with the first payment. Hume refused to sign Hobhouse's instructions. Although the other two commissioners (Ellice and W. Loughman) had signed, Hobhouse said he would not go until all three had given approval. In a letter to Hobhouse,

---

[70]Hobhouse to Hume, 15 October 1823, BL, Add. MS. 36460.

[71]See John Francis, *Chronicles and Characters of the Stock Exchange* (London, 1849), 184; BL, Add. MS. 56548; University College, London (UCL), Creevey Papers (microfilm), paperbooks 17–24.

[72]Francis puts the amount at over £1,600,000, but Hobhouse says it was £800,000.

[73]Hume to Ellice, 5 August 1824, BL, Add. MS. 36460.

Ellice explained "some people have got it into Hume's head that the Greek loan should be cancelled."[74] When Hume learned of Hobhouse's refusal to leave England he decided, reluctantly, to sign the instructions.[75] While it is an enticing diversion to follow the mishandling (and subsequent chaos) of the Greek loan, we must stay with Hume.[76] His delay in signing Hobhouse's instructions, seemingly the result of high-minded concern for the subscribers, was actually the result of self-interest.

The nature of Hume's self-interest did not come into the open until October 1826. He seemed oblivious to the comeuppance in store for him as he went about preparing strategy for the parliamentary session that was scheduled to begin in November.[77] On 26, 27, and 28 October, *The Times* published accounts of how Greece had been deceived by those in charge of the Greek loan. Accusations were made against Bowring, Ellice, and Hobhouse; but *The Times* reserved its most telling blows for Hume. The Scotsman, so long a critic of government finagling and mismanagement, made a rather spectacular target. *The Times* described in detail how this "able arithmetician" had used shady methods to avoid suffering a financial loss.

When the Greek bonds were being sold in 1824, Hume subscribed to the issue in the amount of £10,000. The bonds quickly depreciated. This is what aroused Hume's concern early in 1824. As the slide continued, Hume began to look for a way out with as little loss as possible. It was this that caused him to think about cancelling the loan in the summer of 1824. Finally, in 1825 he asked the Greek deputies (Lureottis and Orlando) to relieve him of the anticipated loss. The Greeks were well aware of Hume's influential position on the Greek committee. They also knew that he was an outspoken proponent of Greek independence in the Commons. An agreement was reached and the bonds made repurchased from Hume. He lost only £1300 on the transaction.

Hume had reason to be pleased with the deal worked out on his behalf until the value of the bonds he had just sold moved upward. This was only one month after the negotiations with Lureottis and Orlando. Hume now insisted that Greek agents give him the £1300 he lost. He further requested that the Greeks pay thirty days' interest (£54) on the total! Once again the deputies complied with Hume's demands.[78] They did not wish to risk losing the Scotsman's vocal support. These dealings, like Hume's dealings in India, were not illegal, but they displayed a want of discretion that dismayed Hume's friends. Francis Place was among those who saw serious consequences for Hume. In his diary Place wrote, "It was . . . his love of money which in this case overcame his prudence. . . . He seems to have acted very reprehensibly

---

[74]Ellice to Hobhouse, 7 August 1824, BL, Add. MS. 36460.

[75]Ibid.

[76]See Francis, *Chronicles and Characters*, 285–90.

[77]BL, Add. MS. 35146, Place diary entry for 12 October 1826 and 24 October 1826.

[78]*The Times*, 28 October 1826; Francis, *Chronicles and Characters,* 289–90. The *Leeds Mercury* for 28 October also reported misdeeds by the Greek committee, but had no criticism for Hume. Hume was a favorite in Leeds for his role in the repeal of the Combination Laws. See *Life of Edward Baines* by his son Edward Baines (London, 1851), 135.

and can scarcely fail to have his usefulness greatly impaired by the transaction."[79] Since Hume's "usefulness" in the House of Commons had already reached a nadir in 1826, there was little left to impair.

Hume's reaction to the exposure of his questionable behavior put the lie to those who contended that he was impervious to ridicule and criticism. He sent explanations to the conservative *Morning Herald* and to the liberal *Morning Chronicle*. Place was not satisfied and said that Hume had done nothing more than confirm the details written in *The Times*. In self-defense Hume pleaded, "The worst, I think, that any man in candour can say against my conduct in this affair is that I may have evinced an over-anxiety to avoid a pecuniary loss, forced upon me by conduct of others. . . ."[80] These were weasel words and Hume must have known that his rationalization convinced no one. Hume then tried to turn opinion in his favor by offering to repay the £1300 with interest if two impartial men of his choice should think it necessary. *The Times* took note of Hume's offer and suggested that he act on his own and pay back the money.[81] *John Bull* also recommended he return the money. The paper, to the surprise of its readers, did not condemn Hume, but rather attributed his behavior to the "frailty of human nature" and his Scottish upbringing.[82]

At Hume's instigation, James Mill and Place met at Hume's Bryanston Square residence on 5 November to discuss the situation. Place records that Hume seemed greatly "agitated." He maintained that he had done no wrong and resolved to return the money. Hume mentioned that his wife had urged this course of action and so had *John Bull* and *The Times*. Mill agreed with this plan. There were, he said, a considerable number of "well meaning and weak-minded persons who would be satisfied with Hume's conduct if he returned the money. . . ." Place had an opposite view. He argued that returning the money amounted to an admission of wrongdoing. People would know with "Mr. Hume's attachment to money he would never have paid so large a sum had he not been quite conscious that he had no just right to hold it." Hume eventually decided to delay for one day any repayment until he could better judge what the public expected from him.[83]

The three men met again the next day for a final verdict on repayment. Mill reported that he had debated the issue with several persons, including Brougham and George Grote, and they had said that Hume should not repay. Each thought that by doing so he would "lessen his utility" and therefore do more harm to the public. Then, too, many might say that he paid back the money to keep Lureottis quiet on other "deals."[84] It was then agreed that Hume would not return the money. All three men hoped that no permanent damage had been done to Hume's career. One week later Place noted in his diary that Hume was "recovering his spirits" and that he

[79]BL, Add. MS. 35146, Place diary entry for 4 November 1826.
[80]Ibid. See *The Times*, 4 November 1826.
[81]*The Times*, 4 November 1826.
[82]*John Bull*, 4 November 1826 and 20 November 1826.
[83]BL, Add. MS. 35146, Place diary entry for 5 November 1826.
[84]Ibid., Place diary entry for 14 November 1826.

intended to proceed with his plan to move an amendment to the king's address at the opening of Parliament on 21 November.[85]

Weeks before any of the Greek scandal appeared in the newspapers, Hume had planned to use the king's opening speech as an opportunity to demand a variety of reforms. He had discussed his intentions with Place and Mill and they thought he would "be able to show very important matters to the people through the House."[86] All three men knew that the House would be nearly empty while Hume presented his amendment, but the purpose was an appeal to the people, not to the Commons. After the Greek scandal became news, Hume's determination to amend the king's speech quite naturally flagged. But by the middle of November he had decided to carry on. He imagined that such a rejoinder to the government would prove that he could not be shamed into silence by the recent revelations. He met with Place on 20 November and went over his proposed speech word for word. Place relates that they made every effort to keep it "short and clear to the public." Place ought to have realized that for Hume to achieve either brevity or clarity would have been accomplishment enough, but to suppose that he could succeed at both was surely asking the impossible.[87]

The next day, 21 November, the king's address was read to the Parliament. There was debate on the speech but nothing very noteworthy. Brougham made a rather perfunctory criticism to which Canning responded, and the debate seemed at an end. At that point, according to Canning,

to the great disappointment and dismay of the House, Mr. Hume presented himself and moved an amendment twice as long as the address . . . which branched into all imaginable subjects. Mr. Hume's amendment, which recommended all kinds of reforms, including that of the House of Commons, was seconded by Mr. Marshall, the new member from Yorkshire. . . .[88]

What Canning did not know is that, at the last moment, a number of Hume's radical colleagues tried to convince him to give up his reform resolutions. The Scotsman paid no attention.[89] It was near midnight when the House voted 58–24 against the Hume amendment. Among those voting in opposition to Hume on this occasion were Brougham, Robert Waithman, and Charles Callis Western. The last two men were prominent radical reformers and their vote might reflect an attempt to punish Hume for the Greek scandal. Brougham had been voting more and more regularly with the Whigs since the early 1820s and they, as a group, would not support anything Hume proposed.

Place applauded Hume's speech as "excellent" and blamed its lack of success on "the paltry, juggling whigs—these mean pitiful panderers, these false friends to the people, not one was found to support Mr. Hume's motion. . . ." Place especially criticized Hobhouse and Brougham for not

---

[85]Ibid., Place diary entry for 12 and 24 October 1826.
[86]Ibid., Place diary entry for 20 October 1826.
[87]Ibid., Place diary entry for 20 November 1826.
[88]Canning to George IV, 21 November 1826 in A. Aspinall, *Letters of George IV*, 3: 185.
[89]BL, Add. MS. 35146, Place diary entry for 22 November 1826.

showing any enthusiasm for Hume's efforts. Hobhouse thought Hume was not the right man to present the case for reform, although, as Place noted, Hobhouse admitted that Hume was the only one who would do it. The Whigs would never make such a bold pronouncement in favor of reform, and neither would they support anything not proposed by themselves.[90]

Place contended that Brougham and the Whigs knew of Hume's intention days before the opening of Parliament. Furthermore, Hume had explained to Brougham that he would not speak at all if someone else agreed to raise important reform issues. Brougham simply told Hume that it would be a mistake to challenge the king's address. He had not been very critical of Hume over the Greek affair, preferring to see the Scotsman's demand for his £1354 as nothing more than "a little Humeism."[91] Brougham did, however, explain to Hume that others did not share this sympathetic view and that he "should confine himself to his usual notices and speeches but avoid thrusting himself forward in existing circumstances."[92]

It was no wonder that Brougham gave vent to his famous temper when Hume ignored his advice. "Nothing could be more absurd and wrongheaded," wrote Brougham to Lord Grey, "than Hume's amendment . . . but we should have voted most of us for it had not his behavior been still more unbearable—his bringing it on was in spite of my urgent remonstrance to him in private." Brougham reported that he, Burdett, and Hobhouse tried, before a vote was taken, to get Hume to separate the reform resolutions in his amendment. They wanted to vote on retrenchment and reform in Ireland "on which we all agree" apart from Hume's demands for parliamentary reform and repeal of the Corn Laws. But Hume refused. "He was," wrote Brougham, "as obstinate as a mule. . . . All felt angry at Hume—whose behavior was a mere piece of personal vanity and so felt by everyone—Folkestone, Althorp, etc." Brougham also told Grey that "half the House went away when he [Hume] began." Only 24 voted for the amendment, but Brougham thought the number could have been "certainly above 70—probably above 80" if Hume had "done as he ought." Brougham expressed surprise that Viscount Howick (Grey's eldest son) voted for the amendment. "He probably was not aware," explained Brougham, "of the nature and tendency of the proceeding adopted by us to punish Hume and protect ourselves." The punishment of which Brougham wrote was a consequence of Hume's indiscretion on the Greek committee, and his failure to assent to Whig advice.[93]

Hume was well aware that his speech had not been well-received in the Commons. This was not unusual in itself, but he detected in this instance an angry disdain from his colleagues. Perhaps, under the stress of the Greek Loan Scandal, his imagination played tricks on him to some extent. Yet, it cannot be said that he completely misread the attitudes of his fellow

[90]Ibid.
[91]Brougham to Grey, 20 November 1826, Brougham Papers, UCL.
[92]Brougham to Grey, 26 November 1826, Brougham Papers, UCL.
[93]Ibid.

members. Place did not seem troubled at all by the events in the House of Commons. He observed to one unhappy M. P. that it "was of no consequence, [for] it was not to the House that Mr. Hume spoke . . . but to the people. . . ."[94]

Hume agreed with Place that the reaction of "the people" was more important than the reaction in the Commons. Still, the Scotsman seemed depressed by the fact that he could not easily escape from the effects of the Greek affair. Following his speech in the Commons, the newspapers reopened the business of his dealings with Lureottis and Orlando. *The Times* insisted that he repay the money immediately. The paper stated that Hume appeared determined to "undercut" whatever standing he had in Parliament. The continuing barbs in *The Times* greatly upset Hume. He thought his family needlessly hurt, and threatened to take legal action to stop such "infamous calumnies and interpretation." Hume did not mind the needling he took from outwardly conservative papers like *John Bull;* but *The Times,* a paper he had defended many times against government coercion,[95] was another matter.

According to Place, Hume was "almost wearied" of the "present circumstances" that made him "not only doubt his usefulness, but almost determine him to abandon what he sees is no recompense for the [trouble] he undergoes for the public." Place tried to "keep up Hume" by telling him that he remained "the friend of the working people and those who attack him hate the working people."[96] This reassurance did not lessen Hume's pain. He continued to fret about *The Times*'s embarrassing commentary. On 28 November, the *Morning Chronicle,* still friendly to Hume, published his letter claiming that *The Times* assailed his character because of a personal "resentment." *The Times* denied the accusation and said it had been lenient with Hume in hopes of preserving his "usefulness." All it asked was that this "foolish man" return his "ill-gotten gain."[97] Each time Hume responded to *The Times,* he found himself in deeper difficulty. Had he just repaid the £54 interest the matter would have died.

Shortly after his exchange with *The Times,* Hume came under fire from *John Bull.* That conservative journal could no longer refrain from calling its old Scottish antagonist to account. To the tune of "Home, Sweet Home" *John Bull* supplied the following words:

'Mongst Patriots and heroes though freedom may bloom
Be they ever so noble there's no man like Hume
A charm from the sies seems to hallow his mind
Which seek as we may, we elsewhere cannot find

Hume, Hume
Pure, Hume

There's no man like Hume.

---

[94]*Morning Chronicle,* 28 November 1826; *The Times,* 29 November 1826.
[95]As in 1821 when the Liverpool ministry withdrew official advertising from *The Times.*
[96]BL, Add. MS. 35146, Place diary entry for 24 November 1826.
[97]*Morning Chronicle,* 28 November 1826; *The Times,* 29 November 1826.

To Exiles, dear Hume, letters promise in vain
If you give not our pounds and our shillings again
The bonds bring daily when we paid you call—
Give us those, and the interest, that's dearer than all.

Hume, Hume
Pure, Hume

There's no man like Hume.[98]

In the past Hume might have laughed at such abuse, but he saw no humor in any of this in November 1826.

Through it all—depression, bitterness, personal attack—Hume continued to attend the House of Commons. He had always been dogged, but this really went beyond anything his colleagues had witnessed. What made him do it? No doubt it was a combination of a sense of duty with an emotional need to take his mind off questions about his integrity. It had also become a routine part of his life to sit through almost every debate. Beyond this, Hume still saw himself as the only true spokesman for reform in the Commons. Outside of London, newspapers from the manufacturing areas had not ceased to refer to him as "incomparably the most valuable member of the opposition."[99] Moreover, the free-trade radicals, disappointed though they were with recent events, could find no one else who could gain more attention for their "cause."

In late November Hume presented a petition from Robert Taylor, a barrister and a Deist, asking for an end to all penalties based on religious beliefs.[100] Some radicals did not think Hume acted prudently in reading this petition. It seemed to confirm the opinion that Hume leaned toward atheism. But Place defended the Scotsman. He thought his friend had behaved in an "enlightened" fashion. "If no one were important," wrote Place, "there would be no progress."[101] Hume continued to act "imprudently" during the early days of December, but he shied away from his usual lengthy speeches. He had decided to limit himself—in Brougham's words—"to giving notices and reading petitions." For someone so recently chastened, it was still excessive; but knowing Hume as they did, most of his colleagues were relieved that he confined himself to telling them what he intended to do in the future.

[98]*John Bull*, 27 November 1826.
[99]See *Leeds Mercury*, 25 November 1826.
[100]*Hansard*, second series, 16: 171–72.
[101]BL, Add. MS. 35146, Place diary entry for 30 November 1826.

CHAPTER IV.

TAKING GROUND FROM THE WHIGS,
1827–1830

The illness of Lord Liverpool, and his subsequent death in April, 1827, began a period of acute instability in English politics. George Canning, foreign minister under Liverpool, was called by George IV to form a ministry in April. He put together a cabinet not much different from Liverpool's. Canning had the support of many Whigs (Grey and Althorp were notable exceptions), and, in time, he might have convinced Englishmen that the unreformed House of Commons could successfully respond to public demand. But Canning, who had waited in the wings so long, had little opportunity. He died in August 1827.

The king turned to another member of Liverpool's administration, Lord Goderich (Frederick Robinson). Goderich tried to keep Canning's ministry intact, although he did add a Whig here and there. Goderich's government was moribund from the start; it failed by the end of the year.[1] In January 1828, some semblance of order returned when the duke of Wellington formed a ministry which included Robert Peel, William Huskisson, and Viscount Palmerston. The high quality of his cabinet members did not, however, guarantee harmony for Wellington. Huskisson and Palmerston resigned within the first six months and the tension among the ministers was all the talk in political circles. Despite the drawbacks in this situation, Wellington managed to preside over the repeal of the Test and Corporation Acts (1828) and the passing of the Catholic Emancipation Act (1829). These were not mean achievements, but they were far short of satisfying the radical reformers.

The uncertain course of national politics between 1827 and 1830 had little affect on Hume's conduct; he continued to pursue questions that had attracted attention from the free-trade radicals since 1815. While Liverpool was incapacitated in March 1827, he raised the issue of the Corn Laws. He began by pointing to the greed of landowners and concluded by recommending an experiment. He moved that from 5 July 1827 until 5 July 1828 a duty of 15 shillings be imposed on every quarter of wheat brought into England, and that the duty then be reduced by 1 shilling a year until 1833. The tariff would then stand at 10 shillings indefinitely. It was a bold suggestion that deserved consideration, but the motion lost 140 to 16 with one great landowner, Lord Folkestone, giving his support.[2] Place was outraged by the vote on Hume's motion and blamed the "boroughmongers" for the decisive setback.[3]

When Canning came to power in April, Hume was not surprised that the Whigs planned to support Canning, thereby further diminishing the

[1]See William Devereaux Jones, *Prosperity Robinson: The Life of Viscount Goderich, 1782–1859* (New York, 1967), 169–204.

[2]*Hansard,* second series, 17: 95–100.

[3]BL, Add. MS. 35146, Place diary entry for 3 May 1827.

opposition. Hume had once had a rather high opinion of Canning (an opinion that Place did not share), but he did not intend to offer his support. Place told Hume to expect abuse as an "opposer of Harmony."[4]

Hume wasted no time in testing Canning's patience. In the process he also tested the patience of many reformers in the Commons. On 31 May, Hume moved for a repeal of all the remaining Six Acts passed in 1819.[5] He was particularly interested in getting rid of the stamp duty as he felt it restricted freedom of publication. The duty meant that newspapers cost more than they should and worked a hardship on those of low income. Numerous efforts were made to stop Hume from moving repeal. Sir James Scarlett[6] asked him not to move for repeal because the Canning government intended to "clean up" the Six Acts next session. Scarlett said he was concerned about a decline in revenue if the stamp duties were precipitously repealed. Most likely Scarlett's real concern was to prevent, as long as possible, the spread of "irresponsible"—i.e., radical—newspapers. At first, Hume agreed to drop the matter, but then changed his mind. He agreed to limit his repeal motion to small publications if the Whigs and government would promise to support this effort. When neither would accept these terms, Hume proceeded as he had originally planned. Canning was furious. He assumed that Hume's sole purpose was to cause distress for the Whig allies of his administration.[7] Indeed, Canning's Whig friends were dismayed.

Hobhouse and Sir Robert Wilson, who had worked closely with Hume in the early 1820s, were especially annoyed with his decision to go ahead. Wilson was angry because Hume had told him he would not bring in such a bill. Furthermore, both Wilson and Hobhouse were now closer to whigdom than to the radical reformers and they wanted to give Canning a chance: not a chance to reform so much as a chance to integrate more Whigs into his government. Wilson was so disturbed by Hume's conduct that he went from committee room to committee room telling members not to attend the House during discussion of the Scotsman's motion. Most did not have to be convinced to stay away. The Treasury, unaware that the government had nothing to fear, sent a note to loyal members that their presence was "earnestly and particularly required." These factors, rather than any great support for the stamp duty, explain the lopsided defeat (120–10) of Hume's bill.[8]

Hume thought that the actions of the Whigs would bring a "storm of protest" from the people. He wanted to make a state of the nation speech similar to those that had gained him attention in 1821 and 1822. Place

[4]Ibid.

[5]Two of the Six Acts had lapsed. The Seditious Meeting Prevention Act was gone in 1824 and the Search for Arms Act had also expired.

[6]Sir James Scarlett (1769–1844). Scarlett was a conservative Whig who adamantly opposed parliamentary reform and resigned his seat for Malton in 1831 after speaking against the reform bill. He was attorney-general in the Wellington administration.

[7]BL, Add. MS. 35146, Place diary entry for 28 May 1827; Aspinall, *Letters of George IV*, 3: 244.

[8]*Hansard*, second series, 17: 1069–83. Also BL, Add. MS. 35146, Place diary entry for 31 May 1827; Aspinall, *Letters of George IV*, 3: 244.

dissuaded him on this occasion. With trade and manufacturing on the upswing, he predicted the speech would have no impact.[9] Hume, Place, and other free-trade radicals were never pleased with economic expansion because it detracted from the "cause." It was easier to arouse public opinion against the status quo in times of economic distress. It is a dilemma faced by all reformers. They want improved conditions but do not want them before reforms they cherish are brought into effect.

Hume realized that Place's assessment of the nation's attitude was right. Frustrated at every turn, he considered starting his own newspaper in the summer of 1827. Hume believed that the parliamentary debates were not adequately reported; he wanted to devote his paper to improving that situation. The editing of his speeches, which the reporters did more and more often in these days, greatly upset him. His idea for a newspaper collapsed when neither Place nor James Mill gave it any encouragement.[10] Still, Hume did not give up on the scheme. He revived it in the 1830s when Place and other radical leaders seemed more willing to support such a venture.

We have no record of Hume's activities in the autumn of 1827, but he resumed his parliamentary routine in February, 1828. Hume showed more respect for Wellington's ministry than he had for Canning's, because the new prime minister did not oppose the repeal of the Test and Corporation Acts. Respect or not, Hume had no intention of allowing Wellington's Tory regime to get by unscathed. Besides his usual efforts to force the government to retrench on military spending, to attack problems in Ireland, and to repeal the Corn Laws, Hume became involved in a rather ugly debate over whether the government should pay substantial debts acquired by Canning's family. The Wellington administration proposed, among other payments, to grant Canning's son £3,000 per year in "gratitude" for his father's labors. This was not a unique proposal since almost the same thing had been done for William Pitt the Younger more than twenty years earlier.

The precedent of Pitt notwithstanding, Hume bristled at the proposal. He demanded to know what Canning had done for the country except to push unconstitutional measures on the public. Even Wellington had done more by consenting to revoke the Test and Corporation Acts. "When had Canning," Hume exclaimed, "shown himself the friend of liberty and the enemy of oppression?" He suggested that any grant to Canning's son ought to come from the king's Civil List. When Hume had finished berating Canning, the pension plan passed by 161 to 54.[11] Nine days later, on 22 May, Hume tried again to alter the terms of the pension, but without success.[12]

The only other notable endeavor for Hume in 1828 was his continuing interest in bringing the issue of voting by ballot before the House of Commons. He hoped to attach a ballot clause to Charles Tennyson's bill to

[9]Hume to Place, 4 June 1827; and diary entry for 9 June 1827.
[10]Ibid. See also diary entry for 14 June 1827.
[11]*Hansard*, second series, 19: 695–97.
[12]Ibid., 881.

disfranchise East Retford and give representation to Birmingham. Tennyson, a radical M.P. for Bletchingley, contended that all electors in East Retford were bribed by candidates for the lower House. Most received £20 to £40 from the winning candidates. Tennyson thought this reason enough to disfranchise East Retford and give Birmingham an opportunity to have its much-needed representation. Hume supported this effort, but he wanted to go further than Tennyson. He wrote to Place and told him to "draw me up a clause to be introduced with [Tennyson's] Bill authorizing the voters at Birmingham to vote by ballot. . . ."[13] Hume explained that Ricardo had encouraged the ballot as a means to limit corruption. Eventually, Place agreed to produce such a clause, but Hume never introduced it. The East Retford bill had no chance for success, and Hume apparently lost interest in it as the weeks passed. Place had been slow to respond to his request for a ballot clause, and he sensed that the "radical tailor" doubted the moment was right to propose the ballot. When the session ended in June, Hume complained that Wellington cared more about paying Canning's debts than he did about purposeful reform. He was now certain that the people must actively—even militantly—demand extended voting rights, the ballot, and free trade.[14]

Hume's tactics in the 1829 parliamentary session varied little from 1828. He applauded Wellington's acceptance of the Catholic Emancipation Bill, but wondered if this might cost the radical reformers some support outside of Parliament. He need not have worried. Wellington had succeeded in alienating his natural political allies, without winning any permanent support from the reformers. By agreeing to the Catholic Emancipation Bill Wellington had unwittingly set the stage for the end of Tory domination.[15]

Hume's favorite subjects for debate in 1829 were religious freedom and the Corn Laws. In April he asked for the abolition of all laws disqualifying Jews from their civil rights. His proposal brought a laugh in the Commons from the government and Whig benches.[16] Undaunted, Hume then protested against continued government support for the Society for the Propagation of the Gospel in Colonies and Foreign Parts. Since 1814 the government had spent over £58,000 to assist this society and all it had done, according to Hume, was to give the members of one religion a monopoly of public money. Furthermore, the Society's operations in North America had apparently encouraged, rather than discouraged, religious animosity.[17] On several other occasions Hume presented petitions asking for the end of all restrictions based on religious belief. These efforts were interpreted as "proof" that Hume was an atheist.

The Corn Laws were also on Hume's mind. As a free-trader he resolutely believed that once the tariff on grain disappeared there would be

---

[13]Hume to Place, 5 February 1828, BL, Add. MS. 35148.

[14]Hume to Place, 13 May 1828, BL, Add. MS. 35148.

[15]For a different view—and for a discussion of Whig attitudes toward the Wellington government—see Mitchell, *Whigs in Opposition,* 216–22.

[16]*Hansard,* second series, 21: 445.

[17]Most particularly in local elections in the 1830s.

a great burst of prosperity in England. Hume saw that freedom in the economic sphere was just as important as civil and religious freedom. From his perspective free trade in grain was an "absolute necessity." On 19 May 1828 he moved for a committee of the whole House to discuss the Corn Laws. He wanted to end Huskisson's sliding scale (in effect since 1828) and replace it with a low, fixed duty on grain. This was similar to his proposal in 1827, although considerably less complicated. To support his motion, Hume gave one of his longest speeches in the Commons. He discussed the political economists from Smith to Ricardo; he traced the history of the export and import of grain; and finally, and incredibly, he read page after page of statistical tables. Only twelve of Hume's supporters remained at the end of his speech.[18] Henry Warburton, one of Hume's followers who stayed to the bitter end, told Place that he feared Hume had taken, or was about to take, leave of his senses. Warburton could not deny, however, that Hume's popularity in radical sections of London seemed higher than ever. The less support Hume had inside the House the more he had outside. His backers were just as likely to be opposed to free trade as they were to be free-traders. It was Hume's obvious contempt for established authority, and not the principles he followed, that won him favor. His parliamentary antics always made good reading in the newspapers. His outlandish behavior appealed to the malcontents.

Encouraging those of radical inclination to work together seemed uppermost in the minds of most radical reformers in the summer of 1829. Alexander Galloway, a London businessman, urged Place to do whatever he could to encourage cooperation among the radicals. He thought that Hume, O'Connell, Cobbett, Alderman Wood, and Poulett-Thompson[19] "could do wonders for the people if they would pull together."[20] Pulling together had never been easy for the radicals. With men as strong-willed as Hume, O'Connell, and Cobbett, coordination of effort was rare indeed. Each man had thrived for many years by virtue of an independent spirit. It was hoping for a great deal to expect the leading radicals to suppress such independence. Even Galloway, who recommended a united front, did not shrink from criticizing some reformers for what he considered "backward" behavior. He thought Hobhouse a great disappointment. He is, wrote Galloway, "really nobody in the House after the high expectations that were formed of him. He is not the cut and come again man, whom the people want at such a crisis as the present."[21] In 1829 Galloway thought Hume, Robert Otway-Cave,[22] and Poulett-Thompson were the most useful men in the Commons.

The problem of divided opinion in the radical camp also caused Hume

[18]*Mirror of Parliament,* 3: 1718–38; *Hansard,* second series, 21: 1464–87.
[19]A merchant, Edward Charles Poulett-Thompson (1799–1841), sat for Dover 1826–1832 and later for Manchester 1832–1839. He was an outspoken reformer, but poor health kept him from achieving greater prominence.
[20]Galloway to Place, 19 August 1829, BL, Add. MS. 37950.
[21]Ibid.
[22]Robert Otway Cave (1796–1844) sat for Leicester borough 1826–1830 and later for Tipperary county.

discomfort. He could see why free-trade radicals and anti-free-trade radicals might have a divergence of opinion, but there appeared to be needless animus among the free-traders. In the summer of 1829 his concern was over the lack of support given to John Bowring's radical publication, the *Westminster Review*. Bowring had been editor of the *Review* since it was founded by Jeremy Bentham in 1824. Bentham wanted James Mill to edit the journal, but Mill refused and Bowring accepted the responsibility. The *Westminster Review* was the radical answer to the whiggish *Edinburgh Review*. Mostly for personal reasons the Mills, James and John Stuart, refused to have anything to do with the *Westminster Review*. Hume could never quite understand the ill-feeling that kept the Mills and Bowring apart. He wrote to Place in September,

I saw Bowring [and] I had some conversation with him about the *Westminster Review*. I think it a matter of great regret to the friends of liberal and good government that both the Mr. Mills's should have set themselves against the review and not only have refused to contribute to its pages; but actually say everything in their power against it.

Hume hoped to get the Mills to oppose the *Edinburgh Review* and support the *Westminster Review*.[23]

There is no account of how Hume intended to persuade the Mills to alter their opinion of Bowring. In any event a more immediate political matter seized his attention. From the time he reentered politics in 1818, Hume had been content to hold his parliamentary seat for the Scottish border burghs. It was not a prestigious constituency, but it created few problems for Hume. The seat never cost him much money; he did not need to canvass to any great extent; and the electorate seemed to appreciate his independent behavior in the Commons. He had carried out his promise of 1818 to be "free and unshackled," and to expose the "system of profane expenditures."[24] In early October 1829 Hume learned that Sir James Carnegie planned to contest his seat for the Angus burghs at the next election. Sir James had been visiting the magistrates to "pay his respects." Carnegie hoped to undercut Hume's support in Brechin. In 1820 and 1821 Hume had won in Arbroath, Montrose and Brechin, but had not done well in the other districts that comprised his constituency.[25] Brechin, however, always required close attention; the magistrates there backed Hume only because he had strong support from the residents. In 1820 troops had to be called in to calm the crowd when it appeared the magistrates were going to desert Hume. In 1829, Hume feared that Carnegie's power and influence might be enough to offset his popularity. Sir James had a rent roll of over £15,000 per year in Brechin, and thus could bring considerable pressure to bear in the burgh.

Place advised that Hume take steps to blunt Carnegie's efforts. Hume should emphasize to the people of Brechin that he (Hume) was indepen-

[23]Hume to Place, 16 September 1829, BL, Add. MS. 35145.
[24]*Caledonian Mercury*, 16 July 1818.
[25]Hume to Place, 4 October 1829, BL, Add. MS. 37950.

dent and not controlled by any political party. Place thought Hume should stand on his record, and tell his constituents that Sir James could only make promises. Furthermore, it might be wise for Hume to remind the magistrates that Sir James's interest as a landowner might not coincide with the interests of the burgh.[26]

Hume agreed with Place on the need to counteract Carnegie's appeal. He told Place he would follow the suggestion of emphasizing his independence. Although there seemed little likelihood of an election in the near future, Hume wanted to be prepared. "Many things may occur before a new election," he wrote to Place, "therefore, procedure is necessary."[27] As the autumn wore on Hume saw that whatever he did in the Scottish burghs might not be sufficient to save his seat.

If his situation continued to deteriorate in the north, there was always the possibility that Hume could find a relatively "safe" district in England. His colleagues already considered him an English radical who sat for the Angus burghs because it cost less than challenging for a seat south of the Tweed. In October of 1829 Hume was mentioned frequently as a potential candidate in Westminster. Many radicals, including Place, were disenchanted with Westminster's current representatives, Hobhouse and Burdett. Hume did not discourage speculation about his standing for Westminster, but he much preferred to hold on to the Scottish burghs. He did not like to canvass, and he did not like to spend money on elections. In the burghs his campaigning had never amounted to much, and his spending had never gone beyond the minimum. What spending and canvassing he had done was mostly in Brechin. If the Carnegie challenge meant that he would need to spend heavily in Scotland, Hume thought it might be a good time to establish an interest elsewhere. Westminster, or possibly Middlesex, might prove a natural home for his radical ideas.[28]

Hume's future with the Scottish burghs remained uncertain as he prepared for the reopening of Parliament in 1830. Place pressured him to drive hard in the upcoming session. He wanted Hume to attack the newspaper Stamp Act, to move for reform of municipal corporations, and to head off any conservative attempt to change the laws relating to masters and workmen.[29] Place wanted Hume to strike fast in 1830 because he could sense, and so could most other radicals, that the country was ripe for another surge of reform agitation.

There had been economic recovery in 1829, but urban workers in some areas, particularly Birmingham, found almost no improvement. This left them ready to join in demands for reform. More significant perhaps was the grim situation in agriculture. The winter of 1829–1830 saw nearly every farming community in a state of serious depression. In January and February there were county meetings on a scale reminiscent of 1821–1822, and petitions were drawn calling for action from Parliament. Once again,

[26]Place to Hume, 9 October 1829, BL, Add. MS. 37950.

[27]Hume to Place, 10 October 1829, BL, Add. MS. 37950.

[28]Place to Hume, 17 October 1829, BL, Add. MS. 37950.

[29]Place to Hume, [?] November 1829, and 7 January 1830, BL, Add. MS. 35148.

as in the early 1820s, there were speeches warning of revolutionary consequences if something was not done to relieve distress.[30]

The rejuvenation of reform interest inspired Hume to become more aggressive than ever in the House of Commons. He planned to carry through on some of the issues recommended by Place; his primary concern, not surprisingly, was retrenchment. Excessive spending was one abuse that Hume thought could only be corrected by parliamentary reform. On this occasion the Whigs were more than willing to join in the demand for economy. They saw Wellington on the ropes and hoped to use economic distress, and the ministry's refusal to cut spending, as a way of forcing him out. We can understand, then, why the Whigs and radicals were stunned when the government announced reduced expenditures on 19 February. The Whigs did not know whether to praise the cuts or contend that they did not go far enough.[31]

Hume and the free-trade radicals had no such dilemma. The ministry could never do enough to satisfy them. Hume thought that the reductions were a lame concession intended to deceive the public into thinking that the administration really wanted to bring spending under control. When the army estimates were debated on 22 February Hume gave his most daring speech in years. It was one of the rare times since 1822 that he held the attention of the House on a budget matter.

He began by saying that his friends had told him any protest against the appropriations would be futile. He had concluded that they were right; only "force" could compel the ministry and the House of Commons to improve the economy by "significantly" reducing spending and taxes. In listing areas where large reductions might safely be undertaken, Hume charged that many members voted for the army estimates to keep relatives on the payroll. He also claimed "when ministers . . . were capable of procuring a corrupt majority; no other recourse remained for the people— except an appeal to arms." It was time, he said, for the people to come out of their lethargy. He acknowledged that his comments were inflammatory, but he made no apology. Shouting and waving his roll of statistics above his head, Hume blustered that he wanted everyone to see the necessity of "the people" taking "matters into their own hands." At this point cries of "Order!" were heard from Whig and Tory benches, but Hume went right on. He did not care who wanted "Order!"—he thought the people had a "right to act."[32]

Although the Tories had usually followed the policy that nothing Hume said had to be answered, there was no way to ignore this extraordinary outburst. The home secretary, Robert Peel, responded for the government. He said he listened with "emotion and astonishment." He had never before heard such words in the assembly. Peel defended the ministry against charges of corruption and he condemned Hume for telling people to take up arms. Hume had only done this, Peel said, because parliamentary privilege

[30]Mitchell, *Whigs in Opposition*, 222–23.
[31]Ibid.
[32]*Hansard*, second series, 22: 807–12.

made him immune to charges of treason. The home secretary did not fail to put his finger on the true cause of Hume's rantings. He noted with more than a little irony that Hume had probably been disappointed by the ministry's plans to lower spending.[33]

Hume interrupted Peel several times, and when the Home Secretary sat down he had a few more things to say. He wanted members to know that officials of government were the true agitators. If violence and rebellion ensued they must be ready to take the blame. How much the free-trader Hume of 1830 sounded like Marx and Engels of eighteen years later! As for his immunity from charges of treason, Hume said he was glad to be safe from the attorney-general, James Scarlett. He would take "especial good care" that law officers did not catch him outside of Parliament. With the House now cheering and laughing he declared his intention not to be "taunted out." He had, after all, always believed that prudence was better than valor.[34] Hume's rebuttal to Peel, tempered as it was by the Scotsman's rare display of tongue-in-cheek humor, took the edge off the excitement caused by his earlier remarks. He tried to disguise it as much as possible, but Hume had high regard for Peel. He thought Peel one of the least objectionable ministers during the 1820s. Not only had he promoted a number of limited reforms, he had used restraint in dealing with malcontents. Peel had tried to prevent the attorney-general from undertaking any frivolous prosecutions. For these reasons, Hume had no desire to come down hard on Peel. Whether Hume's attitude toward the home secretary was reciprocated in 1830 is difficult to tell, but in later years Peel seems to have developed a genuine affection for Hume.

After his rousing speech in February, Hume settled into the routine of opposition he had established since 1819. Questions concerning Ireland and Canada occupied much of his time. He moved to eliminate the office of lord lieutenant in Ireland arguing that for political and economic reasons the position could not be justified. He had made a similar proposal in 1823. His 1830 motion lost 229 to 115, a margin that Hume found encouraging. Quite a few Whigs had supported his effort.[35] On the matter of Canada he spoke glowingly of Henry Labouchere's (later Lord Taunton) motion to reform the government in Canada. Labouchere sought to restrict the power of the ministry (through the Crown) to appoint office-holders to legislative councils in Upper and Lower Canada. There was no likelihood the House would approve such a proposal, but Hume insisted that Labouchere's motion be put to a vote. He wanted "the people of Canada" to know that the radicals in Parliament cared.[36] Later in the 1830s Hume was the chief proponent in the House of Commons for reform in Canada.

There were no significant victories for the radicals in the first five months of 1830, but Hume could see that the cause of parliamentary reform was gaining strength. Not only the numerous reform meetings lifted

[33]Ibid., 817–21.
[34]Ibid., 827–30.
[35]*Hansard*, second series, 24: 555–64.
[36]Ibid., 1093–1109.

his spirits; there were also concrete developments in the House of Commons. At one point, Lord John Russell moved to enfranchise Manchester, Leeds, and Birmingham. Russell went so far as to argue that failure to resolve the evils in English society would lead to violent rebellion.[37] It was virtually the same position Hume had taken during debate on the army estimates. For the most part Russell's reform proposals were moderate when compared with those desired by radical reformers; yet, they did show that middle-of-the-road Whigs understood the need for action.[38] Hume seemed resigned to accepting "half a loaf" rather than none, but even "half a loaf" was not possible in the spring of 1830. The moderate recommendations of Russell and other Whigs still fell over one hundred votes shy of a majority. The reformers, Whig as well as radical, hoped to gain ground at the next general election. Fortunately for them, and for the country, such an election would occur during the summer.

On 26 June George IV died and was succeeded by William IV. George IV had never favored the reformers—moderate or radical—and had done everything in his power to retard reform on all fronts. William IV, on the other hand, appeared more congenial toward moderate reformers in general and toward Lord Grey in particular. The new king's attitude, plus the interest in reform during the early months of 1830, convinced the Whigs that they had a chance to gain a majority in the election required by the death of George IV. They, and the radicals, were anxious to test the depth of reform spirit in England.

Several weeks before George IV died, Hume still had not decided where he would stand for reelection to Parliament. Since 1818 he had never seriously considered campaigning in any area other than the Scottish border burghs. But as we have seen circumstances in 1830 were quite different. He faced a challenge in Scotland; simultaneously, radicals in Westminster and Middlesex tried to attract him to their districts. Hume's popularity had reached such a level during the 1820s that he was a natural and desirable candidate for either of these large and reform-minded constituencies. This ought to have been an enviable situation for any politician, but Hume managed to make it one of anxiety and confusion for his friends and for himself.

Despite the anticipated problems from Sir James Carnegie, Hume, in the first days of June, leaned toward seeking a return from the burghs. He knew what to expect in Scotland, and he imagined that he could stave off Carnegie with just a little more canvassing than usual. Furthermore, he had improved his reputation for being independent during the recent parliamentary session, especially with his inflammatory remarks on the need to take up arms. About the time he had made up his mind to stand again for the Angus burghs, an opportunity developed in Middlesex that caused Hume to reconsider.

Samuel Charles Whitbread, one of the Middlesex members, told Hobhouse that he had to give up his seat. Whitbread, first elected for Middlesex

[37] *Hansard*, second series, 22: 860–61.
[38] Mitchell, *Whigs in Opposition*, 225–26.

in 1820 with Whig support, had been ill for some time. Hobhouse immediately talked with Burdett and Place about whom the reformers should recommend for the Middlesex vacancy.[39] Hobhouse suggested Hume, and Burdett and Place agreed that he was the best choice. Place, however, saw an ulterior motive in Hobhouse's endorsement of Hume. He believed that Hobhouse feared Hume might become a candidate in Westminster and offer a serious challenge to Hobhouse's seat for that constituency. Place might well have been right. Many Westminster voters were disenchanted with both of their representatives, Hobhouse and Burdett. Some openly sought an alternative candidate. In late May or early June a group offered to nominate Hume and provide him with up to £1000 if he agreed to run. The Scotsman refused, but Hobhouse probably feared he would change his mind if more problems occurred in the border burghs.

Place thought Hobhouse persuaded Whitbread to quit in order to provide an opening other than Westminster for Hume to pursue. Most of Place's reasoning revolved around his conviction that no Whig, and Hobhouse clearly fit that category, would offer to support Hume on principle. "The Whigs hate Hume," wrote Place, "even more than the ministers hate him." They hated him because each time the Whigs tried to convince the people that they were doing them a service, Hume would go further and take the ground from them. "It was not therefore from any respect to Hume," Place concluded, "that [the Whigs] now proposed him from Middlesex, nor from any desire to see him in Parliament that they were willing to assist him. The sole object was to get him out of the way at Westminster." His concern about motive notwithstanding, Place thought Hobhouse ought to approach Hume about Middlesex as soon as possible. Place did not think Hume would win in Scotland, and he did not see how he could lose in Middlesex. Although he preferred to see Hume contest Westminster, Place knew that his Scottish friend had no interest in challenging Hobhouse or Burdett. Besides, such an effort might cost a huge amount of money—money that Hume had no intention of spending.

Most politicians of Hume's popularity would have jumped at the chance to win a seat for the largest constituency in England, but "Old Joe" surprised Hobhouse by hesitating. He told Hobhouse that he was fairly sure of his seat in Scotland (not true) and he did not wish to use personal funds to compete in an election he might not win. He did agree to meet with Hobhouse, Place, and Henry Warburton (radical M. P. for Bridport) to further discuss the prospects in Middlesex. This meeting occurred on 18 June. The three men tried to overcome Hume's resistance to the plan. Hobhouse told Hume that Lord Althorp thought the scheme a good one and was confident of his success in Middlesex. Despite such reassurances, Hume continued to fret about the potential cost of the campaign. He also complained that his wife opposed surrendering the "Scotch" burghs. Since

---

[39]Discussion of the 1830 Middlesex election has been drawn from John Cam Hobhouse's "Account of the 1830 Election," BL, Add. MS. 56554, and from Place's "Account of the 1830 Middlesex Election," BL, Add. MS. 27789. We shall provide references to these sources only when it is not clear which "Account" we are following.

the election in Scotland was scheduled later than the one in Middlesex, Hume wondered whether he could get the results in Middlesex before declaring himself in Scotland. Although several members had found this a useful tactic, Place told Hume it would not work for him. Most likely he would lose both elections if he tried this strategy. Hobhouse thought all such talk quite silly because Hume could, in his opinon, win Middlesex for less than £500. Warburton avoided predictions, but he did remind Hume that sitting for Middlesex was much more impressive than sitting for the border burghs. Finally, Hume acceded to the wishes of his friends. A room would be rented in Pall Mall to house his election committee.

With Hume's acceptance secured, Hobhouse broke the news to other reformers. According to Hobhouse, Althorp, Tavistock, Shaw Lefevre, Edward Ellice, Lord Milton, Sir James Graham, and numerous "Westminster friends" were "delighted" with the project. Grey and Brougham were not so enthusiastic. Both men considered Hume excessive in zeal, and both found his constant lecturing in the House of Commons exasperating. Nevertheless, Grey let it be known that if the reformers wanted Hume the Whigs would not offer any opposition.[40] It was good politics for Grey, especially in view of his need for radical support in 1830. After further discussion, Brougham also reluctantly consented to back Hume's candidacy.

While Hobhouse made these arrangements, Hume began to have second thoughts. He worried anew about finances. Place told him that Hobhouse, Warburton, and Burdett would contribute £500 to his cause, and that he could count on at least £2500 from other friends. These pledges did not satisfy Hume. When he arrived at his committee rooms on 21 June, Place reports that he seemed shaken and unsteady. He lacked sufficient resolve to go ahead with the campaign. All attempts to rally him out of his insecurity had no effect. Hobhouse noticed this as well and grew impatient with Hume's "shilly-shallying." Hobhouse was further disquieted by a conversation he overheard between Hume and Brougham. Brougham casually asked whether Place (a man he disliked) had anything to do with Hume's campaign. To which, according to Hobhouse, Hume "without change of expression" said "No!" Hobhouse "marvelled" at how well Hume lied.[41]

On the morning of 22 June, Place reported that Hume was "more frightened than ever." Colonel Davies[42] had told Hume's wife of the added work and expense a county seat would entail. He explained to Mrs. Hume that she and her husband would have to support all local charities and that this was only a small portion of the extra costs they could expect. It was not the price of the election that now troubled Hume—Grey's support almost surely meant there would be no opposition—but rather the anticipated expense of maintaining the seat. When the Scotsman expressed his new fears to Place, the latter commanded him to stop equivocating before he did

[40]Hobhouse, "Account."

[41]Place, "Account."

[42]Colonel Thomas Henry Hastings Davies (radical) sat for Worcester from 1818–1835. He was defeated in 1835, but returned again in 1837 and sat until he retired in 1841.

irreparable damage to his reputation among the radicals. James Mill and Daniel O'Connell also urged Hume to remain firm in his decision to contest Middlesex. Mill said he ought "to be proud" to spend the money. O'Connell "vehemently" pressed Hume to continue. Place, meanwhile, carefully went over the financial situation again with Hume. In the course of this discussion Place predicted that there would only be one more election between 1830 and 1837. Seeing Place's obvious irritation, Hume promised that he would reach a definite decision within three or four hours.[43]

When he returned to give Place his "final word," he was still not close to a decision. Hume pleaded for another twenty-four hours. Place told him if he did not run for Middlesex he would be ruined. People would call him a "sneaking, cowardly, mean fellow." They would say he was "governed by his wife." Place was now ready to close down the committee rooms.[44] Hobhouse had also determined that Hume would not run and complained to Place over his "reprehensible" conduct. Hobhouse was convinced that the reformers had made a "mistake" and that Hume was a "shabby fellow" and "done forever" if he backed out.[45]

Under mounting pressure and criticism, Hume temporarily removed himself from all discussion of his political future. He went into retreat for two days, 23 and 24 June, and would talk to no one. Then, on the night of 24 June he told Warburton that he would probably stand for Middlesex. Warburton relayed the message to Hobhouse. Hobhouse was anything but enthusiastic. In his diary he wrote,

I said it was too late and that now I should have to give consent at least if I was to take an active part. The nomination had originated with me and Hume had shown a marked want of confidence and consulted O'Connell and other objectionable persons without considering that his real supporters ... were compromising themselves all the time.

Warburton asked Hobhouse not to withdraw his support until the matter could be fully debated by those directly concerned.[46]

The following day, 25 June, Warburton, Whitbread, Shaw Lefevre and Hobhouse met at Althorp's house. Warburton brought two letters from Hume—one accepting the invitation to campaign in Middlesex and the other declining. The acceptance was conditional; Hume reserved the right to retire at any time. Hobhouse wanted to drop Hume immediately, but the others worked to persuade him otherwise. Warburton said he would take responsibility for £2500 of the election expenses, and Althorp insisted that Hume remained the best candidate available to the reformers. Hobhouse, although reiterating his disdain for Hume, consented to support the effort as long as his dealings were limited to Althorp and Warburton. He wished no further association with Hume.

[43]Place, "Account."
[44]Ibid. Compare with Hobhouse, "Account."
[45]Ibid.
[46]Hobhouse, "Account."

Place's reaction to Hume's latest dallying was even more severe than Hobhouse's. He wanted Hume to withdraw because he thought his esteem could sink no lower. Place later changed his mind when he learned that Hume's vacillation had not yet become general knowledge in the country. There was every reason to believe that Hume would have no serious trouble if there were no further delays.

On the morning of 26 June George IV died, and Hume showed his first trace of enthusiasm for the contest in Middlesex. He began to prepare lists of "useful persons" and freeholders to assist his campaign. He also collected references and endorsements to be used in canvassing the district. On 28 June Hume complained to Place that his election committee still did not have its full complement of members. Mostly because of Hume's uncertain status, Warburton had found it difficult to recruit individuals who would allow their names to appear on a committee list. Place was unconcerned about the committee. He told Hume that all decisions in any election were made in a private room by two or three persons. As it developed, there never were any formal meetings of Hume's election committee before the polling. There were *ad hoc* meetings of those who happened to be in Hume's committee rooms when a decision had to be made. Warburton and Hume asked Place to go to the Pall Mall headquarters two or three hours every day to see that all ran smoothly. Place did try to appear once or twice a day, but routine affairs were left in the hands of John Wallis and Place's son Frederick.[47]

By early July Hobhouse had begun to soften his opinion of Hume. On 4 July he praised the Scotsman for telling Lord Grey and other Whigs in the House of Commons that, if they expected support from the people, they had better declare an interest in cutting down the number of sinecures and in providing more substantive reform measures. Hume's comments, said Hobhouse, were the "only sensible thing I heard in the Commons today."[48]

Throughout the month of July Hobhouse did his share to solidify Hume's image as the people's advocate. He wrote circulars and private letters of support to key electors. Hume did not like to canvass, but he did make successful appearances before large gatherings of Middlesex voters. These meetings were carefully arranged by Hobhouse, Warburton, and Wallis to guarantee a favorable reception for their candidate. With Hume's popularity among the constituents this posed little problem. Only once in July did Hume look wistfully toward the Angus burghs. *The Scotsman,* always a friend to Hume, reported on 21 July that Brechin was ready to come into line for Hume after all. The paper predicted it would be too late to bring Hume back, and concluded that Scotland did not deserve to be represented by such an outstanding reformer: "Mr. Hume is more emphatically even than Mr. Fox, the man of the people; and he is, besides,

[47]Place, "Account."

[48]Hobhouse, "Account." See also Lord Ellenborough (Edward Law), *A Political Diary 1828–1830,* ed. Lord Colchester (London, 1881), 2: 301.

the man of sense, and the man of business."[49] If this article had appeared a month earlier, Hume would surely have abandoned Middlesex; but he was now too deeply committed to the county to back away.

By the end of July Hume had a full head of steam and the likelihood of any opposition had almost disappeared. This is exactly what Place and Hobhouse had said would happen. Hume's requisition, written by Hobhouse, was printed on 28 July. On the day of the election Place arranged a huge procession for Hume by land and by water. Hume arrived at the election meeting with seventy-three carriages and hundreds of supporters. At 2 P.M. the sheriff declared Hume and George Byng[50] elected. There was no challenge.[51] Hume addressed the gathering and adhered to his usual practice of speaking longer than he ought. His remarks were mostly about the turmoil in Paris. He suggested that England might suffer the same fate if reform of Parliament were not quickly undertaken. At the conclusion of his speech the Scotsman acknowledged the cheers of the crowd and went home. Place records that "neither Mr. Hume nor anyone else paid more than £50."

With his own election now over, Hume turned his attention to other contests not yet complete. Place asked him to canvass for several radical reform candidates, but Hume drew back from such an assignment. As he explained to Place, "I question the propriety of my doing more than attending meetings at the several districts. . . . I think of addressing the electorate generally and leaving it to them."[52] In all, Hume recommended five men, including Benjamin Disraeli for High Wycombe, at various reform meetings. He supported only those persons who were pledged to vote for reform of Parliament. "As I consider it important to get in good men," Hume wrote to Place, "I only regret that I cannot do more good. . . ."[53]

At the end of August, Hume returned to Scotland for a few weeks of relaxation. He was hailed as a hero in most places. In Arbroath he received a rousing welcome. He was called a "true representative of the people" and "Scotland's gift to the world."[54] A giant dinner in his honor was given in Glasgow. More than two hundred attended the gathering and a toast to parliamentary reform highlighted the occasion. Hume was praised as a genuine "radical reformer" whose moment of triumph could not be long denied. There was optimism that the duke of Wellington, if he wished to stay in office after the recent elections, would need to accept the inevitability of electoral reform.[55]

Hume did not share this optimism. He was prepared to join forces with anyone who called for the ouster of the Tory ministers. In October 1830,

---

[49] The Scotsman, 21 July, 1830.
[50] A Whig who sat for Middlesex from 1790 until his death in 1847.
[51] Place, "Account" and Hobhouse, "Account."
[52] Hume to Place, 26 August 1830, BL, Add. MS. 37949.
[53] Ibid.
[54] The Scotsman, 1 September 1830.
[55] Ibid., 18 September 1830.

Hume applauded Althorp's condemnation of the Wellington government.
Many radicals in the House of Commons looked upon Althorp as a
moderate, and refused to lend support. Hume, however, thought Althorp
more radical than Whig.[56] Hume's support for Althorp's attack on
Wellington was clearly justified by the events. As the days passed in the
autumn of 1830 the prime minister stubbornly insisted that no alteration of
the representation was necessary. Thus he doomed his ministry. When
Brougham, in November, offered a motion in support of electoral reform,
Wellington decided to avoid a showdown and resigned. William IV then
asked Lord Grey to form a ministry. For the first time since 1806 a king
had called upon the Whigs to take charge of the government.

[56]Denis Le Marchant, *Memoir of John Charles (Viscount Althorp), third Earl Spencer*
(London, 1876), 254–55.

CHAPTER V.

WORKING WITH THE WHIGS, 1830–1834

The new Whig ministry under Lord Grey had a distinctly aristocratic cast, but Hume seemed pleased with it. On 22 November, after moving that the appointed officers of the crown not receive a salary in excess of that paid in 1796, he withdrew the motion to show that he had confidence in the new administration.[1] At the same time, he warned that the radicals would oppose the ministry unless economic retrenchment, parliamentary reform, and the adoption of a free-trade policy were undertaken. This statement was less a threat than a display of faith in the ministers' commitment to these objectives.[2]

Hume's reluctance to press the Whigs contrasted with Place's suspicions. In Place's memory the Whigs had betrayed reformers in 1806 (under "All the Talents") and had failed to act when it was timely in 1818, 1819, and 1820. To avoid future deceptions Place had advised Hume to test the Whigs now that they were in office. He proposed to do this by having Hume raise the ballot question.[3] But Hume ignored Place's suggestion. He preferred to give the Whig government a chance. In fact, Hume was quick to praise the ministers. He was especially pleased when the ministry abolished the post-master general's office in Ireland. It was an indication, he thought, of the government's desire to practice economy.[4]

While praising the conduct of the ministers in Parliament, Hume and other radicals continued to hold public meetings to push for reform. These gatherings in Middlesex and other metropolitan areas were aimed at putting pressure on the government. Since the Whigs appeared solidly in power, Hume hoped to sustain popular enthusiasm through these meet-ings. The crowds addressed by Place and Hume were much less "wild" than those goaded by the rhetoric of Hunt and Cobbett.[5] The free-trade radicals thought of themselves as intermediaries between the Whigs and "the people." Unlike the followers of Hunt and Cobbett, they hoped to persuade "the people" that the Whig government would respond to reasonable demands. Even while he urged moderation on the public, Place confided to Hume that he did not expect a satisfactory reaction from the ministers.

Place's doubts were well founded. Grey preferred to make changes without being pressured. He thought the government, and not "the people," should reform the constitution.[6] On the other hand, such ministers as Althorp, Ellice, and Durham were open to broader reform measures. They hoped to cooperate with the radicals as much as possible. It remained

---

[1]*Hansard,* third series, 1: 630.
[2]Ibid.
[3]Place to Hume, 22 November, 1830, BL, Add. MS. 35148.
[4]*Hansard,* third series, 1: 747.
[5]T. R. M. Butler, *Passing of the Great Reform Bill* (London, 1835), 253.
[6]George M. Trevelyan, *Lord Grey and the Reform Bill* (London, 1920), 262; Butler, *Passing of the Great Reform Bill,* 157ff.

to be seen whether these more reform-minded men could sway the rest of the cabinet.

The government did not ease radical concern when it undertook to prosecute several persons for seditious utterances and writings in December of 1830. The indictment of Richard Carlile, editor of the *Prompter,* elicited an angry response from the radicals and threatened their relations with the government. Place, while agreeing that Carlile tended to be extreme, thought the prosecution foolish and dangerous. "Look at the words prosecuted, look at the barbarous sentence," he wrote in his diary, "and find, if you can, since the time when Castlereagh put an end to his own existence, any one who has been prosecuted and sentenced for such words."[7] Place used the occasion of the Whig indictment to demand repeal of all taxes on newspapers and any other laws that restricted freedom of publication. He pressed Hume to take up the battle. But Hume demurred. He did not think it the right moment to ask for a reduction in the newspaper tax or to do anything else that might anger the ministers. Place then accused Hume of working hand-in-glove with the "ministerial people." In a note of 12 January 1831, he warned Hume to stay at arms length from the Whigs. "Have they not played you false," he wrote to Hume,

have they not shirked you, have they not divided your most useful efforts, shrunk from you at times as if you were inflicted with some plague, have they not taken pains to magnify small errors into "big blunders." Have they not said that you never could be anything but a "damn apothecary." Have they not called you Old Joe. Have they not in fact treated you much worse than the Tories treated you?[8]

Place's petulant (though truthful) comments reveal the degree of Hume's openness to Whig cooperation. To this extent, he was a wiser politician than Place. In following a narrow course, Place limited his tactical options; Hume had greater maneuverability. His continued confidence in the ministry was aimed at encouraging the Whigs to act liberally while never precluding opposition to selected measures. Even when Hume dissented, his criticism was so astute that it frequently became a reference point in the ministry's preparation of bills.[9] In the past, his thorough studies of fiscal and reform measures had aided Whig reformers. Warmer relations in 1831 made the Whigs more receptive to his advice.

Hume believed that the government's commitment to economic retrenchment offered greater proof of Whig intentions than their treatment of radical agitators. When the civil list was presented on 4 February 1831, Hume questioned Althorp about the abolition of more pensions and sinecure offices, but retreated after learning that William IV would suffer no reductions. Hume did take exception to the size of the army estimates, but Althorp's budget generally pleased him.[10] In reporting to Place on the

[7]BL, Add. MS. 35146.

[8]Reported in Place's diary, 12 January 1831, BL, Add. MS. 35146. See also Place to Hume, 6 February 1831 and Hume's reply, 8 February 1831, BL, Add. MS. 35146.

[9]See William Harris, *The History of the Radical Party in Parliament* (London, 1885), 413.

[10]*Hansard,* third series, 2: 164–68, 429, 466, 694.

budget, he advised that the radicals wait until 1832 for greater reductions.[11] This was strange talk coming from the well-known champion of retrenchment. Place was incredulous. "You are a remarkably odd man," he told Hume, "and as a legislator are good for nothing unless your opponents 'show fight,' the moment they become civil your good nature gets the better of you, and the fight is all taken out of you."[12] Place may have had a point about Hume's "good nature," but it is more important to understand that Hume was closer to the parliamentary scene than his old friend. He sensed the precarious condition of the ministry, and he wanted to be certain that the administration had a fair chance to produce reform proposals.

Hume's patience was rewarded when Lord John Russell brought in his reform bill on 1 March. The Scotsman declared that the bill went far beyond his expectations as a radical reformer. He was prepared to give it his hearty support.[13] Although most radicals agreed with Hume, there was some consternation over the failure to include a provision for the ballot. Place called a meeting of radicals at the Crown and Anchor to demand its inclusion.[14] But Hume's approval of the bill was unconditional. He thought the government sensible to defer the ballot until a later time. He assured Russell privately of his full support and said he would "vote black white in order to carry the measure."[15]

Hume's unguarded enthusiasm for Russell's bill did not lessen his esteem among his radical associates. This was reflected in talk of his nomination as chairman of the new Parliamentary Candidates Society. This society was organized to inform electors of the character and background of candidates standing for the anticipated reformed Parliament. Hume welcomed the Society's formation, but questioned the wisdom of probing into the personal activities of members of Parliament. Although such older radicals as Burdett and Bentham endorsed the organization, Hume's caution was understandable.[16] At the time (mid-March), he was uneasy about the chances of the reform bill at the second reading.[17] He was right to be concerned. The measure passed its second reading on 22 March by only one vote. This meant that a future alliance of former ministers, ultra-Tories, and waverers might lead to the bill's outright rejection.[18] Clearly, radical support for the bill, together with eagerness to rid the Commons of anti-reformers through the agency of the Parliamentary Candidates Society, would rankle many members of Parliament. According to Place, when news of the Society's intentions became known to the public a howl went up from the Tories and also from many Whigs. Fearing a conservative reaction, Hume worried that his connection with the organiza-

[11]Hume to Place, 12 February 1831, BL, Add. MS. 35149.
[12]Place to Hume, 16 February 1831, BL, Add. MS. 35149.
[13]Hansard, third series, 2: 1156.
[14]Broughton, Recollections, 4: 88; Le Marchant, Earl Spencer, 292–93.
[15]Lord John Russell, Recollections and Suggestions, 1818–1873 (London, 1875), 72.
[16]Hume to Place, 13 March 1831, BL, Add. MS. 35145 and Place's diary, 6 March 1831, BL, Add. MS. 35146.
[17]Butler, Passing of the Great Reform Bill, 196.
[18]See Norman Gash, Sir Robert Peel: The Life of Sir Robert Peel (Totowa, N.J., 1972), 27–29.

tion (let alone if he became its chairman) would diminish his influence in the House of Commons.[19]

The close vote on the second reading made it obvious that the reform bill had virtually no chance to leave the Commons. After it suffered a defeat in committee on 19 April, Lord Grey asked the king to dissolve Parliament.[20] The electorate would again have an opportunity to express itself on constitutional reform. Hume favored this course of action and urged his radical colleagues to facilitate the dissolution. In the parliamentary campaign that followed, Hume made no strident demand for reform. He had considered working with the Parliamentary Candidates Society in exposing anti-reformers to the electorate, but changed his mind as the weeks passed. In an election alive with the expectations of reform, the Society's assistance proved unnecessary.[21] Hume, who again had the support of the Whigs and the radicals, was reelected for Middlesex and joined a majority of more than one hundred reformers who assured easy passage for the government's reform bill through the Commons.[22]

Although faithful to Whig reform throughout the summer of 1831, Hume was careful to maintain his credentials as a radical. During June, July, and August, he opposed the administration's enforcement of laws against publishers, presented a petition to abolish the newspaper tax, and appealed to the government to accelerate the progress of the reform bill. He warned the ministers that the public had the impression they were losing their enthusiasm for the measure. At the same time, Hume made it clear that demands from the ultra-radicals (especially Hunt) for the ballot, annual parliaments, and universal suffrage were also responsible for slowing the bill's advance.[23]

Despite fears that the day might never come, on 21 September 1831, the reform bill received final approval in the House of Commons and was sent to the Lords. There were few who expected the bill to last very long in the upper House. Over the objections of a few radical peers (principally Lord Radnor), the Lords defeated the measure on 8 October.

The rejection moved some radicals to call for drastic action by the Whigs. Place warned that unless the Whigs asked the king to create peers panic would result. Indeed, riots already were occurring in Bristol and Nottingham.[24] "Down with the Lords" was heard with ever-greater frequency. More than one nobleman pondered Cobbett's oft-repeated warning that the lack of reform had put the country on a course toward revolution. The ministry itself was shaken by the reaction in the country, and word was passed to the radicals that a sterner effort in behalf of reform would soon be made. The demand for reform was so acute that it could not be safely

---

[19]Hume to Place, 16 March 1831, BL, Add. MS. 35149.

[20]General Isaac Gascoyne's motion, opposing the reduction of seats for England and Wales, passed by eight votes.

[21]See Wallas, *Francis Place,* 262; Butler, *Passing of the Great Reform Bill,* 209. The Parliamentary Candidates Society was disbanded after the 1831 election.

[22]Russell, *Recollections and Suggestions,* 77.

[23]*Hansard,* third series, 4: 10–11, 871–75.

[24]Place to Hobhouse, 11 October 1831, BL, Add. MS. 35149.

ignored or resisted. It was a situation that Place viewed favorably. He was convinced, as he later wrote, that "physical force, or the threat of physical force" had been at the "bottom of all the great changes" in the English government.[25] Months of parliamentary maneuvering seemed now to pale before the pressure from outside. It was in this trying circumstance that Hume and other parliamentary radicals joined the majority in favoring a vote of confidence in the ministry.

Place, with his deep-seated distrust of the Whigs, was appalled by the radicals' support for the administration. He was especially annoyed with his Scottish friend. But Hume had a reason for his action. He was pleased that Lord Grey had pledged, shortly after the second reform bill failed in the Lords, to bring in as soon as possible a third measure of equal extent. For Hume, this offered hope that reform could still be achieved through the traditional order of king, Lords, and Commons. On 12 December 1831, Lord John Russell fulfilled Grey's pledge by producing another bill in the Commons. As the legislation moved through Parliament, Hume's modera- tion was accented in an atmosphere of anger and frustration. Place ridiculed Grey's management of the bill, but Hume understood the prime minister's difficulties. He admitted that the government had gone as far as it could under the circumstances.[26] Hume had high regard for most of the men in the Grey cabinet. He knew that Brougham, Durham, Althorp, and Holland were genuinely committed to substantial reform.

The bill moved through the Commons with unusual speed during the early weeks of 1832. Hume's voice in these days was nearly always a moderate one. His anxiety showed itself only when anyone, radical or Tory, did something that he thought might impede the progress of the measure. Most members, fearful of rebellion in the country, were desperate to get the bill to the Lords. Hume shared this concern.

It appeared that the upper House might finally have realized the danger in further opposition. In April the peers approved the bill in principle. But the victory was not yet won. The conservative bishops and noblemen began to tear the bill apart in committee; and Grey, exasperated by this turn, asked the king to create peers or accept his resignation. Hume and other parliamentary radicals approved of this action. Faced with the prime minister's ultimatum, William IV attempted to replace Grey with Welling- ton. This immediately set off a series of protests and demonstrations that made rebellion seem imminent. Hume despaired of this situation and used whatever influence he had in an effort to calm angry crowds in Marylebone and St. Pancras. He had advocated direct action in 1829 when he knew there was little chance for it, but now he feared England was truly on the doorstep of revolution. Fortunately William IV, proving he had more savvy than his immediate predecessors, told Grey he could have his new peers. With that threat the Lords embraced the reform bill without revision. Through it all, Hume had steadfastly resisted Place's exotic plans to boycott taxes, barricade key cities, and appeal to the army to join hands

---

[25]Place to William P. Gaskell, 4 March 1840, BL, Add. MS. 35151.
[26]*Hansard*, third series, 9: 546.

with the protestors. Like Bentham, Hume did not see the 1832 bill as the end of parliamentary reform. It was, rather, a necessary beginning. He hoped many other needed reforms (economic, political, and legal) would soon follow.

Taken together, Hume's parliamentary conduct from the beginning of 1830 to the passage of the Reform Act in 1832 had an unmistakably moderate tone. His actions were wholly expedient. Grey's reform was the best that Hume could expect in 1832. Once he accepted this premise it was strategically appropriate for him to temper his position on other questions to safeguard the progress of reform. This tactic, questioned at times by fellow radicals, reveals Hume as an astute parliamentarian. His desire to maintain good relations with the Whigs testifies to his political realism. Unlike younger radicals (and such older ones as Hunt, Place, and Cobbett), Hume had learned his craft in the unreformed House of Commons. As a member of a distinct minority, and subject to ridicule for thirteen years, he had learned the art of patiently advancing motions, refining them in committee, and marshalling votes for divisions. He had experienced defeat so often that he could accept something less than total triumph.

Hume's cooperation with the Whigs after the success of parliamentary reform depended on whether the government moved to fulfill his hopes for further reforms. Such expectations were not unrealistic considering the interest shown in the past by men like Althorp, Russell and Durham in economic retrenchment, reduction of import duties, and the adoption of the ballot. With the addition of John Cam Hobhouse at the War Office and Charles Poulett Thomson, a friend of Jeremy Bentham, at the Board of Trade, the radicals had even more allies in the cabinet. Place, for one, did not find much solace in this potential radical influence. He wanted immediate proof that the ministers meant to carry through on a wide variety of reforms. Place demanded action on the secret ballot, the shortening of parliaments, the abolition of slavery, fiscal reform, Church reform, and legal reform.[27] In addition he hoped for repeal of the Stamp Act. Hume shared all of Place's long and short range goals, but he thought the summer of 1832 was a bit too soon to prod the Whigs. Everyone in government needed a respite from the reform bill crisis. During the remaining weeks of the 1832 session he saw little value in pushing the ministers.

Like most politicians Hume was looking beyond the 1832 session to the December elections. As in the past, he had the dual task of standing for Middlesex as well as promoting other candidates in other districts. In 1832 he made a special effort for John Arthur Roebuck, a zealous follower of John Stuart Mill. Roebuck had been encouraged to seek a parliamentary seat for Bath, and his radical supporters were anxious for a recommendation from Joseph Hume.[28] At first, Hume was reluctant to assist Roebuck's campaign. He thought the Bath constituents might be alarmed at

[27]Place to Hobhouse, 2 June 1832, BL, Add. MS. 35149; Wallas, *Francis Place,* 326-29, n. 3.

[28]Roebuck to Place, 19 September 1832, BL, Add. MS. 37949.

Roebuck's republican opinions. But Hume finally came to Roebuck's support. He sent a letter to the Bath electorate approving of the candidacy, and he also agreed to attend a dinner for Roebuck on 13 September.[29] His backing for Roebuck was made awkward by the fact that his sometime ally, John Cam Hobhouse, had a brother who also sought Hume's endorsement in Bath.[30] This caused Hume to be sparing in his appearances with Roebuck.[31] Despite this caution, Hume was bitterly attacked by Hobhouse for his disloyalty, thus widening a rift between Hobhouse and Hume that had begun with the Scotsman's indecision during the 1830 Middlesex election.[32]

Although Hume was embarrassed by the affair in Bath, it did not seem to affect his candidacy in Middlesex. Only his indolence threatened to stand in the way of certain success. Henry Warburton, Hume's campaign manager, had set down as prerequisites for victory the compilation of voters, three weeks of visits to various parishes, letters to friends announcing Hume's availability and the scheduling of large meetings in key districts near London.[33] True to his penurious ways, Hume carped about putting up the £1500 necessary to meet election expenses. He never spent money willingly and Warburton had to cajole him for every shilling. In the end, all potential opposition disappeared and Hume won his seat uncontested.[34]

Hume's victory in Middlesex was one of a wave of radical triumphs. At least fifty radicals, including such "new" men as J. A. Roebuck, George Grote, Charles Buller, William Molesworth, and William Ewart, won seats in the House of Commons. These victories, coupled with the impressive showing of the Whigs, seemed to reflect a growing appetite for reform in the country. Yet not all reformers interpreted the election as a mandate to push ahead. Sir James Graham thought "it was time to steady the direction and check the velocity of the irresistible machine."[35] Lord Grey, meanwhile, came out in favor of an Irish policy that was not nearly so conciliatory as the parliamentary radicals had advocated. These moderate tendencies in the Whig hierarchy were bound to create problems for the Whig-radical alliance that had worked so well in the spring and summer of 1832.

Hume was quick to realize that the success of reformers in the 1832 election might very well make cooperation between Whig-reformers and radicals more difficult. Cooperation between 1830 and 1832 had been based on the radicals' desire to promote the Whig reform bill while keeping

[29]Hume to Place, 23 August 1832, BL, Add. MS. 37949; Hume to Place, 24 August 1832, BL, Add. MS. 37949; Hume to Place, 3 September 1832, BL, Add. MS. 37949; and Hume to Place, 7 September 832, BL, Add. MS. 37949.

[30]Roebuck to Place, 19 September 1832, BL, Add. MS. 37949.

[31]Hume to Place, 10 September 1832, BL, Add. MS. 37494.

[32]Hobhouse to Place, 10 October 1832, BL, Add. MS. 37949.

[33] Warburton to Place, 28 August 1832, BL, Add. MS. 37949.

[34]From Denis Le Marchant's diary, 13 December 1832 in Aspinall, *Three Early Nineteenth Century Diaries*, 283.

[35] Southgate, *Passing of the Whigs*, 39.

the Tories out of office. In 1833, the paucity of Tory numbers in Parliament prevented them from being a serious concern to the Whigs. The old political lines between Whigs and Tories might fade, and the radicals emerge as the new opposition. The Tories seemed to be dying as a group, leaving the field to the Whigs (moderate reformers) and the radicals. As Albany Fonblanque, editor of the *Examiner,* noted in December 1832, "the contest will be solely between the stationary principle and the Progressive; between the spirit of Toryism, whether under its own or Whig colors and the spirit of Reform."[36]

Between the election and the opening of Parliament in late January, the radicals actively planned their strategy for the coming session. It was decided that George Grote should take up the ballot question; Warburton should move for the repeal of the tax on journals.[37] In this connection, there were meetings in early January to discuss the formation of the Society for the Diffusion of Practical and Moral Knowledge and the publication of an inexpensive journal. Place and Roebuck provided the main force behind the project, but Hume played a key role by assuming the presidency of the Society as well as acting as a solicitor of subscriptions. Moreover, he became the chief go-between with those liberal Whigs who were welcomed into the Society.[38]

Hume took the initiative when Parliament opened. In the first session on 29 January, he surprised most of the members by moving that Edward John Littleton be made Speaker of the House instead of the long-time Tory Speaker, Charles Manners-Sutton. The Whigs, fearful that Littleton was too much a reformer, supported Sutton. Hume argued that it would be inconsistent for a reformed Parliament to have as its Speaker an anti-reformer. To prove that the House of Commons was serious about reform, it ought to elect a man like Littleton.[39] Hume's effort failed. Few came to his assistance in debate. Burdett outspokenly opposed Littleton and forced Hume to admit that Manners-Sutton had acted impartially during the reform bill controversy.[40] When the motion was put to a vote only thirty-one diehard radicals voted in favor. Hobhouse wrote rather gleefully, "thus ended Joseph Hume's first attempt to head and lead a party."[41] The problem, it appears, did not lie with Hume alone, but with the radicals' inability to be led. They were, wrote Edward Lytton Bulwer, " a motley, confused, jarring miscellany of irreconcilable theorists."[42]

Hume suffered another setback when he attempted to organize radical support behind O'Connell's motion to study the causes of violence in Ireland. O'Connell was dismayed by the government's insistence that a coercion bill was required to suppress protests carried out by Irish radicals.

[36] Aspinall, *Three Early Nineteenth Century Diaries,* xxx, n. 5.

[37] Bain, *James Mill,* 368. See also Place's diary, 14 January 1833, BL, Add. MS. 35154.

[38] Memorandum of Place, 6 January 1833, BL, Add. MS. 35154, and Place to Roebuck, 27 December 1832, BL, Add. MS. 35154.

[39] *Hansard,* third series, 15: 37–44.

[40] Ibid., 49.

[41] Broughton, *Recollections,* 4: 279.

[42] See quotation in Hamburger, *Intellectuals in Politics,* 117.

Hume defended O'Connell's view by pointing out that it was unrealistic for Irish dissidents to cease their demonstrations until the ministry undertook some redress of their grievances. When ministers brought justice to Irish Catholics peace would follow. He warned the administration that the Irish could not be expected to show trust until reform pledges were redeemed.[43]

Hume was undoubtedly responding to the ongoing agitation and violence occurring in Ireland. Instead of satisfying Irish Catholics, the winning of Catholic Emancipation had only whetted their appetite for more concessions. While Catholic Emancipation had represented a great victory in providing civic equality, it came with some cost. A parallel act disenfranchised the 40 shilling freeholder by restricting the county vote to £10 freeholders. Similarly, as part of the bargain, O'Connell's Catholic Association was suppressed. Hence, along with the well-earned Emancipation there arose new grievances. This fact was dramatized by the growth of such groups as the Irish Volunteers for the Repeal of the Union and the Irish Society for Legal and Legislative Reform. Efforts to suppress these societies were undertaken by the Tory lord lieutenant in 1829, and later by the new Whig administration of Lord Anglesey and E. G. Stanley. Stanley's unconciliatory, even taunting attitude, precipitated more violence and prepared the way for the ministry's revival of coercion measures.[44]

The reaction to Hume's support for O'Connell's motion was adverse. Some of his friends, such as Edward Ellice, twitted him for attaching himself to another losing cause. Others accused him of trying once again, from vanity, to lead the radicals. It was reported that fifty or sixty of Hume's friends and constituents organized a meeting to criticize his conduct. O'Connell's motion eventually lost by a margin of 428 to 40. This lopsided defeat was made more bitter by the fact that Warburton, Roebuck, Grote and Molesworth voted with the majority.[45] The division was not a fair indication of support for the Irish cause either among the radicals or within the ministry. Such cabinet officers as Russell, Durham, and Althorp favored a conciliatory approach toward the restive Irish, but they were not ready to support an investigation of the scope proposed by O'Connell.

These early triumphs over Hume and O'Connell may have given the ministers a false sense of security. The support for continued reform, whether moderate or extreme, was still great within the House of Commons. Hume could not command a distinct radical block, but he could excite the interests of a large number of reformers when he raised the issue of retrenchment. His motion of 14 February, calling for the abolition of sinecures in the army and navy, appealed to many in the reformed Parliament.[46] He reminded the ministers that he had not pressed this question in 1832 because of his concern for parliamentary reform. With

[43]*Hansard*, third series 15: 325, 332.

[44]R. B. McDowell, *Public Opinion and Government Policy in Ireland, 1801–1846* (London, 1952), 140–41.

[45]Arthur Aspinall, "Le Marchant's Reports of Debates in the House of Commons, 1833," *English Historical Review*, 58 (1943): 91.

[46]*Hansard*, third series, 15: 459–61.

that goal achieved he thought it was time for the administration to give the people cheap government.[47] Although this motion failed by a vote of 232 to 138, the Whigs were concerned about their narrow majority.[48] Not only had the division revealed a desire for retrenchment, but it also placed some members of the ministry in an extremely difficult position. John Cam Hobhouse, secretary of war in Grey's cabinet, was given the task of defending the retention of sinecure offices. During the 1820s Hobhouse had joined Hume in leading a campaign against the very offices he now had to defend. His humiliation caused him to consider resignation.[49] He was not alone. Durham, Althorp, and C. Grant were also inclined to favor Hume's motion, but decided to hold the line rather than risk serious damage to the government.[50] The vote on sinecures revealed fissures within the cabinet as well as an opposition more potent than anticipated.

The ministry was not strengthened by the continuing disagreement among the leading Whigs over the Irish question. When Grey decided to deal firmly with Irish dissidents, he put liberals like Althorp in an uncomfortable position. Althorp's predicament was much the same as that faced by Hobhouse on Hume's sinecure motion. In introducing the ministry's Irish Coercion Bill on 27 February, Althorp exposed his embarrassment by fumbling through its presentation to the House. It was small wonder that shortly after this Althorp began to muse on the virtues of country life. Since Althorp was the glue that held the Grey government together, his despair over Irish policy threatened the existence of the administration. By early March there was talk of a government collapse.[51] It managed to struggle on, but divisions in Whig ranks intensified.

Ireland was still alive with excitement, most of it focused on opposition to Church tithes. Unlike such general demands as Catholic Emancipation and Repeal of the Union, the grievance against tithes dealt with a concrete problem affecting owners, occupiers, Catholics, dissenters, and anyone who bristled at the inequity of a minority church taxing the great majority. In such places as Clare and Galway, there were nightly raids against the gentry and huge gatherings of people to denounce the tithe. Irish newspapers including the *Comet,* the *Dublin Evening Post,* and the *Northern Whig* spoke for a cross section of Catholics and Protestant Irishmen in criticizing what the *Comet* called "wealthy prelates," and "pheasant shooting parsons."[52] The displacement of the Tories by the Whigs offered some hope for tithe reform, but strings would always be attached. Not all Whig ministers agreed with the conciliatory stance taken by Althorp and Russell. If tithe reform were accepted, it was almost certain that a coercion bill would be its corollary.

Hume blamed the chief secretary for Ireland, E. G. Stanley (later Lord

[47]See Abraham D. Kriegel, "The Politics of the Whigs in Opposition, 1843-45," *Journal of British Studies,* 7 (1968): 68. Also *Hansard,* third series, 15: 670-71.

[48]*Hansard,* third series, 15: 712.

[49]Broughton, *Recollections,* 4: 285-87.

[50]See Aspinall, *Three Early Nineteenth Century Diaries,* 302-3.

[51]Ibid., 311-12.

[52]McDowell, *Public Opinion and Government Policy in Ireland,* 144-45.

Stanley and Earl of Derby), for the government's unenlightened Irish policy. He saw the conservative Stanley as the "evil counselor" in the Whig ministry and urged that he be promptly removed. Hume did not like to oppose any of Grey's ministers with such vehemence, but he found the Irish coercion bill intolerable. He compared the measure with the Six Acts; it was, he said, an irony that the Whigs, who had damned the Tory repression in 1819, now proposed a similar measure of their own.

Although he thought Grey's administration derelict where Ireland was concerned, Hume persisted in the view that this government was still better than anything that had preceded it in the nineteenth century. He never failed to remind the parliamentary radicals that, say what they will about Grey's deficiencies, the Whig ministry had achieved more in three years than the Tories had in thirty. Even while he attacked the government's plans in Ireland, he praised Graham for the savings he had made at the Admiralty and Althorp for the budget he introduced on 19 April. In both instances Hume thought he saw signs that ministers were finally ready to recognize the importance of retrenchment to the success of any reform effort.

The government's good intentions, however, did not slow the opposition. On 25 April, Sir John Ingleby's motion for a reduction in the malt duty was approved by a group of radicals and agriculturists after a number of ministerialists had left the House. Since the Whigs had opposed this measure, ministers again talked of resigning.[53] Hume supported the motion, but he seemed to fear the consequences of the vote. He told a gleeful colleague, "If you knew what you had done you would not cheer."[54] Concerned about the possibility that the government would collapse, Hume wrote to Ellice that the radicals had no desire to turn out the Whigs. He advised Ellice that the Whigs would gain greater support from the public if they showed more interest in reform.[55] Althorp attempted to help the situation by moving an amendment to Ingleby's motion requiring a rise in property and income taxes if the malt tax was reduced. Hume opposed Althorp's amendment, but he expressed only mild displeasure with the Whig position. The problem was not with the ministers alone, he said, for "they had to contend against a system the whole machinery of which was of the most complex and pernicious character."[56]

This incident testifies to the ambivalent course followed by Hume in the 1833 session. He thought constant pressure was necessary if the radicals hoped to achieve far-reaching goals; yet if the liberal Whigs were the most likely agents of reform, their place in government had to be preserved. The Whigs had survived the test on tax reductions in April but were still uncertain of their strength. Outside of Parliament the signs were not more favorable. There seemed to be a growing sentiment in the country that the government had abdicated its responsibilities. The Birmingham Political

[53] Aspinall, *Three Early Nineteenth Century Diaries*, 322.
[54] Broughton, *Recollections*, 4: 302.
[55] Hume to Ellice, 27 April 1833, Ellice Papers, National Library of Scotland (NLS).
[56] *Hansard*, third series, 18: 776–82.

Union passed a resolution asking that the ministers be dismissed for having "proved themselves utterly unable or unwilling to extricate the country from the difficulties with which it is surrounded."[57] The administration was not reassured to learn that a public meeting was planned to prepare for a national convention for the purpose of "overthrowing the government, and substituting another for it."[58]

Hume could have mirrored this extra-Parliamentary disfavor in the Commons by reminding the Whigs of their past promises. Certainly he had reason to be dissatisfied. Althorp's refusal to consider the repeal of the tax on journals, the ballot, triennial parliaments, or an enlarged electorate left Hume with the impression that the Whigs were unresponsive to the will of the people.[59] Despite this he could not bring himself to condemn the backsliding Whigs. As in 1832, Hume decided to accept whatever reform crumbs the government offered and hope for bolder efforts in 1834.[60]

Hume's role in the 1834 Parliament did not vary much from what it had been in 1833. He still saw himself in a dual capacity: as a liaison between Whig leadership and the parliamentary radicals and as a gadfly in the cause of reform. Hume continued to maintain that he acted as an independent in all parliamentary business, but his conciliatory attitude obviously worked to the benefit of the Whigs.

The Grey government needed all the help it could get in 1834. The cabinet was seriously divided, especially over Irish matters, and some Whigs expected the radicals to exploit these differences.[61] From Hume's perspective, however, the Whig government made encouraging strides in 1834. He continued to grumble about the lack of retrenchment (a refrain that bored everyone except Hume); but he saw much to applaud in Althorp's promise of tax reductions, reform of ecclesiastical abuses, and a new poor law.[62] In addition, the Whigs appeared open to investigating the questions of national education and abuses in parliamentary elections.[63]

Hume was most pleased with the ministry's effort to reform the Poor Law. This was an issue dear to the heart for all free-trade radicals. In 1833 Grey had established a Poor Law Commission to study the many deficiencies in the old Poor Law. The commission was packed with individuals hostile to the Law. Two of the commissioners, William Nassau Senior and Edwin Chadwick (both laissez-faire economists), were responsible for gathering information on poor relief management in England. They drew up the questionnaire that was distributed to parish leaders throughout England and from which the commission acquired most of its data. The questions were phrased in such a way as to predetermine the answers. In March 1834 the commissioners produced an extensive report of their

[57]Molesworth, *History of England,* 250.

[58]Ibid.

[59]See *Hansard,* third series, 20:608–36.

[60]Hume to Place, 21 July 1833, BL, Add. MS. 35149.

[61]Place to John Smith, 10 August 1833, BL, Add. MS. 35149; Hamburger, *Intellectuals in Politics,* 132–33, n. 48.

[62]See Althorp's speech at the opening of the session, *Hansard,* third series, 21: 71–73.

[63]Ibid., 137–39.

findings, which clearly reinforced all the opinions of the free-traders. Although it had been virtually abandoned by the early 1830s, the Allowance System received severe criticism from the commission. In addition, it concluded that outdoor relief encouraged low wages, population growth, and unemployment. The commissioners, bound by preconceived ideas about the poor, were not above altering the evidence to fit those ideas.[64]

As the government had hoped, the commissioners included in their report recommendations for amending the old Poor Law. In suggesting changes, the commission followed the principle of "less eligibility" for outdoor assistance. This principle is most closely associated with Jeremy Bentham, who had advocated the building of workhouses for all able-bodied paupers, including children. Historically, indoor relief always had wide support from Englishmen, who felt it was the only way to stamp out sloth. In fact the feeling that paupers should not be cared for out of doors, except for widows with children and those who were ill, is traceable through several centuries in Britain.[65] Another recommendation of the commission was also influenced by Bentham: the commissioners called for a central governing board to increase efficiency and to eliminate abuses.

On 17 April 1834, Lord Althorp brought forward a Poor Law Amendment Bill in the Commons. The bill called for the curtailment of allowances in aid of wages and the virtual elimination of outdoor relief. The backers of the measure supposed this would provide an incentive for all able-bodied men and women, under threat of being sent to a workhouse, to find a place in the free market.

The Amendment Bill earned rapid approval in the reformed Commons, where upper-middle-class values now had a strong hold. As an old follower of James Mill and Bentham, Hume enthusiastically endorsed the proposed revision of the Poor Law. He thought the Whigs "deserved the praise of every man for the present attempt, which, if not perfect, ought not to be stopped unless the House was disposed to put an end to all improvements in the Poor Law."[66]

Hume's appreciation of the Poor Law Amendment Bill stood in contrast to his criticism of the administration's spending policies. But his repeated calls for retrenchment (especially in military appropriations) made almost no impact in the Commons. The House was usually empty when he appealed for greater prudence, and those who were there paid scant attention. The Grey ministry had nothing to fear from these weekly tirades, and Hume knew this as well as anyone. There were other issues, however, on which Hume could, and did, prove troublesome. The question of Irish Catholics was one such matter.

Government policy toward the established Church and Catholicism in Ireland had created trouble for the Whigs since 1830. The ministers were

[64]See J. R. Poynter, *Society and Pauperism: English Ideas on Poor Relief, 1795–1834* (Toronto, 1969), 310–321. See as well Mark Blaug's excellent "The Poor Law Report Re-Examined," *Journal of Economic History* 24 (1964): 231.

[65]Poynter, *Society and Pauperism*, 133–37.

[66]*Hansard*, third series, 23: 836–37.

seriously divided over what action to take, and Hume did all he could to exacerbate such internal divisions. For all of his concern about the Whigs being replaced by Tories, he did not hesitate to embarrass Althorp and Russell by insisting on a more liberal policy toward Irish Catholics. At the heart of Hume's criticism was his disdain for the political role of the established Church. This excessive political influence delayed needed reform in Ireland. Accordingly, on 13 March, he spoke in favor of a bill to strip the bishops in the House of Lords of their judicial and legislative functions. This proposal attracted only fifty-nine votes.[67] Hume pushed his opinion in the House of Commons because he knew that several men in Grey's cabinet agreed with his view, and because he thought conditions in Ireland required a clarification of the Church's position. He hoped he might be able to force Althorp and Russell to take a firm stand in support of Church reform.

Whether or not Hume helped to inspire the liberals in Grey's administration, during the first week in May Lord John Russell declared in favor of the use of Church tithes for secular purposes. The issue of lay appropriation of tithes made the fissures in the ministry into chasms. Stanley, Graham, the earl of Ripon, and the duke of Richmond all resigned.[68] Hume could scarcely contain his glee. He thought the moment had arrived when the liberal Whigs would take control. He anticipated that the crisis in May would allow reformers like Russell, Durham, and Brougham to assume leadership.[69] Hume therefore applied immediate pressure for more positive treatment of the Irish Catholics. In this instance, the Scotsman's political antenna failed him. He seemed not to realize how the May defections had devastated the Grey ministry. The desertion of the conservative Whigs was one thing, but the suspicions that remained behind were equally pernicious.

By the middle of June, Althorp and Russell had reached the conclusion that Lord Grey stood in the way of Irish reform. On 9 July, Althorp announced to the Commons that the ministry was at an end. Hume was surprised and dismayed.[70] Up to this point he had not understood the precarious state of the Grey administration. Hume worried most about the departure of Althorp. He had always considered Althorp the most reliable of the Whig reformers. In fact, Hume and O'Connell later presented a petition to Althorp (signed by over two hundred members) urging him to stay in government.[71] When the Whig ministry was quickly refashioned under Lord Melbourne, Hume expressed relief that Althorp had returned to the Exchequer.

By his own actions in the House of Commons, Hume encouraged the radicals to go easy on Melbourne in the first weeks of his administration. When, for example, the matter of disturbances in Ireland came before the

[67]*Hansard,* third series, 22: 151, 153.
[68]See Hamburger, *Intellectuals in Politics,* 134–35.
[69]Hume to Place, 3 June 1834, BL, Add. MS. 35149.
[70]*Hansard,* third series, 24: 1341–42.
[71]Broughton, *Recollections,* 4: 354; Hume to Althorp (then Earl Spencer), 28 January 1835, printed in Le Marchant, *Earl Spencer,* 351.

House, Hume spoke in unusually moderate tones. He also allowed one of his favorite targets, the militia bill, to proceed without his customary diatribe. Hume had every reason to be pleased with the new Melbourne government. Not only had Althorp returned as leader of the House of Commons, but Duncannon was made home secretary and Russell became paymaster-general. With obstacles like Ripon and Stanley removed from the ministry, it appeared certain that major reforms, especially those relating to Irish Catholics, would be introduced in the next session. Hume now thought that England had a government which "would prove itself a firm, steady, and liberal one."[72]

Hume's optimism proved to be unfounded. Melbourne's ministry did not last through November. The most serious blow came when Lord Althorp's father, Earl Spencer, died in November. With his death Althorp advanced to the earldom and into the House of Lords. It provided him with an opportunity to do what he had wanted to do for a long while—retire from politics. "You must be aware," he once wrote in a letter to Brougham,

that my being in office is nothing more or less than misery to me. I am perfectly sure that no man ever disliked it to such a degree as I do; and, indeed, the first thing that usually comes into my head when I wake is how am I to get out of it.[73]

Althorp's departure from the House of Commons caused Melbourne to offer his resignation to the king. At the same time he suggested to William IV that Russell might assume Althorp's role in the House. This did not suit the king. He had never trusted Russell, and he wanted to be certain that there would be no softening of policy toward Ireland. In fact, it was probably his concern over Ireland that led him to accept Melbourne's resignation and send for Peel to form a Tory government.

Hume was naturally disheartened by these developments. He had great admiration for Althorp, and it distressed him that this genuine reformer was lost to the cause. But Hume's disappointment in the autumn of 1834 did not blind him to the possibility of some good coming from the return of the Tories. The events seemed to confirm that the radicals needed the Whigs and that the Whigs needed the radicals. There was reason to hope for greater cooperation in the future as all reformers would see the necessity for removing the Tories and keeping them out.

[72]*Hansard,* third series, 25: 1116.
[73] Le Marchant, *Earl Spencer,* 527.

CHAPTER VI.

THE WHIG-RADICAL ALLIANCE AND ITS PROBLEMS, 1835–1841

When the Melbourne government collapsed in November 1834, Hume was quick to see the need for all reformers, Whig and radical, to unite against the Tories. His friends, especially Place and John Stuart Mill, wanted no more to do with the Whigs, but their position was unrealistic. Most reformers agreed with Hume that unseating the Peel ministry could be achieved only through continued cooperation. In December 1834 Hume tried to overlook differences that existed among the reformers. He wrote optimistically to Brougham, "all reformers, Radicals and Moderates are forgetting their differences and uniting against the tories, it is reform or no reform."[1] Later, he asked Brougham to use his "powerful assistance" to counteract the "illiberal and bigoted Tory administration."[2]

Lord John Russell did not need to be convinced. He was one of the first of the Whigs to be inclined toward a union with the radicals in order to defeat the Tories.[3] His motives were not altruistic. He realized that the radicals, as champions of reform, might readily profit from the apparent weakness of the Peel government and thereby capture the public's favor. To prevent this the Tories must be defeated with dispatch; this required combining forces in opposition.[4] Moreover, if Russell intended to continue advancing such proposals as tithe reform, he certainly could not rely on the alienated Stanley-Graham connection. These "hesitant" Whigs were not likely to be interested in opening liberal questions. Russell could, however, find support among the radicals.

Movement toward forming a united front against the Tories followed a tortuous course. Hume and the free-trade radicals met several times before the end of January in an effort to form a party of seventy to eighty reformers and to select a leader. They hoped that this group, combined with the Whigs and liberal Irish members, would join in providing formidable opposition to the Tories.[5] On 28 January, Hume asked Lord Spencer to stay in politics by helping all "reform-minded men" elect the liberal Scotsman, James Abercromby, as Speaker of the House of Commons. Hume wanted to oust the Tory Speaker, Manners-Sutton.[6] Spencer responded that should Abercromby lose, it might very well weaken the reform cause while strengthening the hand of the Tories. Russell also wondered whether an attack on Manners-Sutton might backfire.[7] Such a move could alert the Tories to danger and cause them to plot counter-

[1]Hume to Brougham, 10 December 1834, Brougham Papers, VCL.
[2]Hume to Brougham, 13 December 1834, Brougham Papers, VCL.
[3]Russell to Grey, 19 November 1834, Grey Papers, University of Durham.
[4]Walpole, *Life of Lord John Russell*, 1: 223–24.
[5]Lord Lansdowne to Russell, 1 February 1835, Russell Papers, Public Record Office (PRO), 30/22.
[6]Le Marchant, *Life of Lord Spencer*, 530–31.
[7]Russell to Grey, 30 January 1835, Grey Papers, University of Durham.

strategy. It was also unclear as to just how many Whigs would support this effort. Manners-Sutton had been a popular and able Speaker since 1817. He was respected for his fairness and propriety. Despite doubts raised by several leading Whigs, Hume decided to push the candidacy of Abercromby as an issue around which radicals and Whigs could unite.

Discussions over the speakership eventually led to the meeting at Lord Lichfield's house on 18 February. The Whigs initiated this gathering, but it was the radical Henry Warburton who circulated invitations.[8] The response heartened those who favored cooperation. The Lichfield House meeting had the support of all the important parliamentary radicals, including Hume, and also earned the endorsement of O'Connell's "Irish Brigade."[9] The goals of the Lichfield House conferees were limited. Their long range purpose was to remove Peel from office, but the factions represented only pledged themselves to vote for Abercromby. There was talk of closer alliance in reforming the tithe system, but no formal plans were developed.

It was generally agreed by Whigs and radicals that they ought to "go slow" in forcing out Peel's government. The Whigs preferred to amend Tory proposals judiciously. This would gradually erode confidence in the government. A direct attack on the administration might cause "waverers" in the Commons to draw back.

The Whigs saw the Lichfield House compact as a temporary expedient, but it significantly affected the future of parliamentary politics for the next six years. The union of Whigs and radicals successfully achieved the election of Abercromby as Speaker by a vote of 317 to 307; and thereafter it was difficult for Peel to attract waverers to his side.[10] He struggled until April, but the cooperation shown by reformers in these early votes indicated that a majority could be mustered against the Tories at any time. Beyond this immediate effect, the Lichfield House compact reinforced the idea that the Whigs and Tories were still the primary rivals in the Commons. The agreement set back the desire of radicals to emerge as a majority party. By cooperating with the Whigs, the radicals effectively blurred their separate identity and partially tied their reform hopes to Whig leadership. Hume had been advocating such a "liberal phalanx" since 1832. No party to the compact had committed itself to a list of specific issues, but the fact that there was a general desire to keep out the Tories made it difficult for the radicals to take an independent line on most issues.

The Lichfield House compact provided a solid foundation for the formation of a liberal faction in the House of Commons.[11] Prior to February 1835, liberal Whigs and radicals had followed a coincidentally liberal direction in favoring parliamentary reform, revision of the tithe system, poor law reform, and factory legislation. The next logical step was for like-minded reformers to agree expressly to cooperate. The Lichfield

---

[8]Walpole, *Life of Lord John Russell*, 1:231–32.
[9]Hume to Charles Babbage, 19 February 1835, BL, Add. MS. 37189.
[10]*Hansard*, third series, 26: 56–61, 410–15.
[11]Gash, *Reaction and Reconstruction in English Politics*, 169–70.

House compact, therefore, represents the high point of Whig-radical amalgamation.

Hume was more than pleased with the arrangements made at Lichfield House, but he found it difficult to abide by the "go-slow" policy supported by most of his associates. In his first major speech of the session on 27 February, he spoke of the opposition's willingness to turn out the Tories "as soon as possible." He then moved an amendment to the Address, expressing regret that the king chose ministers who lacked the confidence of the nation.[12] It seemed premature for a vote of no confidence against the ministers, and the Scotsman was urged by friends to reconsider. Although he eventually withdrew his motion, Hume's effort embarrassed Russell and the Whigs. The apparent lack of coordination in opposition continued when Hume attempted to limit supplies. Troubled by this unforeseen action, Russell complained to Grey,

In this state of things I feel much embarrassed. Many of our friends have been sent for from the country, and I can hardly avoid, if we do not *vote* with Hume, calling a general meeting of all shades of opposition—if on the contrary we support the limited supplies, I fear we shall be defeated both in number and what is worse, in opinion.[13]

In short, if Hume's motion failed it might boost Peel's confidence and thereby reverse the effect of the opposition's victory on the speakership.

Despite Russell's reservations, Hume continued to badger the government with querulous attacks on the army and navy estimates. On 16 March, dissatisfied with information supplied to him on the navy estimates, he moved an amendment referring the matter to a select committee. The motion failed miserably, 146 to 66.[14] Such harassing tactics, ineffectual in themselves, seemed to frustrate Peel as he attempted to impress the country with his parliamentary achievements.[15] J. C. Herries, Peel's secretary of war, revived a complaint most familiar to Hume when he accused the Scotsman of obstructing the business of the House of Commons. Hume replied that the representatives of the people should not "place the public money at the disposal of the Ministers without due discussion or strict attention to economy."[16] Hume's view of the situation did not please the Whigs; but they had to agree, contrary to the fears expressed by Russell, that his criticisms wore down the ministers.[17] Without realizing it, Hume was contributing toward fulfilling the Whig-radical intention of slowly destroying the Peel government. That Hume's constant and pedantic criticism weighed heavily on the ministers is probably evidence that Peel's administration was moribund from the start.

The final blow to the Peel administration came on the issue of Irish tithes. Hume eagerly joined Russell's challenge to the Tories on this

---

[12]*Hansard,* third series, 26: 426.
[13]Russell to Grey, 10 March 1835, Grey Papers, University of Durham.
[14]*Hansard,* third series, 26: 1032, 1036, 1046.
[15]Kitson-Clark, *Peel and the Conservative Party,* 244.
[16]Hansard, third series, 28: 316.
[17]Kitson-Clark, *Peel and the Conservative Party,* 244.

question. When Russell announced, on 30 March, that he would bring in a motion regarding the appropriation of Irish Church revenue, Hume knew that the liberal Whigs had decided to bring the prime minister down. After consecutive parliamentary defeats in early April, Peel offered his resignation to the king.[18]

Peel's failure, attributable to the weakness of his ministry and to the joint efforts of liberal Whigs, radicals, and Irish members, not only completed the general objective of those who met at Lichfield House, but it also set back the effort by conservative Whigs to curb their party's shift to the left. Those Whigs who dragged their feet when it came to allying against the Tories were considered out of step and politically impractical. One can imagine the shock to the old Whig guard when, at a dinner held in March, Russell received recognition as a leader of the radicals and the Irish as well as the Whigs.[19] Disagreements with Hume over parliamentary tactics notwithstanding, liberal Whigs seemed to have more in common with the radicals than they did with such conservative Whigs as Stanley, Graham, and Howick. What had begun as an alliance of temporary convenience gave evidence of developing into something more permanent.

A further test of Whig-radical cooperation came when the new Whig ministry was formed in April. Naturally, the radicals expected the Whigs to push those measures that they had favored out of office: lay appropriation of church revenue, municipal corporation reform, the ballot, comprehensive relief for dissenters, and general retrenchment. Hume asked for something more from the Whigs. He wanted the prime minister, Lord Melbourne, to appoint radicals to the ministry. Specifically, he advised that Edward Lytton Bulwer, Dr. John Bowring, Charles Buller, and Daniel O'Connell receive cabinet posts.[20] There was no hope that such concessions would be made. Melbourne virtually precluded any possibility of bringing in radicals when he told Lord Grey in January 1835, "I will have nothing to do with Brougham. . . . I will have nothing to do with Durham. For obvious reasons I forbear to state to you my reasons for this decision; nor need I account for my third preemptory exclusion, which is O'Connell."[21] Melbourne was not quite a conservative Whig, but he was cautious enough not to want members from the extreme left in his cabinet. The rejection of Hume's nominees indicates the limits of the Whig-radical entente.

Ironically, many Benthamites also took the position that radicals ought not to participate in the Melbourne administration. James Mill reasoned that such an affiliation would divide the radicals and discredit them in the eyes of the public.[22] His son, John Stuart, although willing to support the new ministry, agreed that the radicals should not tie themselves to Whig

---

[18]Gash, *Sir Robert Peel*, 117.

[19]Greville, *Memoirs*, 3: 238.

[20]Hume to Ellice, 15 April 1835, Ellice Papers, NLS.

[21]Melbourne to Grey, 23 January 1835, in Sanders, *Lord Melbourne's Papers*, 237. See Bruce L. Kinzer, *The Ballot Question in Nineteenth Century English Politics* (New York, 1982) for an account of the evolution of this major political question.

[22]*London Review*, 1 April 1835.

policy.[23] Albany Fonblanque, editor of the *Examiner,* supported the Mills in contending that the radicals should only act as "a corps of observation."[24] All three of these men still looked forward to the emergence of a majority radical party once the Whigs and Tories weakened. They recognized that the time was not ripe for this to happen, but in the interim they wanted to safeguard the radicals' separate identity.

Hume did not share the concern of his Benthamite friends. He did not seem troubled by his proximity to the Whigs. Even when Melbourne refused to consider putting radicals in his ministry, Hume was not unduly alarmed. As so often in the past, he was content to give the Whigs a chance. This was especially true in the spring of 1835 as the Whig ministers clumsily sought to establish a solid administration. When, for example, Place asked Hume to petition once again for the abolition of the newspaper tax, he refused to do anything until he learned the government's plan for the coming session. "My wish is not to do anything as regards the stamp on newspapers," wrote Hume, "until we know what is to be done by ministers."[25] He had no intention of embarrassing the Whigs on this occasion.

This proved more than Place could bear. It discouraged him to have individuals throughout England and Scotland campaigning for the cause of repeal and not receive assistance from Hume in Parliament. He did not know why Hume waited for the ministers to take the initiative. He knew that the Whigs were unreliable. Place recalled that in 1833 Lord Althorp had promised action on the repeal of the newspaper tax, but then gave it up. "When did any minister, whig or tory, keep his promise to you," Place inquired of Hume.[26] It seemed to Place that his old friend had succumbed to the Whiggish tendency of avoiding controversial questions. He noted that Hume had expunged the word "ballot" from a recent speech he had made to the Middlesex voters.[27] Stung by this criticism, Hume replied that he had done his part for the cause of the stamp tax's abolition by pressing Spring Rice for change. He had, he reminded Place testily, also sent out five thousand circulars demanding repeal.[28]

At the heart of the disagreement between Place and Hume were differing radical views of the trustworthiness of Whigs as reformers. Place accused Hume of suffering from "Lord Johnism" and too much Whig kindness.[29] Could it be, he wondered, that Hume still basked in the success of the Lichfield House compact? How else could one account for the fact that when Parliament reconvened in May, Hume and his colleagues moved to the ministerial side of the House? This was carrying accommodation to extreme lengths. Despite Place's protestations, Hume continued to have a generous regard for the Melbourne government.

[23]Hamburger, *Intellectuals in Politics,* 140–41.
[24]Ibid.
[25]Place to Hume, 2 May 1835, BL, Add. MS. 35150.
[26]Place to Hume, 2 May 1835, BL, Add. MS. 35150.
[27]Ibid.
[28]Hume to Place, 10 May 1835, BL, Add. MS. 35150.
[29]Place to Hume, 12 May 1835, BL, Add. MS. 35150.

The state of the ministry was still uncertain in early May. The situation would not change until by-elections, necessitated by the change in administration, were completed. Hence, important questions were held in abeyance until the Whig ministers were on a firmer footing. Hume played a waiting game, doing little in the month of May except counseling fellow reformers to be patient. William Cobbett, who sought repeal of the new Poor Law, was told by Hume to give the reform more opportunity to work. This advice had no influence on Cobbett, but it does indicate the interest Hume had in keeping Parliament as calm as possible. Similarly, the Scotsman tried to tone down Henry Burton's inflammatory demand that the king call upon all nations to abolish the slave trade.[30]

By June the Whig government was more secure, and Hume looked forward to Russell's promised motion on municipal corporation reform. The groundwork for the motion had been done by Joseph Parkes, so that on the face of it, it was a radical reform effort. Most radicals seemed content with the terms of the measure, but, from his view outside of Parliament, Place thought that the radicals had given away too much in compromise. He wanted Hume to introduce legislation based on his own (Place's) "Principles upon which the Municipal Government ought to be founded." While Russell's bill had many liberal provisions, including the franchise for house-holders who paid the poor rate, Place's proposal went further by allowing for the annual election of town council members, the secret ballot, and complete council control over municipal functions. Hume preferred the features of Place's suggestion, yet he hoped that all factions would pull together behind the Whig bill.[31] He made no attempt to recommend a more liberal measure. Place thought that Hume was overly close to the Whigs and thereby losing his freedom to make demands upon them.[32] Only when the municipal corporation reform bill went to committee did Hume register a mild objection, preferring a two-year rather than a three-year residency requirement. Aside from that, Hume raised no questions about the measure as it sailed through to passage by the House on 21 July.

The debate over municipal corporation reform was not the only prominent issue in the summer of 1835. Irish Church reform, the appropriation of Church revenue for secular purposes, and the Orange Lodges also caused stormy debates in the Commons. When the new chief secretary for Ireland, Lord Morpeth, introduced the Irish Tithe Bill on 26 June, Hume predicted that it would easily pass through the House of Commons and be hailed by the people. Hume wanted comprehensive change in the Church and, while the Whig bill fell short of this goal, he accepted it as a splendid beginning. He did nothing to impede its progress, if for no other reason than his belief that it would help to bring tranquillity to Ireland.[33]

Although nearly all of the parliamentary radicals voted for the bill's final approval, only Hume spoke for the measure in debate. English radicals considered Irish matters a distraction from the serious work of reform in

---

[30]*Hansard*, third series, 27: 1027, 1047–48.
[31]*Hansard*, third series, 18: 541–88.
[32]Grote to Place, 7 June 1835, BL, Add. MS. 35150.
[33]*Hansard*, third series, 29: 885–893.

England. Francis Place encouraged this indifference. He held the view that the Irish should solve their own problems without help from the English.[34] Place was not the only radical to disassociate himself from Irish issues. J. A. Roebuck, exasperated by the failure of the liberal Whigs to press for the ballot, annual Parliaments, and a broadened suffrage, also was annoyed that Irish Church reform should take precedence over important political changes. In his *Pamphlets for the People,* he urged radicals to abstain on the Irish Church question until O'Connell and the Whigs promised to support radical proposals.[35]

It is clear enough from parliamentary debates and divisions that most radicals favored dismantling the ecclesiastical establishment in Ireland while still believing that Irish issues were of secondary importance. Hume was the sole parliamentary radical to offer any proposals relating to reform in Ireland during 1835. It is understandable, then, why a rapport developed between Hume and O'Connell. Moreover, O'Connell's close ties with the Whigs after 1835 were clearly inspired by Hume's loyalty to the ministers and to their new administration in Ireland.

One other matter relating to Ireland drew Hume and O'Connell closer together in the summer of 1835. This was the proliferation of Orange Lodges. In July Hume expressed concern about the violent incidents fomented by these ultra-Protestant societies in Ireland.[36] He told Lord Morpeth that he looked to him as lord lieutenant to suppress the Orange Lodges. Hume continued the initiative in August by moving resolutions declaring Orangeism illegal, and specifically asking the king to direct his attention to the Orange Lodges in the army. These resolutions, requiring that persons connected with the Lodges be court martialled,[37] were based on four reports from a select committee appointed to investigate the societies. Although the committee consisted of twenty-seven members, including eight Orangemen, the drafting of the reports came under Hume's direction.[38] Russell and Melbourne saw the evil in the Orange societies, but they were sensitive to the fact that the king's brother, the Duke of Cumberland, had signed warrants for the formation of Orange Lodges in the army. Rather than outlaw the lodges, Melbourne preferred that they weaken and wither away from their own inertia.[39] Hume did not wish to create problems at court, and told Russell that he would be open to a compromise on the matter.[40] This question, then, was hardly an obstacle to Hume's maintaining good relations with the Whigs.

Hume remained faithful to the Whig ministers through the remainder of 1835, although his enthusiasm waned somewhat in August and September. He objected to the government's acquiescence in changes recommended by

[34]Place to Ensor, 27 May 1835, BL, Add. MS. 35150.

[35]Leader, *Life and Letters of John Arthur Roebuck,* 74.

[36]*Hansard,* third series, 29: 694–97.

[37]Ibid., 320.

[38]*Hansard,* third series, 30: 1439–40; Hereward Senior, *Orangeism in Ireland and Britain, 1795–1836* (London, 1966), 267–68.

[39]Russell to Grey 13 October 1835, Grey Papers.

[40]Hume to Russell, 2 November 1835, Russell Papers, PRO 30/22.

the House of Lords for the tithe and corporation bills. For a time, Hume seemed prepared to break his alliance with the Whigs unless the ministry forced a showdown with the Upper House. It took considerable persuasion from Russell and O'Connell to convince Hume that a direct confrontation between Commons and Lords was not in the country's best interest.

By early September Hume appeared to have forgiven his Whig associates for their "spirit of compromise" with the peers. He directed his attack less against the ministers and more at Peel and the Tory noblemen. In fact, when the Municipal Corporation Bill finally passed on 7 September, Hume praised the Whigs for moving this significant measure while taunting Peel for proposing amendments calculated to split the Whig-radical entente.[41] Hume defended his cooperation with the Whigs not only to the Tories but also to his moderate radical friends. He took this course, he explained to his colleagues on the floor of the House, "only from a conscientious conviction that it was now the best to be pursued."[42] Hume's quarrel was not with the Whigs but with the Lords who were frustrating the intent of the Great Reform Act and the broader reform movement that followed.

There were some radicals who blamed the Whigs for not applying more pressure to the House of Lords. "Ought the ministers," asked Francis Place,

to have to put up with the kicking the Lords bestowed on them? I say no. . . . The Lords will not be reformed, not they, but it is good to make every one see that they must either be reformed or abolished, that whenever the time comes, the abolition [of the Lords], cost what it may, may be perfect.[43]

Roebuck also had harsh words for Russell and the Whigs. He questioned the value of supporting the ministers. He thought the Whigs "resisted popular reform" almost as much as the Tories.[44] Despite the opinions of Place and Roebuck, such opposition to compromise remained a minority view among the radicals. Although he stayed on reasonably good terms with the ultra-radicals, Hume continued to preach to his parliamentary associates against any disturbance of the tenuous Whig-radical alliance. While Place and Roebuck feared losing the support of "the people," Hume feared jeopardizing the life of the Melbourne ministry.[45]

At the same time, Hume worried about the depth of commitment any Whig administration could have to reform. He spent much of November and December fretting over what to expect from Melbourne. Maybe he had anticipated too much. By the beginning of 1836 Hume seemed to be of two minds about the future of the Whig alliance. He agreed with Edward Ellice, the former Whig whip, that the Whigs could not survive without

[41]*Hansard*, third series, 30: 1414–18; Parkes to Ellice, 6 September 1835, Lambton Papers, Lambton Estate office, County Durham; Place to Parkes, 6 September 1835, BL, Add. MS. 35150.

[42]*Hansard*, third series, 30:1418.

[43]Place to Parkes, 30 September 1835, BL, Add. MS. 35150.

[44]*Hansard*, third series, 30: 1158.

[45]On the general subject of the Lichfield House agreement, see A. H. Graham, "The Lichfield House Compact, 1835," *Irish Historical Studies*, 12 (1960–61): 219.

radical assistance, yet he wondered whether the ministers properly understood this reality. Could they be persuaded to advance a genuine radical
cause, or would they forever be satisfied with half-way measures? Since
1832 Hume had accepted the principle that "half-a-loaf is better than
none"; but was it possible that the radicals would never get beyond
"half-a-loaf"? Perhaps there was more to the complaint of the ultra-
radicals than he had cared to admit.

The first test of the Whig-radical alliance came early in the 1836
parliamentary session. The issue was a renewed campaign to eliminate the
duty on newspapers. There seemed to be greater enthusiasm for repeal.
Aroused by the government's rigorous prosecution of pamphleteers and
publishers of cheap journals, Hume formed part of a deputation including
Place, O'Connell, Warburton, and Grote to petition Melbourne for
abolition of the tax and mitigation of the penalties against those accused.[46]
Hume told Melbourne that the public wanted elimination of the tax, or at
least proposals for its reduction. He pointed out that the interest "felt by the
smaller shopkeepers, by persons of small income, and the more intelligent
of the working people was intense."[47] In light of these circumstances,
Hume warned of the possibility that the radicals might desert the
government if no action were taken. Melbourne responded cautiously,
promising only that he would consider what Hume had said.[48] On 15
March, the attorney-general announced that the ministers would agree to
reduce the stamp duty to one penny. It was a half-way measure, but Hume
accepted it as a sign of good faith from the government.[49]

There were many parliamentary radicals who could not agree with
Hume on this issue. They wanted an immediate end to the newspaper tax,
and showed signs of rebelling against the Whig leadership.[50] In early May,
O'Connell, Ewart, Duncombe, Grote, Warburton and several others
planned a second deputation to see Melbourne and his chancellor of the
exchequer, Spring Rice. The deputation hoped to convince the prime
minister that there was nothing to be gained by retaining the penny tax on
newspapers and pamphlets. Hume agreed to join this deputation, but he
did not intend to berate the ministers. He hoped to bring the two sides
closer together by arguing a point that both Whigs and radicals could
understand: to stay in office and keep out the Tories the government must
have radical support. Spring Rice and Melbourne knew this to be true, yet
they insisted that total abolition of the tax would jeopardize the government's revenue and would not be acceptable to the great majority in
Parliament. The ministers stood their ground; the radicals gave way. When
the bill was discussed in committee on 20 June, not a radical voice was
heard against it.[51]

Paralleling his efforts against the newspaper tax was Hume's participa-

[46]Reported by Place, 20 February 1836, BL, Add. MS. 35146.
[47]Ibid.
[48]Ibid.
[49]Hansard, third series, 32: 351, 359, 361.
[50]Place to Hume, 10 April 1836, BL, Add. MS. 35150.
[51]Hansard, third series, 34: 663–65.

tion in an attempt to wed the Whigs officially to the radicals. This was to be achieved through the creation of a reform club that would, at least in theory, supply all reformers with a forum for their ideas. Molesworth, Grote, and Parkes were among the leaders in trying to form such a club. Molesworth urged Hume to take an active role and, once having convinced the Scotsman that the club could succeed, assigned him the task of persuading his Whig friend, Edward Ellice, to join the association. At first, Hume did not have much success. Ellice had reservations. He feared that a club would be too controversial and that many would view it as a Whig-radical conspiracy. He wrote at the time to Parkes,

I *have serious doubts* whether any attempt to carry this club system further would be popular, and how far many of the Town Councils would be frightened by the cry that would immediately be set up of "club government." Suppose some of the liberals . . . think one way, some another. Would a division be a good thing or tend to give the enemy a more wholesome opinion or apprehension of our strength?[52]

Eventually, Ellice consented to become a member of the club; and it was established that the organization's central committee would include several Whigs.[53] By March 1836 some two hundred and fifty members of Parliament as well as a thousand other persons were enrolled as members.[54] Included in that number were E. J. Stanley, the Duke of Norfolk, the Earl of Mulgrave, and most of the members of Melbourne's cabinet.

The apparent success of the Reform Club brought jubilation to the radical camp. Molesworth exclaimed, "It will be the best club in town, and the effect will be to break up the whig party by joining the best of them to the radicals."[55] But a cynic may well wonder whether Molesworth was more interested in a Whig-radical stew or in haute cuisine. From the start he appeared to have greater concern for the requirements of good dining than he had for political strategy. He wanted the Reform Club to have dining facilities equal to those in the Athenaeum Club. Luxury requires money, and this, more than any other consideration, may account for Molesworth's determination to recruit Whig aristocrats. Molesworth had never seen any contradiction in socializing with the Whigs while damning them politically. When the Reform Club opened in May 1836, Molesworth was the only one who gained much satisfaction. The club never fulfilled the political hopes of many of its founders, but it did employ an outstanding chef.

Despite the marginal success of the Reform Club, Whig-radical harmony did not turn to dissonance in 1836. There were a number of strains and rifts between the government and its radical backers, but not one of them posed a serious threat to the working arrangement. Hume was the chief reason they did not. He championed cooperation at every turn;

---

[52]Quoted in Norman Gash, *Politics in the Age of Peel* (London, 1953), 405–6.
[53]Ibid., 408–9.
[54]Hume to Brougham, 12 February 1836, Brougham Papers; Parkes to Durham, 1 March 1836, Lambton Papers, Lambton Estate office, County Durham; *Politics in the Age of Peel*, 409–10.
[55]See Gash, *Politics in the Age of Peel*, 409–10.

and as long as he remained loyal to the alliance, the impatient radicals, principally Place, Molesworth, and Roebuck, found their hands tied. This is not to say that Hume never criticized the Whig ministers. He frequently chided Russell for not pushing reform measures with greater vigor, but he never lost sight of the reason for Whig-radical cooperation. "No man is more sensible to the necessity of union amongst reformers than I am," he said on 2 August, "and I have made and am proposing to make great use of opinion for that purpose, being convinced that there is imminent danger of division among the reformers; and if so, of the triumph of the tories for a time."[56] Unlike some radicals, Hume had not lost hope in Whig leadership. He thought that the Whigs had done more since 1830 than could ever have been achieved by Tory administrations.

At the same time, Hume was never blind to reality. In his assessment of the work of the 1836 session, he said he was mortified that scarcely one-tenth of the needed reforms were passed. He complained to Ellice that he found it lamentable "to be obliged to support ministers" who refused to "take off the tax on newspapers in violation of Lord Althorp's promise." He also cited misrule in the Colonial Office that he predicted would force the colonies, particularly Canada, to seek independence. Hume did not, however, place all the blame on the Melbourne government for this situation. He directed most of his criticism toward the conservative interests in the House of Lords that discouraged action in the Commons. When the Irish Tithe Bill was stripped of its important clauses in the upper House, Hume said he was happy to join Russell in refusing to accept the amended bill even if it meant that no legislation would be enacted in 1836.[57]

His defense of the government notwithstanding, no one with Hume's radical connections could remain immune to the calls from his old friends for greater demands on the Whigs. He knew that the Irish contingent in the Commons, as well as such men as Molesworth, Ewart, Baines, and Grote, wanted him to heed the advice of Place for more demonstrable opposition to what appeared to them to be a very staid and comfortable Whig administration. Hume resisted these appeals. He still clung to the opinion that the Whigs could, however slowly, be brought around to accepting more extensive reform. There was another reason. Hume was shrewd enough to know that in 1836 public opinion was simply not sufficiently excited about tithe reform, the newspaper tax, or Irish questions for the radicals to make a direct appeal to the country. Circumstances were much different from what they had been in the months immediately preceding the passage of the Great Reform Bill. Hume had appealed to "the people" many times during the days of the unreformed Parliament, thus he had a well-developed sense of timing on popular causes. He knew that the summer of 1836 was not the moment for the radicals to threaten dire consequences if the public's interests were not served. He was content to wait for the Whigs to take the lead.

---

[56]Hume to Joseph Strutt and Samuel Fox, 2 August 1836, Miscellaneous MSS., University College, London.

[57]*Hansard,* third series, 34: 795–802.

In the autumn of 1836 Hume did try to assuage the militant radicals to some extent. He became involved in the founding of a newspaper, the *Constitutional,* designed to "advocate those principles which are essential for the welfare of the people and for their good government." He explained to Place that he wanted a paper that would

oppose the arbitrary and unconstitutional, i.e., anti-liberal tory party, that will support the whigs in all good measures but to point their faults and advocate measures that would promote good government and reform in every branch of the state—to be in fact the paper of the people. . . .[58]

Specifically, the paper would argue for shortened parliaments and the ballot. The *Constitutional,* which called itself "the first fruit of the penny tax," began publishing on 15 September, the day the newspaper duty went from 4d. to 1d. Hume asked Place to help manage the paper, but he declined. Place used the excuse that the new paper did not have sufficient financial backing, but his real reasons were more philosophical. He wanted no part of any journal that gave support, however qualified, to the Melbourne government.[59]

The extent of Hume's influence over the newspaper is unclear, but in succeeding weeks the *Constitutional* presented views on the Corn Laws, Canadian independence, and parliamentary reform that were basically his. It also discussed the relationship of Hume and O'Connell with the Whig government. The paper made it plain that they were not "contented" radicals as some had claimed.[60] The *Constitutional* told its readers that Hume was fond of quoting Bentham's "simple but profound maxim" that the only way to secure justice to the many is to make "the ruling few uneasy."[61]

Throughout October, November, and December, the *Constitutional* attacked the conservative newspapers. The *Globe, Herald, Courier,* and *Times* received heavy criticism. There was also a denial that a radical could be a Tory. "Tory-Radicals," wrote the *Constitutional,* "are creatures of the fancy." In general the paper pointed to Hume as the most worthy proponent of reform legislation. But it did not always support his views. It was especially slow to adopt his favorable opinion of the new Poor Law. "The *Constitutional* newspaper is thoroughly liberal," Hume wrote to Edwin Chadwick on 11 November, "and I am trying to get it right about the Poor Laws."[62]

Whatever good the *Constitutional* did for the cause of reform, it did little good for Hume. His support for the Whig cabinet, always frustrating to the militant radicals, was now verging on the intolerable. Roebuck, spurred on

---

[58]Hume to Place, 20 September 1836, BL, Add. MS. 35150.

[59]*The Constitutional,* 15 September 1836.

[60]*The Constitutional,* 17 September 1836. See Joel H. Wiener, *The War of the Unstamped: The Movement to Repeal the British Newspaper Tax, 1830–1836* (Ithaca, N.Y., 1969), 27, 45, 273.

[61]20 October 1836.

[62]Chadwick Papers, UCL. The *Constitutional* never gained more than one thousand official subscribers and it died in the summer of 1837. The Penny Tax helped to push the price too high for its likely purchasers.

by Place, planned to force the hands of the Whigs early in the next session. He hoped Hume would join his effort, but they were ready to go ahead without him. Unless radical advice was accepted, Roebuck and his associates planned to desert the Whigs and lead the opposition against a new Tory government.[63] It is also apparent that Roebuck envisioned the emergence of the radicals as an enlarged party able to preempt the Whigs as sponsors of true reform. He did not elaborate on how this was to be accomplished, but he saw the radicals following an independent course.[64]

Roebuck reflected Place's view that there was no reason for maintaining the alliance with the Whigs if the only objective was to keep the Tories out of office. Comparing the Whig-radical alliance to the old Fox-North coalition, Place told everyone he could that Hume had been cowed by Lord John Russell for fear that the Whigs might resign. Hume, he said, should have "cut the whigs" long ago.[65] Place had no faith that Hume would take the lead in demanding more reforms, and he expected the 1837 parliamentary session to be as dismal as that in 1836. Molesworth also believed that Hume had been contaminated by the Whigs and that his usefulness was at an end.[66]

While Place, Molesworth, and Roebuck talked of going on alone, other radicals, even when espousing radical views, were loyal to the Whigs. Joseph Parkes, whose channel of communication remained open to the cabinet, assured Russell that all reform parties would pull together. He and other "sober" radicals were sensitive to the ministry's embarrassment in trying to follow a course between backsliding and radical reform.[67]

The emerging conflict came to a head in January 1837 just prior to the opening of Parliament. William Molesworth had thrown down the gauntlet in an article in *The London and Westminster Review,* where he argued that unless the Whig ministers accepted the ballot as an open question for debate, the radicals should follow an independent line. This would permit the Tories to take office. In the short term, such a development would no doubt retard reform, but Molesworth reasoned that there would be long-term political benefits. It would allow the more conservative Whigs to gravitate to their natural allies, the Tories, while liberal Whigs would join company with the radicals. Molesworth reasoned that radicals had little to lose if the Tories came in since no significant reforms were expected from the Whig ministers.[68] The militant radicals had seized the initiative in demanding that their moderate colleagues reassess their association with the Whigs.[69]

The division between militant and moderate radicals reached a new level when a testimonial dinner was planned in January 1837 for the Middlesex parliamentary representatives, Hume and George Byng. Place, who was

[63]Roebuck to Brougham, 7 September 1836, Brougham Papers, UCL.
[64]Hamburger, *Intellectuals in Politics,* 175–76.
[65]Place to Roebuck, 3 October 1836, BL, Add. MS. 35150.
[66]Molesworth to Place, 5 October 1836, BL, Add. MS. 35150.
[67]Parkes to Russell, 6 October 1836, Russell Papers, PRO 30/22.
[68]See Hamburger, *Intellectuals in Politics,* 171–72, 179.
[69]Ibid.

asked to be a steward at the dinner, refused the invitation because he
disliked Byng. He considered him a false reformer. He also feared that
ministers would use this dinner (and Hume's presence) to indicate unity
among radicals and Whigs. It might also serve as a platform to trumpet
praises for ministerial accomplishments. He knew that Hume would
attend; but he hoped that instead of celebrating his alliance with the Whigs,
he would challenge the ministers to take up greater reforms. If Hume did
this, Place promised that the public would rally to his side. Place thought
the radicals and Whigs had reached another turning point. He told Hume,
"this meeting will be a crisis of great importance to the nation, and much
may depend on what you . . . may say."[70] Roebuck agreed with Place that
the dinner could spell disaster for reform, and he castigated Hume for
cowardice.[71]

Hume's defense against such accusations was to say that no Whigs could
keep him from speaking like a radical, and if the dinner lacked a radical
flavor it was because men like Place refused to attend.[72] Hume's opinion
was shared by others. T. Perronet Thompson thought the dinner would not
damage the radical cause. He viewed it as a time for radicals and those they
"least disliked" to gather together. The most that Thompson planned to
demand from the Whigs was contained in a toast he offered calling for the
ministers to "continue in power so long as they advance the cause of the
people."[73] Place and Roebuck found this objectionable because it implied
that the Whigs had performed well in the past.[74]

Most speakers at the dinner on 27 January spoke in praise of the
Whig-radical alliance. Hume unequivocally committed himself to the
government. "We had nothing to expect from the Tories but evil," he said
at one point, "while we can have nothing from a liberal government but
good."[75] He recognized that a need still existed for more reforms, but he
thought that the Melbourne administration would accomplish this unfin-
ished business.[76] Warburton and Buller followed the same theme; they
commended the Whig-radical alliance while expressing hope for future
reforms.

The upshot of the Middlesex dinner was that most radicals continued to
support the Whig ministry. Place, Roebuck, and Molesworth were shown
to represent a militant minority who were ready to risk a break with the
Whigs. There were some radicals, like George Grote, caught between the
Hume moderates and the Roebuck militants. Grote sympathized with
Roebuck's call for aggressive tactics, but could not bring himself to help
undermine the Whig government. Grote talked as if he were a militant, but

[70]Place to Joseph Davies of the Middlesex Reform Club, 12 December 1836, BL, Add. MS.
35150, and Place to Hume, 30 December 1836, BL, Add. MS. 35150.

[71]Roebuck to Place, 4 January 1837, BL, Add. MS. 35150.

[72]Hume to Place, 1 January 1837, BL, Add. MS. 35150.

[73]Thompson to Place, 1 January 1837, BL, Add. MS. 35150, and Thompson to Place, 7
January 1837, BL, Add. MS. 35150.

[74]Place to Thompson, 8 January 1837, BL, Add. MS. 35150.

[75]See The Examiner, 29 January 1837.

[76]The Constitutional, 24 January 1837.

he acted as if he were a moderate. The radicals were, as Donald Southgate aptly describes them, "individualists, not lacking in energy and zeal, but differing in their interests and emphasis, and they had no general staff and no leader, so that they fought as irregulars in uncoordinated skirmishes."[77] The challenge posed by Roebuck and Molesworth only underscored this divisiveness.

The disarray in the radical camp continued when Parliament opened on 31 January. Prior to this date, leading radicals had all agreed in principle that the 1837 Parliament ought to consider such issues as free trade, the ballot, shorter parliaments, and equality of civil and religious rights.[78] But the ranks broke almost immediately. Roebuck led the way for the extremists by attacking the Whigs for standing still and doing nothing. The time had arrived, he said, for the radicals to form a separate party even if it meant driving the Whigs into the arms of the Tories.[79] Hume thought such suggestions were rash. He argued that he had "the same objects in view" as Roebuck, but he did not think the member from Bath knew the best way to obtain them.[80] The most suitable way to obtain radical goals, contended Hume, was to remain united with the Whigs despite past disagreements. Rather than attack the Whigs, he preferred to "pat them on the back and urge them on." He knew that the ballot had support from a majority of the public, but that did not suffice if only a minority favored it in the House of Commons. His role was to encourage the government to see the ballot as a proposition that all reformers could support.[81]

Roebuck made no effort to hide his frustration with his Scottish friend. It was Roebuck's opinion that the Whigs respected Hume and, therefore, if he made greater demands on them they would listen.[82] If Roebuck's position had represented the ground swell of opinion among radicals, it might have been advisable for Hume to follow the recommendations of the militants. Most parliamentary radicals found Roebuck's view extreme; few were in a mood to break step with the Whigs. Place was furious at the lack of support for Roebuck. He called Hume a "dawdler" who should be "put away to hibernate the rest of his days."[83] Not having been a member of Parliament, Place could not understand Hume's reluctance to scream out against the Whigs.

At the beginning of the 1837 session, Hume found that he could support the Whig government on specific issues, while opposing the ministry's general policy and principles. He backed all of the cabinet's major bills. Applauding both men and measures, he endorsed the ministry's bill to abolish Church of England rates in order to relieve Protestant dissenters of this burden. He had suggested this change four years earlier and was

[77]Southgate, *Passing of the Whigs*, 68.

[78]These demands were contained in a document signed by Hume, Grote, Molesworth, Roebuck, T. P. Thompson, and other radicals, BL, Add. MS. 35150.

[79]*Hansard,* third series, 36: 28.

[80]Ibid., 45.

[81]Ibid., 43–50.

[82]Roebuck, *The Life and Letters of J. A. Roebuck,* 92.

[83]Place to Roebuck, 1 February 1837, BL, Add. MS. 35150.

pleased that the Whigs had, in principle, adopted his plan. Hume stressed that he did not want to embarrass the ministers by asking for too much. He thought the Whig bill would probably satisfy most dissenters. This is yet further evidence that Hume was still following his philosophy that "half-a-loaf is better than none."

With the public at large, if not with the militant radicals, Hume managed to maintain his radical credentials by supporting every reform that he thought might win acceptance. He consistently voted for any parliamentary reforms moved in 1837. In February he supported Moles-worth's motion for the abolition of property qualifications for election to Parliament.[84] Grote's motion for the ballot on 7 March received less attention from Hume, and he refused to speak on the question or help Grote publicize the issue. Yet he voted with the minority in favor of the proposal. The militant radicals were not pleased with Hume's reaction to Grote's motion, but no one could deny that the Scotsman was consistent in his effort to keep the Whigs happy without surrendering his "radical" label.

Hume managed to keep his "radical" conscience clear by quietly voting for nearly all reforms proposed by members of the radical camp, but on only one occasion in 1837 did his old-time spirit rise to the fore. The issue was Canada, and his efforts made him a hero in that North American outpost. The matter of Canada came before the House of Commons in early March. The House of Assembly of Lower Canada had refused to grant supplies to the Crown until the Legislative Council, modeled after the House of Lords, was made an elective body and the Executive Council was made responsible to the Assembly. This issue had festered in Canada for many years. The Assembly wanted greater independence. Lord John Russell responded to developments in Lower Canada by moving a series of resolutions denying the Canadian Assembly its demands and empowering the governor of the province to appropriate money for the government's maintenance. Russell viewed the Assembly's requests as wholly incompati-ble with Canada's relations with the mother country. It would deny the king his proper authority and allow the Assembly to control the province. He pointed out that the governmental structure established by the Cana-dian constitution of 1791 followed the British system with an elected lower house, an appointed upper house, and an executive who followed the king's direction.[85]

Russell's stand triggered an eruption from all the radicals. John Temple Leader, for example, quickly moved that it was advisable to make the Legislative Council of Lower Canada an elective council. Leader appealed to all enemies of authoritarian rule, especially those in Ireland, to do justice to Canada. O'Connell agreed with the analogy to Ireland and supported the Canadian cause. Roebuck, reared in Canada and at one time a paid agent of the Canadian Assembly, carried on Leader's analogy to Ireland

---

[84] *Hansard*, third series, 35: 544–45, 618.
[85] *Hansard*, third series, 36: 1289–94, 1304–6.

and chided the ministers for supporting reform in Ireland and not in Canada.[86]

When debate on this issue resumed on 8 March, Hume revealed his intimate acquaintance with the subject. In 1836, he had supported a motion by Roebuck to amend the Canada Act of 1791, only relenting when Russell promised that Canadian grievances would be treated in the near future.[87] Hume and Roebuck remained in touch with various members of the government in Upper and Lower Canada. In fact, Hume was accused (by a select committee of the House of Assembly of Upper Canada) of sending inflammatory statements to dissident Canadians. The incident in question was a letter of 30 March 1834, to W. L. Mackenzie, an M. P. for York in Upper Canada. In the letter Hume speculated that Canadians would one day win their freedom. This statement was published by a London newspaper which charged him with treasonable opinions.

When he spoke on this question on 8 March, Hume revealed the full context of his letter to Mackenzie in which he warned that the conflict with the American colonies should not be forgotten.[88] To show that his views were supported by many Canadians, he produced resolutions from the Toronto Common Council and various other towns and counties approving his statements. The brunt of his speech was not a defense of his actions, but an attack on the government for allowing the grievances of the French Canadians to simmer for nearly twenty years. Hume did not directly threaten to abandon the government on this issue, yet he made no attempt to hide his disappointment. He predicted a Canadian civil war if the Whigs continued to ignore the situation. In the divisions that followed, including votes by Hume to delay proceedings, the radicals were easily beaten. Since the radical onslaught on Russell's Canadian resolutions posed no threat to the ministry's existence, Hume enjoyed the luxury of ventilating his radical views without fear that it would damage the Melbourne ministry.

Hume had resolved to maintain his working association with the Whig government however slow it might be to move reforms. And it was slow. By mid-June not one significant reform had earned approval.[89] The government had made no effort to extend the franchise or to bring in a ballot bill. Even the bills left over from the 1836 session (Irish tithe reform, Irish corporation reform) were not passed. Hume knew that he had infuriated the ultra-radicals by his failure to come down hard on the ministers for these failings. Molesworth, Grote, and Ewart within Parliament, and Place without, had expected that Hume would eventually help to take up the lead for the militant radicals. He had, after all, joined with them before the session in calling for a whole series of reforms, with the implication that they would test Whig sincerity.

Throughout the session Hume showed that he had no interest in leading

---

[86]Ibid., 1313–14, 1325, 1333, 1336.

[87]*Hansard,* third series, 38: 942, 945, 953.

[88]See Lillian F. Gates, "The Decided Policy of William Lyon Mackenzie," *Canadian Historical Review,* 40 (1959): 185–208; Gerald M. Craig, *Upper Canada: The Formative Years 1784–1841* (Toronto, 1963).

[89]*Hansard,* third series, 38: 1593.

the left wing radicals. Nor was he, strictly speaking, a leader of the moderate radicals.[90] No specific group owed allegiance to Hume. He had influence through his popularity in the country, but his influence was a personal one and it varied from issue to issue. This is not to say that Hume's role in the Commons lacked importance. Since he was the most well-known radical sitting in the House, it was difficult for the militants to attack the Whigs without his help.

Hume's determination to remain a liaison between the Whigs on the one hand and the impatient radicals on the other was again put to the test in the summer of 1837. The death of William IV on 20 June meant that the consequent general elections would be conducted during July and August. Just before the dissolution Hume had asked the Whigs to be prepared to debate in the next parliament such issues as a national system of education, emancipation of the Jews, the secret ballot, and extended suffrage. He promised that the parliamentary radicals would press the initiative with greater purpose than in previous sessions. There were some who dismissed this as Hume's usual "end of the session" posturing; a time when he spoke boldly because he knew nothing would come of it. Hume's subsequent behavior in the summer of 1837 makes this view a bit overly cynical.

Hume wanted to encourage the Whigs to do something on the major reform questions. If only the government would initiate a full discussion of issues dear to the radicals, some progress might be made in bringing all reformers together. He saw the upcoming elections as an opportunity to impress on supporters of the government the need to show some consideration for the wishes of the radical reformers. On 16 July, Hume told Lord Brougham,

We will bring forward all motions we consider necessary and leave the members of the govt to vote as they like—we will at the same time strongly urge the Electors of Manchester, Nottingham . . . and other places not to reelect men who will not support in the House the questions they pledged on the Hustings.[91]

One reason for writing to Brougham was to induce him to persuade the ministers to allow for open questions. He told Ellice in early July that he still favored the cooperation of all reformers rather than having the radicals go off by themselves. He hoped that Ellice and Brougham could help in this cause. When certain radicals refused to attend dinners in honor of liberal Whigs, Hume thought that it was "detrimental to the great Object of Union of Reformers to keep out the Tories." The Scotsman did whatever he could to prevent these silly protests. "There are always forward characters amongst us," wrote Hume to Ellice, "and it is well there are, but the generality of reformers are sound and anxious to support the ministry . . . if they will but help themselves." By "help themselves" he meant that the ministers could improve their strength in the elections if they opened the door to liberal reforms.[92]

---

[90]For another view, see Thomas Archer, *William Ewart Gladstone and His Contemporaries: Fifty Years of Social and Political Progress*, 4 vols. (London, 1883), 78. Also Platt, "The English Parliamentary Radicals," 333–37.

[91]Hume to Brougham, 16 July 1837, Brougham Papers, UCL.

[92]Hume to Ellice, 17 July 1837, Ellice Papers, NLS.

If they did not do this, they could expect defeat at the hands of the Tories. As Hume explained to Brougham,

I say now that unless measures are brought forward such as the people want, the people will not long care for men. You seem to talk of the majority of 20 or 30 or 40 as not enough to bring forward good measures with—if not when do you expect more of a majority.

Hume's comments did not mean that he was giving up on the Whigs. It is clear, however, that he worried about the future of the reform cause, or, as he called it, the "great Object of Union of Reformers." The outcome of the general election did nothing to relieve his concern.

According to Lord John Russell's estimate, the Whig majority was reduced to twenty-seven in the 1837 election.[93] The actual working majority may have been two or three less than that.[94] Just as Hume had predicted, the Whigs were weakened. As he had not predicted, the radicals were decimated. J. A. Roebuck, Thomas Perronet Thompson, and William Ewart all went down to defeat. More startling was Hume's loss in Middlesex.[95] The enormous nationwide publicity given to the Middlesex election made this a most ignominious development. Hume attributed his defeat to the huge influx of newly registered Tory voters in the past two years. He blamed the Whigs for not using their influence in his behalf and predicted (yet again) that "unless there is further Household Suffrage and the Ballot, the whigs must give way to Tory intimidation and competition."[96]

While the Tories exalted in finally getting rid of "Old Joe," the radicals recriminated over who should be held accountable for this humiliation. The liberal *Morning Chronicle* thought Hume bore responsibility for his defeat since his support for the Chandos clause (£50 tenantry) had helped it to pass in the House of Commons. The Chandos clause, argued the *Morning Chronicle,* worked to the advantage of Tory landlords who could readily control their tenants-at-will.[97] In response to the *Chronicle,* Hume wrote on 12 August,

I voted for the 50 pound tenantry clause on the broad principle of extending the suffrage as much as possible; and those who recognize property as a qualification for suffrage can scarcely affirm that a tenant of 50 pounds per annum is less entitled than a 40s freeholder or a ten pound householder to a vote in the choice of his representative. We are legislating for a nation, not for a party—for all time—not for the present days only.[98]

[93]Russell to Melbourne, 13 August 1837, Russell Papers, PRO 30/22.

[94]Noted by Gash, *Reaction and Reconstruction,* 134, n. 3.

[95]Grote to Place, 16 August 1837, BL, Add. MS. 35150. Grote retained his City of London seat by just six votes. For a discussion of the 1837 election in Middlesex and elsewhere see D. H. Close, "The General Elections of 1835 and 1837 in England and Wales," PH.D. dissertation, (Oxford, 1966), 370–521.

[96]Hume to Brougham, 12 August 1837, Brougham Papers, UCL. See *Middlesex Voters Register* (1834–37), Members Library, County Hall, London.

[97]Reported in BL, Add. MS. 35150.

[98]Ibid.

The blame, he reiterated, properly belonged on the shoulders of the Whigs who failed to follow up the Reform Act with amendments providing for the ballot and household suffrage.

In any event, Hume did not think his loss in Middlesex could be attributed to the £50 tenants. Besides being burdened with a registration system that favored the conservatives, the Tories had "the best tactics and the longest purses" when it came to recruiting 40s. freehold voters. With near admiration, Hume pointed out that the Tories had registered over four thousand of their friends since 1834 whereas the reformers had accounted for only five hundred. Hume may have exaggerated the numbers somewhat, but not by very much. Moreover, the Whigs did nothing while the Tories imported hundreds of "out-voters."[99] It made the Scotsman furious to contemplate such stupidity and treachery. "From the Vice-Chancellor, downwards," wrote Hume to a London acquaintance, "every public officer, generally speaking, voted against me, or refrained from voting and thus the influence of the government, legitimate and proper in favor of a liberal, was lost."[100]

While Hume traced his defeat to a lack of Whig support and to the efficiency of the Tory registration effort, Place faulted Hume himself. He contended that his friend had been overconfident in Middlesex, and that this complacency led him to shirk the obligations of a candidate. He did not, said Place, conduct a proper canvass; he did not organize his election committees; and he did not spend any money. He chose instead to hook himself on to "the old hypocrite," George Byng, in order to save expenses.[101]

Place's criticism of Hume was not entirely justified. The Scotsman never had been a great campaigner, and this was something well-known to Place. Hume had been forced to make a monumental effort to hold his seat in 1835; he was so "done up" by that election that he had vowed never again to put himself through such misery.[102] It was expecting too much for Hume to work that hard in 1837. He made the required stops at various gatherings and banquets, but he told his supporters that merit, not money and canvassing, would have to win the election.[103]

Neither Place nor Hume considered radical opposition as a cause of Hume's defeat. But radical opposition there was, and it probably contributed to the Scotsman's downfall. At least one radical newspaper, the *London Mercury*, urged radicals in Middlesex to work against Hume and his free-trade ideas. Hume is an "incarnation of the spirit of shopocracy,"

[99]Ibid. See John Prest, *Politics in the Age of Cobden* (London, 1977), 10–45, 50–51, 133.

[100]Hume to John Childs, 8 August 1837, BL, Add. MS. 2521. See D. A. Hamer, *The Politics of Electoral Pressure: A Study in the History of Victorian Reform Agitations* (London, 1977), 9–20.

[101]Place to Grote, 23 August 1837, BL, Add. MS. 35150, and Place to Roebuck, 10 September 1837, BL, Add. MS. 35151; *Morning Chronicle*, 12 August 1837.

[102]Grant, *Random Recollections*, 265.

[103]Place describes a meeting with Hume and several others in December 1836 in which Hume was told that £500 would secure him the county in the next election. Hume responded that he would not spend money for such a purpose. See BL, Add. MS. 35150 for 16 December 1836.

wrote the *Mercury*. The paper took "Old Joe" to task for his support of the new Poor Law and exclaimed, after the election results were in, that Hume's loss was more a triumph for the radicals than it was for the Tories. The "working masses," contended the *Mercury*, who were the "intended victims of the New Poor Law withdrew from him. . . ." Yet even the *Mercury* found it difficult to exult in the Middlesex result, and ultimately concluded that it was "melancholy" that a Tory was elected from Middlesex.[104]

The Tories were still celebrating Hume's Middlesex debacle when it was learned that the Scotsman would be returned for Kilkenny. Daniel O'Connell had arranged for his election from this Irish city. Place was annoyed that Hume had accepted O'Connell's invitation to stand in Kilkenny. He was certain that Hume would be controlled by O'Connell, a man whose fidelity to the Whigs had never wavered.[105] Place imagined that Hume would now become tied not only to the government, but to hopeless Irish causes as well.[106] Roebuck also had harsh words for O'Connell in 1837. He was certain that if the Tories managed to take office, "Dan will acquiesce and perhaps sing a song of praise if a catholic barrister or two be well treated and one or two catholics put into place."[107] Even Hume, when expressing his frustration with the Whigs' failure to advance reform, privately criticized O'Connell for supporting the ministers with excessive dedication. Despite these moments of doubt, Hume evinced no inner conflict over accepting the seat for Kilkenny.[108]

Hume was back in Parliament, but the future for organic reform was no brighter. The key ministers, Melbourne and Russell, were adamant in refusing to compromise with their radical allies. As early as July Melbourne made it clear that he was not inclined to make any concessions to the radicals. Neither radical men nor radical measures would be countenanced. He would not hear of the offer of a ministerial position to Lord Durham, a man who was looked to by some radicals as their natural leader. "I have no personal objection to any man," Melbourne told Russell on 7 July, "but everybody, after the experience we have had, must doubt whether there can be any peace or harmony in a cabinet of which Lord Durham is a member."[109] Charles Buller (a wealthy radical who sat for Liskeard) was also thought to be in line for a place in the government, but Melbourne had no use for him in the summer of 1837. The prime minister thought Buller as unpredictable and unmanageable as Lord Durham.[110] When Edward Ellice requested that Buller be considered for high office, Melbourne explained to Russell, "This after what I have caused to be said

---

[104]*London Mercury*, 13 Aug. 1837. See also *Morning Chronicle*, 14 August 1837; *Morning Post*, 7 August 1837; *The Country Chronicle*, 3 August 1837.

[105]Place to Grote, 23 August 1837, BL, Add. MS. 35150, and Place to Roebuck, 10 September 1837, BL, Add. MS. 35151.

[106]Place to Hume, 6 January 1837, BL, Add. MS. 35151.

[107]Roebuck to Brougham, 9 Aug. 1837, Brougham Papers, UCL.

[108]Hume to Ellice, 17 July 1837, Ellice Papers, NLS, and Hume to Brougham, 12 Aug. 1837, Brougham Papers, UCL; *Kilkenny Journal*, 19 August 1837.

[109]Walpole, *Life of Lord John Russell*, 1: 297.

[110]New, *Lord Brougham*, 310–11.

to Lord Durham about not wishing to give the Government a more Radical character at the present moment . . . would be impossible."[111]

Melbourne simply had no interest in reform. In his victory message to his constituents at Stroud he had said, "I must declare to you freely and frankly that I see no sufficient cause for altering the ancient constitution of the country."[112] Russell also offered scant hope. He argued that many people were not adequately prepared for the vote, therefore education must come first. He and his ministerial colleagues preferred to sponsor a general education bill which would make the people fit for suffrage. As matters stood in 1837, Russell thought the public's idea of legislation was only "skin deep."[113] Russell did not, however, fool himself about the strength of the Whigs and the reliability of the radicals as allies. He admitted to Melbourne, "It is certainly of no use to conceal the difficulty of our situation. I do not at all think, as some do, that the members of the new House of Commons will be more steady than the last. On the contrary, the best was pledged to the last." He was not pleased by the prospect of having to deal with the radicals. He hoped that they would "drop some of their unpalatable schemes and really act with us," so that Whigs and radicals could have a broader base of support.[114] By "unpalatable schemes," Russell presumably meant the ballot and other electoral reforms.[115]

A clearer statement of the intended conduct of the Whigs was contained in an anonymously written pamphlet entitled, "Domestic Prospects of the Country under the New Parliament." The pamphlet's central point was that all matters must be subordinated to the maintenance of the Melbourne government.

All parties or combinations of persons—those for the ballot—those for extended suffrage—those for the abolition of church rates—those for the grand plans of education—those for the appropriation clause—those who are in favor of Municipal Institutions in Ireland—those who are for yielding a more democratic form of government for Canada than at present exists there, should one and all, enter upon the new session, with the conviction impressed upon their minds, there is not one of these questions, no, not one, which is not secondary to the great object of maintaining Lord Melbourne's cabinet as the great object of future improvement, free from any species of present embarrassment.[116]

Place and Roebuck reacted angrily to the "Domestic Prospects." It proved to them that the Whigs could not be expected to do any better in the next parliamentary session. Not even the projected Russell scheme for national education pleased Roebuck. He saw it as no substitute for giving the people what they wanted: namely, the ballot and extended suffrage. If the ministers granted these concessions, the people, he claimed, would "rise up

---

[111]Walpole, *Life of Lord John Russell*, 297, n. 2.

[112]Russell to Brougham, 1 Aug. 1837, Brougham Papers, UCL; Southgate, *Passing of the Whigs*, 71, 91–92; and Walpole, *Life of Lord John Russell*, 296.

[113]Russell to Brougham, 24 Aug. 1837, Brougham Papers, UCL.

[114]Russell to Brougham, 27 July 1837, Brougham Papers, UCL.

[115]Russell to Brougham, 24 Aug. 1837, Brougham Papers and Russell to Brougham, 15 Nov. 1837, Brougham Papers, UCL.

[116]Quoted by Place in a letter to Roebuck, 10 Sept. 1837, BL, Add. MS. 35151.

in strength as in 1832. The Tories would be put down and the Whig's term of power would be indefinitely increased." But the Whigs would never do this, for "though they love Place much they love aristocracy more. They endeavor to conciliate two things wholly irreconcilable, viz. the present aristocratic dominion and a whig government."[117]

Even loyal supporters of the Whig-radical alliance believed that the Melbourne administration would need to yield to some liberal demands. Joseph Parkes said that unless Melbourne permitted the ballot as an open question, the liberals would split away. This judgement was based on information from "many quarters" indicating that two hundred liberal members would vote for a ballot motion in the next session.[118] His willingness to insist on reform from the Whigs did not necessarily portend Parke's abandonment of the ministers, but his views further revealed the fragile state of the Whig-radical connection.[119]

Although Hume desired more in the way of reform promises from Melbourne, his attitude toward the Whigs remained ambivalent in the autumn of 1837. Place, Roebuck, and Molesworth had already given up on the Whigs as well as those "willing slaves" of the ministers.[120] In November Hume hinted at moving to the opposite side of the House because he was so disappointed with the Whigs' performance in recent years. He thought the loss of seats in the summer elections pointed to the pressing need for reforms such as the extension of the suffrage and the secret ballot. The ministers must realize that "it was essential to their existence as a ministry that they should support the ballot, not merely by leaving it an open question, but by zealously making it a cabinet question."[121] He also wanted the government to clarify its position on Canada, to show how the ministry intended to conciliate the Canadian people. Hume then concluded by making it clear that he pressed reforms to help maintain the Whigs in office.[122]

Despite Hume's reassurance that he had not yet forsaken the administration, the issue was being drawn between the Whigs and radicals. When Melbourne failed to mention any proposal for constitutional reform at the opening of Parliament on 20 November, Thomas Wakley moved three resolutions calling for consideration of the ballot, extension of the franchise, and repeal of the Septennial Act. Hume had reservations about the timing of Wakley's effort, but gave his backing. So did Molesworth and Grote. Lord John Russell interpreted the proposals as destructive of the 1832 Reform Act, and tried to close the door to new experiments with parliamen-

[117]Roebuck to Brougham, 9 Aug. 1837, Brougham Papers, UCL.

[118]Parkes to Ellice, 24 Aug. 1837, Lambton Papers, Lambton Estate office, County Durham.

[119]Parkes to Durham, 26 Aug. 1837, Lambton Papers, Lambton Estate office, County Durham.

[120]Place to Hume, 14 Nov. 1837, BL, Add. MS. 35151. See Molesworth's article, "The Terms of the Alliance between Radicals and Whigs," referred to by Hamburger, 192. See also Roebuck to Place, 18 Sept. 1837, BL, Add. MS. 35151.

[121]Hansard, third series, 39: 58, 81, 87, 99–102.

[122]Hansard, third series, 39: 51–55.

tary reform. He responded to Wakley by saying that so far as he was concerned the 1832 Act was "final."[123]

The radical reaction to Russell's speech was predictable. He became "Finality Jack." Grote believed that any hopes that radicals might have held out for Melbourne's government were destroyed by Russell's "declaration." John Leader thought "the last hope of obtaining really popular measures from the present government has been taken from us."[124] Outside of Parliament Roebuck raged that "the finality of Lord John Russell is the Toryism of Sir Robert Peel with a newfangled name, and to support him and his colleagues is to support Toryism in reality."[125] Mrs. Grote wrote smugly to Place, "Now we know what to expect from a liberal cabinet,—viz.'O'—as you and I knew all along but which we could never persuade people to see."[126] Russell's finality statement seemed to be proof positive that the dissident radicals were correct in judging the Whigs untrustworthy.

It would, however, be inaccurate to leave the impression that the parliamentary radicals in general, and Hume in particular, thought Russell's speech a turning point in their association with the Whigs. There were twenty members (Hume among them) who voted for Wakley's resolutions to extend the franchise, but this was scarcely of any consequence. The small majority showed that most radicals were not ready to vote against the ministers.[127] Hume voted for Wakley's motion because he made it a point always to vote for the ballot. Certainly, Russell's "Finality" speech created no ground swell of indignation among the parliamentary radicals. Mrs. Grote would have been disappointed to learn that the radicals were still not persuaded that the Whigs were as evil as the Tories.

The weakness of the radicals was shown anew when Canada became an issue again in December. During 1837 there had been disturbances in every Canadian province. The unrest was led by W. L. Mackenzie, a political journalist, in Upper Canada and by Louis Papineau in Lower Canada. The British government forces readily suppressed the malcontents, but Melbourne saw the events as a grave attack on the honor of Great Britain. He was determined to prevent a recurrence of these outbursts. The radicals interpreted the unrest as the desire of Canadians (French and English) to have a greater role in decisions affecting their lives. Hume accused the government of fomenting the rebellions of 1837 by not heeding the warning in the last session against ministers infringing on the Canadian constitution of 1791. He considered rebellion defensible when human suffering had reached its limit, or when a government taxed a majority against its will. He did not think, however, that the situation was beyond redemption. He pointed to the achievements in Ireland and recommended that similar steps be taken in Canada. Then, as if to mitigate his criticism of

[123]Ibid., 47–48, 51, 58–59, 70.
[124]Ibid., 91, 109.
[125]Roebuck, 123.
[126]21 November 1837, BL, Add. MS. 35151.
[127]*Hansard,* third series, 39: 58, 81, 87, 99–102.

the Whigs, he turned on the Tories and said he had no hope that members on the opposite side would assist the cause of the Canadians.[128] On the other hand, he held out hope that the Whigs might do some good if the Tories would let them.

His words were moderate, but Hume was thoroughly annoyed with the Whigs over Canadian policy. Writing to Place on 1 January 1838, he complained that the conduct of the ministers was scandalous. He even went so far as to conclude that little separated the Tories and the Whigs. His past loyalty to the Whigs notwithstanding, he contemplated alternatives for the radicals. "I think the state of Ireland has restrained many of the liberals from turning out the whigs," he explained to Place, "but there seems to be a limit now fixed to that forbearance."[129] Hume knew, however, that political realities had to be weighed before any drastic steps were taken. He worried about the reaction of his Irish constituents if he turned against the Whigs.

Place had a simple solution for Hume. He told him to oppose the Whigs without fear of the consequences. Place believed that "the people" would support anyone who called Melbourne inadequate. The Whigs, according to Place, had "benumbed the people" while members of Parliament were afraid to do their duty, thereby allowing the ministers to do what they wanted. To maintain the momentum of criticism against the Whigs, Place urged the radicals to meet at the Crown and Anchor to plan strategy on the Canadian question.[130] The meeting, though it produced a good deal of rhetoric, did not bring the radicals to a common ground on Canadian policy. They decided to wait for the Whigs to announce their plans for North America.[131]

On 16 January, Russell explained the next steps to be taken by the Whig government. The Canadian constitution would be suspended indefinitely, and Lord Durham would be sent to the colonies to report on the situation. Melbourne sent Durham to appease the radicals and to get a potential rival out of the country. Hume praised the prime minister for sending Durham, but condemned him for moving so abruptly to suspend the Canadian constitution. He thought more time was needed to discuss the matter. Russell replied by teasing Hume that the radicals had plenty of time for debate at their Crown and Anchor meeting. Hume's criticism of the Whigs also exposed him to Peel's mocking reminder of the Whig-radical alliance. Peel called upon Hume to help return the Tories to office in the face of a "most factious combination." There was, in fact, never any concern among the Whig leadership that the Canada question would bring Tories and radicals together.[132]

The government had no cause to worry, but Hume's Irish constituents were obviously fretful over any possibility of a Tory-radical alliance.

[128]*Hansard*, third series, 39: 1455.
[129]BL, Add. MS. 35151.
[130]Place to Edward Baines, editor of the *Leeds Mercury,* 4 January 1838, BL, Add. MS. 35151, and a notation found in memorandum of 3 January 1838, BL, Add. MS. 35151.
[131]Baines to Place, 2 Jan. 1838, BL, Add. MS. 35151.
[132]Hansard, third series, 40: 43–55, 71, 92–95.

Richard Sullivan, a member of the Irish repeal party, wrote to O'Connell on 5 February,

I hope that Mr. Hume will not join the Tories on any question that may endanger the present government. As an Irish member it would not be the wish of his constituents that he would not dissever himself from you in your support of the Administration.[133]

Keeping faithful to his Irish friends, and especially to O'Connell, did not prove easy for Hume. Many of his radical acquaintances ridiculed O'Connell for refusing to join them in the attack on the ministry's Canadian bill. Roebuck spoke for most when he asked,

Where were the Irish members? Where was Mr. O'Connell? When the liberties of Ireland were attacked by the very Whigs whom Mr. O'Connell is never tired of praising—when the Irish Coercion Bill was going through the House of Commons in 1833—I never was absent one night.[134]

As a member for Kilkenny, Hume was constantly reminded that the Irish radicals wanted nothing to do with a Tory regime. In late February William Molesworth planned to move for the removal of Lord Glenelg as secretary for war and colonies. This effort appeared to have the potential for uniting Tories and radicals against the Melbourne government. It was really a very remote possibility, but the Irish radicals were alert just the same. The Kilkenny radicals hoped "that all liberal representatives of the Irish constituents including our City Representative Mr. Hume, will uphold Ministers when principle cannot be sacrificed by so doing."[135] *The Pilot*, an Irish radical publication, warned Hume that he should remember "that he is the chosen representative of an Irish constituency and that Ireland will be the greatest sufferer should Sir William Molesworth succeed in bringing in the Tories." *The Pilot* knew there was talk of Hume allying with Molesworth in this effort, but credited the Scotsman with having too much sense for such a venture. "There has been some mention," explained *The Pilot*, "of getting up an address to him on the subject from his constituents. We hardly think it necessary for we are sure he will do nothing that may be calculated to leave Ireland again at the mercy of the Orangemen."[136]

Hume's immediate response to this pressure is unknown, but the message from the Kilkenny radicals had its effect. When Molesworth moved for Lord Glenelg's dismissal on 6 March, Hume did not speak on the matter. The Tories saved him from having to vote in a division. Viscount Sandon moved an amendment which castigated the Canadian rebels for their behavior in 1837. This perverted the meaning of Molesworth's resolution, and he then withdrew it from consideration. When the Sandon amendment was allowed to stand on its own, Hume, along with

---

[133]O'Connell Papers, N. L. of Ireland, 16348.

[134]Place Collection, BL, Add. MS. 35151. See Lawrence McCaffrey, *Daniel O'Connell and the Repeal Year* (Lexington, Kentucky, 1966), 30–110.

[135]*Kilkenny Journal*, 21 Feb. 1838, no. 865.

[136]*Kilkenny Journal*, 3 March 1838, no. 868.

many other Whigs and radicals, voted it down.[137] Hume was thus able to keep faith with his followers in Kilkenny and still remain an outspoken critic of the Colonial Office.

The vote on the Sandon proposal showed again that Whigs and radicals were still more likely to vote together than Tories and radicals. For this reason, Melbourne had no trouble maintaining an ample majority throughout the 1838 session. There were many Whigs who supported political reform in principle, and somewhere down the road it was not inconceivable that a Whig leader would take up that cause in earnest. There was no chance a Tory government would support the ballot. On the local political level, radical candidates could expect some meager support from a Whig government; they could expect none at all from a Tory ministry. This was far from an ideal situation for the parliamentary radicals. The Whigs gave them crumbs and the Tories gave them nothing.

The radicals also made life difficult for themselves. There were many instances of reformers lashing out at one another in 1838. One of the best examples may be found in Hume's involvement in the February by-election in St. Marylebone. The district had been represented since 1832 by a reformer, Sir Samuel Whalley. Early in 1838 Sir Samuel was forced to resign when he could not prove his qualification after being returned in the 1837 election. Colonel T. Perronet Thompson, an old acquaintance of Hume, immediately declared his intention to become a candidate. As a former proprietor of the *Westminster Review* and a long-standing opponent of the Corn Laws, Thompson's credentials as a radical were well-established. He had represented Hull from 1835 to 1837. His friends considered him a promising candidate in Marylebone.

It was at this point that Hume entered the picture. He took an "informal" poll of electors in Marylebone and deduced that Thompson could not beat his Tory challenger, Lord Teignmouth. With this "knowledge" Hume put forward the candidacy of William Ewart, a reformer who had lost in Liverpool and in Kilkenny in 1837. Thompson was enraged. He accused Hume of a conspiracy with O'Connell to use Ewart to help maintain a Whig-radical alliance in the Commons. Thompson described himself as an "independent" radical who would not mind if the Melbourne government collapsed.[138]

Hume defended his support for Ewart by telling Thompson that his (Thompson's) friends had put his name in nomination without consulting any portion of the electorate. "The object I have in view," wrote Hume, "is to carry a Radical. If you had any chance you should have had my support. . . . "[139] In the end, Hume's assessment of Thompson's chances proved correct. The electors gave Teignmouth 4,166 votes; Ewart 3,762; and Thompson 186. His lopsided defeat did not prevent Thompson from blaming Hume for the Tory victory in Marylebone. He told *The Times,*

[137]*Hansard,* third series, 40: 629; 41: 525–37, 684–88.

[138]See L. G. Johnson, *General T. Perronet Thompson* (London, 1957), 219–20; W. A. Munford, *William Ewart, M.P.: Portrait of a Radical* (London, 1960), 95.

[139]Hume to P. Thompson, 25 Feb. 1838, in Johnson, *Perronet Thompson,* 219.

"Joseph Hume and the Middle Classes have trampled on me."[140] The uncompromising radicals had been betrayed by Whig-radicalism. O'Connell, Ewart, and Hume had "masterminded" his defeat, and in the process had cost the radicals another place in Parliament.[141] Left to himself Thompson was certain he could have beaten Teignmouth. There was no question that Hume campaigned harder against Thompson than he did against Teignmouth. In the midst of being ridiculed and mocked by the Whigs and Tories, the radicals always had time to challenge each other and to call each other a variety of epithets.

The condition of the radicals was further complicated by the publication of the People's Charter in May 1838. Support for the Chartist cause grew steadily over the summer in working-class districts. Hume saw much to applaud in making workingmen aware of their interests, but his opinion of the Chartists was not yet fixed. He liked most parts of the People's Charter (which Place had helped to write); yet he worried that it erred in its broad-scale attack on the status quo.[142] Hume had, as well, misgivings about the Chartists' demands for more factory legislation.

The Chartist cause also complicated Hume's relationship with Irish radicals. O'Connell urged Hume to stay away from any direct association with the Chartists. He feared the English radicals might merge their efforts with those of Feargus O'Connor. "If they go with O'Connor," wrote O'Connell, "we cannot in too strong language reprobate their conduct and express our digust at it."[143] The problem for Hume was that most English radicals no longer had much use for O'Connell. In September, Hume suggested to Place that English and Irish radicals should work together in pushing for political reform. He hoped to achieve this without pledging loyalty to the Charter. Place responded that since Irish politicians, and particularly O'Connell, had shown themselves to be completely self-serving, he had lost interest in them. It would be wiser, he thought, to allow the Irish to solve their own problems rather than permit them to act as a drag on the English. He and Lovett had just finished simplifying the language in the Charter, and he wanted Hume to give his support.[144] The Scotsman promised that he would give the matter consideration in the weeks ahead. It was just one of many things he needed to reflect upon. He still had not made up his mind on what to do about the recalcitrant Whig government.

Throughout the autumn of 1838 Hume consulted with various radicals over what approach he should take in the upcoming parliament. Should he pledge his loyalty to the Whigs immediately; should he put them to the test again on suffrage reform; or, should he lead a radical revolt against the ministry? Place and Roebuck begged him to see the light and do whatever

[140]Johnson, *Perronet Thompson*, 220.

[141]See *The Sun*, 15 October 1838.

[142]Hume to Place, 13 September 1838, BL, Add. MS. 35151; Place to Hume, 13 September 1838, BL, Add. MS. 35151.

[143]*Kilkenny Journal*, 1 December 1838.

[144]Place to Hume, 13 September 1838, BL, Add. MS. 35151.

was necessary to bring down Melbourne and Russell. O'Connell, Warburton, and Hobhouse continued to argue that a radical revolt would prove to be self-defeating. Hume eventually decided to do all he could to maintain his association with the Place-Roebuck faction without trying to undermine the Whigs. When the session opened in January 1839, he attacked the ministry on the Address from the Crown. Hume frequently made such speeches at the beginning of Parliament, always exaggerating radical demands before retreating to a more moderate position. His language was less yielding this time. He charged that Russell's "Finality" doctrine had provoked Chartist demonstrations and general unrest. Had he not warned the ministers this would happen?[145] Quite naturally Hume was delighted with the discontent; his only concern was that the "unrest" was not as serious as he portrayed it.

The meanness of Hume's assault shocked Melbourne and Russell. The Whig leaders were counting on Hume's support, and they wondered if this was his declaration of war. They knew that he had been put under great pressure to abandon the Whigs, so there was reason to think he might finally have given in. The Scotsman, however, did not plan anything quite so drastic, at least not yet. The speech was his way of preparing the House for a bill to expand the electorate. Hume had decided sometime in December to move for household suffrage. He did not mention his plans to other radicals until he had given notice in the Commons. Then, on 9 February, he wrote to Place, "I am very desirous to see you to consult you on the motion of which I have given notice, for household suffrage in the next month."[146] Place replied that there were already too many ideas on household suffrage and that he and Brougham thought Hume's plan inadequate.[147]

Hume continued to work on his plan through the month of February. As usual, he prepared himself as much as possible. He tried to locate all the previous resolutions on the question of expanded suffrage.[148] Place sent him tracts written on the subject by such eighteenth-century reformers as C. J. Fox and R. B. Sheridan.[149] When Hume introduced his legislation on 21 March, no one knew exactly what to expect. Unlike the ballot issue, a motion for household suffrage was something new in the House of Commons. Neither Hume nor Place gave the proposal a chance, but both thought it was certain to nettle the Whigs.

In arguing for household suffrage, Hume acknowledged that some reformers feared that expanded voting rights might threaten the constitution. He reminded the House that in 1832 Russell had contended that no man should be taxed without his consent. It followed, said Hume with tongue in cheek, that the vote should go to all who pay taxes, including householders. If this action had been taken years ago England could have avoided the Chartist demands. It was a speech to remember, especially as

---

[145]*Hansard,* third series, 45: 80–82.
[146]BL, Add. MS. 35151.
[147]Place to Hume, 9 February 1839, BL, Add. MS. 35151.
[148]Hume to Place, 27 February 1839, BL, Add. MS. 35151.
[149]Place to Hume, 1 March 1839, BL, Add. MS. 35151.

Hume punctuated his words by waving his paper of notes high over his head.[150]

Russell responded by noting that Hume's plan would never satisfy the Chartists. The real issue, he said, was between retaining the present system of representation or adopting universal suffrage. Hume's motion would satisfy no one. Russell argued that the representation should be based only on the voter's intelligence and property qualifications. Grote and O'Connell came to Hume's defense: the former contending that householders were as fit as anyone to vote, while the latter thought the 1832 experiment had failed and needed to be reformed. But these presentations drew a surprisingly apathetic response in the chamber. Fewer than 150 members participated in the division on Hume's resolution. It went down 85 to 50.

Hume had never imagined that household suffrage would pass; he had hoped, however, for a more excited reaction to his effort. It seemed to upset him that so few Whigs expressed interest in significant reform. He told Ellice that perhaps the time had come to bring down the Whigs, if for no other reason than to punish them for broken promises. But the spectre of a new Tory government was held up as something to dread. O'Connell certainly followed this line in his remarks. "At this moment," he warned, "common sense seems to have gone astray, for there is no rallying point to be found amongst sincere reformers; while on the other hand the triumph of Toryism appears to be approaching." When it was his turn to speak, Hume disappointed O'Connell by saying that despite the Tory danger, he had reached his limit with the Whigs.[151] In stating his position so candidly, Hume risked the wrath of O'Connell as well as the Kilkenny constituents. For once, wrote Roebuck, "Hume has not succumbed to flattery."[152]

Hume was still mulling over what to do next when the government made a misstep. On 3 May, Russell moved to suspend the Jamaican constitution. Lord John characterized members of the Jamaican Assembly as floggers of females, who had no intention of carrying out slave emancipation in a timely fashion. Hume immediately opposed the administration on this issue. He had consistently opposed government intervention in any colonial matter. Peel quickly joined him in attacking Russell's motion as premature and unnecessary. This was unusual. On an issue such as this there was often cooperation between Whigs and Tories. The administration's position was precarious.[153] If Hume and Peel remained adamant there was reason to think Melbourne's ministry was over.

The editor of the Whiggish *Morning Chronicle,* John Black, advised a friend that "It is believed *here* that Hume intends to vote against the Ministers upon the Jamaican Question and *with* Sir Robert Peel. It is considered highly important that this not take place."[154] When Black tried to persuade Hume to change his mind, the Scotsman replied, "I mean to act

[150]*Morning Chronicle,* 23 March 1839.

[151]Hume to Ellice, 12 April 1839, Ellice Papers, NLS.

[152]Roebuck to Place, 2 May 1839, BL, Add. MS. 35151.

[153]See Tavistock to Russell, 13 April 1839 in Spencer Walpole, *Life of Lord John Russell,* 1: 33.

[154]Black to Richard Sullivan, 29 April 1839, Smithwick Papers, Birthfield, Kilkenny.

towards Jamaica as I acted towards Ireland against the coercion act, and to Canada against the Suspension Act."[155] In an effort to convince Hume to remain loyal to Melbourne on this issue, supporters of the government resorted to base flattery. They arranged for a dinner, in Hume's honor, at the Crown and Anchor for 1 May. Some three hundred persons, including Daniel O'Connell, gathered for the event. No explicit reference was made to Hume's opposition to the Jamaica Bill; however, as speakers lauded Hume, there were many allusions to his constancy in backing the Whigs.

When the Jamaican Bill was debated in its first reading on 3 May, Hume argued that he could not defend coercion in Jamaica any more than he could defend it in Ireland. The Whigs, he said, had adopted Tory measures. They had deprived the representative assembly of its power and transferred it to the governor and his council. Freedom for the Negroes had always been his concern, but the ministers' bill was unconstitutional.

The vote on the suspension act showed the government with a slim majority, 296 to 291. Six Tories voted with the majority, while eleven Whigs and ten radicals sided with the opposition. The cabinet agreed to resign.[156] It was thought that the large minority had undercut Melbourne's authority in the colonies. Russell, preparing to leave, thanked O'Connell for his "constant and disinterested support" over the years. No such praise went to Hume, who, his position on Jamaica notwithstanding, deserved it more.[157]

Now that Hume had bolted from Whig cooperation, he found his Kilkenny friends just as cross with him as Roebuck and Place had been when he supported the government. Despite the nasty consequences he remained unrepentant. The Citizens Club of Kilkenny voted a series of resolutions censuring Hume for his behavior and concluding that he should resign from Parliament.[158] Hume responded in a long letter. He cited historical precedence for his action. He was proud, he said, that the electors had placed their confidence in him, but "the charge was confided to me unconditionally." Referring to Burke's position on representation, he reminded his constituents that "your representative owes you not his industry only, but his judgment; and he betrays, instead of serving you, if he sacrifices it to your opinion." Hume recalled that, just as he displeased some of his Kilkenny constituents by his vote on the Jamaica Bill, he had also annoyed his English and Scottish electors in the past by his advocacy of the abolition of tithes and Catholic emancipation.[159]

Hume's Irish constituents need not have bothered themselves to condemn Hume for the Whigs' departure. Their favorites were back in office before Hume had a chance to explain why he helped to drive them out. Under circumstances that might generously be called bizarre, Peel could not form a ministry. This is not the place to recount the details of Peel's difficul-

[155]Black to Sullivan, 6 May 1839, Smithwick Papers, Birthfield, Kilkenny.
[156]*Kilkenny Journal*, 8 May 1839.
[157]Prest, *Lord John Russell*, 146.
[158]*Kilkenny Journal*, 15 May 1839.
[159]Ibid., 25 May 1839.

ties;[160] it is enough to say that Donald Southgate put the situation in perspective when he wrote, "Nothing that the whigs did in office became them so ill as their return to it."[161]

Hume did not welcome the continuation of Whig rule. He was not convinced by Russell's rather desperate promise to reconsider household suffrage and perhaps the ballot. The Whigs also did not convince the Chartists. They increased their anti-government activities during the summer. Hume could give nothing more than limited support for the Chartists. He sympathized with their reform demands, but criticized them for violent behavior. His opposition was directed against the reality of violence, not the threat. Hume had, on occasion, expressed the belief that fear of violence could do wonders by way of encouraging reform.

Hume's major objection to the Chartists had nothing to do with their method of protest; it was their attempt to associate middle class (free-trade) interests with aristocratic interests that troubled him. It also bothered Place. He complained about Chartists who "link the middle class with the aristocracy under the dignified cognomen of murderers of society."[162] Both Place and Hume had tried to establish that free-trade reformers were operating in the best interests of the workingman. All doctrinaire free-traders assumed that adherence to laissez-faire principles would bring prosperity to all classes. In the spring of 1839 the third earl of Radnor, as intense in his free-trade opinions as Hume, assured the country that the adoption of free-trade precepts would make it possible for the worker to enjoy "butter and cheese, roast beef, and plum pudding."[163] Most Chartist leaders did not agree. They warned their followers to dissociate themselves from the free-trade radicals.[164] Feargus O'Connor was especially adamant in saying that those who cooperated with the free-traders were not true friends of workingmen. Hume assigned the Chartists' intractability to "blindness" or intellectual error, the radical explanation for most differences with the working class. The Scotsman thought the workers were so ignorant of their own interests that they were "engaged in agitation for the attainment of abstract rights . . . instead of endeavoring to obtain a repeal of the Corn Laws, from which most of the practical evils under which they labored arose."[165]

The 1834 Poor Law Amendment Act was another point of contention between Hume and the Chartists. In contrast to those workmen who formed anti-new Poor Law associations, Hume had steadfastly defended the changes made in 1834. The revised Poor Law was in perfect harmony with free-trade doctrine, and Hume reacted defensively every time petitions

[160]See Gash, *Sir Robert Peel*, 229–27.

[161]*Passing of the Whigs*, 73.

[162]Place to R. Cobden, undated but internal evidence places it in 1839, BL, Add. MS. 43667.

[163]See R. K. Huch, "Earl of Radnor and Free Trade," *Huntington Library Quarterly*, 39 (February, 1976): 155.

[164]A. R. Schoyen, *The Chartist Challenge: A Portrait of George Julian Harney* (New York, 1958), 25.

[165]*Hansard*, third series, 46: 729.

were brought forward to remedy alleged abuses in the law. In some instances he admitted that there might be problems in the application of the new Poor Law, but he attributed this to poor administration rather than to any defect in the legislation. The Poor Law, he said, served to help the poor to improve their "moral condition" and to "encourage industrious habit." Beyond this, the law protected those "who occupied a station in society just above that of the poor man, from paying for the support of the dissolute and idle." This utilitarian outlook set Hume apart from the Chartists, but in no way did he think it set him apart from the workingman.

Hume's speeches in the 1840 session were laden with references to the grievances of the working classes and the desperate need to respond to their pleas for relief from taxes and political disfranchisement. His comments were not so much for the ears of his colleagues as they were for the eyes of the malcontents outside the House. It was yet another way to create the discontent that he said was so rampant. In recommending a reduction in the allowance for Prince Albert from £50,000 to £21,000, Hume wondered if the ministers realized the effect the news of such a large grant would have on the disaffected. He pointed out that even the queen's Civil List subsidy of £385,000 was excessive and could be better used by providing for some eighteen thousand poor families.[166] He further warned that "the landed proprietors in England were following fast in the course which had been pursued by the old aristocracy of France; everything was laid by them on the shoulders of the people." According to Hume, not only did the working and manufacturing classes subsidize the aristocracy by paying disproportionate taxes, but the Corn Laws monopoly worked an additional hardship on consumers. The Chartists, therefore, had the lines of conflict reversed. The landed interests were the oppressors; the middle and working classes were the groups mutually disadvantaged. Hume hoped that the Chartist leaders might still come to see that cooperation with the free-trade radicals offered the best chance to realize political and economic improvement.[167]

The primary interest of the Whig ministry in 1840 was not in free trade or in assistance to the workingmen of England. Lord John Russell spent most of his time preparing legislation for Canada and in holding back a Tory plan to reduce the electorate in Ireland so that fewer Irish liberals would be returned. Lord Stanley introduced the bill calling for changes in registration procedure in Ireland. It took all the ingenuity Lord John could muster, in addition to some mistakes by Stanley, for the government to stave off defeat on this issue.[168]

Hume opposed Stanley's efforts, but he was not sorry to see the ministers hard pressed. While Russell and Melbourne dealt (or tried to deal) with Canada and Ireland, Hume decided to make some trouble of his own. On 5 May, he moved for the appointment of a select committee on import duties. There was little opposition; liberal Whigs agreed with the free-trade radicals that it was a good idea. Hume had big plans for the

---

[166]See Wallas, *Francis Place,* 384.
[167]*Hansard,* third series, 52: 1081–83.
[168]Prest, *Lord John Russell,* 162–64.

committee. As chairman he was able to guide it any way he wished. He directed committee members and witnesses in a fashion reminiscent of his chairmanship of the select committee on the Combination Laws in 1824.[169] As a result of Hume's influence, the committee consisted of ten free-traders and five protectionists. The manner in which the committee proceeded clearly favored the free-traders. Attendance at the meetings was irregular owing to the inconvenient scheduling during the summer months. Much to the consternation of his colleagues, Hume showed no drop in vitality in the summer. He thought it inefficient for members to leave town so much in July and August. Only Hume, Villiers, Thomas Thornley (M.P. for Wolverhampton), and William Ewart (M.P. for Wigan) religiously attended the hearings. They were all free-traders. The committee report was heavily influenced by James Deacon Hume (no relation to Joseph) and John McGregor, joint secretaries to the Board of Trade.

Hume had no difficulty in getting McGregor to testify that high duties caused smuggling, hurt labor, and undermined England's trade. When the chairman asked James Deacon Hume whether it was his opinion that protection of any commodity operated as a tax on the community at large, he already knew the answer. In addition to extensive questioning of J. D. Hume and McGregor, the committee (especially Hume and Villiers) allowed John Bowring to discuss at length his well-known free-trade views.[170]

The committee's one-sided alignment and its managed use of witnesses made its conclusions predictable. Moreover, the partisan members under Hume's guidance were able to shape the evidence to create the impression that free trade had gained popularity in the country. This was not an altogether false impression in 1840. While the opposition to free trade had been formidable in Parliament in the past two years, there were increasing signs that public opinion was in favor of reduced tariffs. The select committee had the opportunity to reach over the head of the administration to "inform" the people that there was considerable evidence to support removal of protection. By doing this Hume and the committee aided the cause of the Anti-Corn Law League. Hume publicized the committee's report through articles submitted to *The Spectator* just before Parliament was to meet in January 1841. Other papers, such as the *Liverpool Mercury,* the *Leeds Mercury,* and the *Morning Chronicle,* made certain that *The Spectator* articles were widely reprinted.

While Hume generated support for the committee's findings, the government prepared for some changes in its fiscal policies. In December 1840 the ministry considered a revision of import duties along the lines proposed by Hume's committee. There were to be significant reductions of sugar and timber duties and possibly a sliding scale for corn. It is generally accepted that this change in policy was inspired by Hume's report. Earlier in the year the government had favored increased duties. It took Hume's

[169]Lucy Brown, *The Board of Trade and the Free Trade Movement, 1830–1842* (Oxford, 1958), 72.
[170]Ibid., 72–74, 145–52, 167–70, 182–83, 215–16; *Report of the Select Committee on Import Duties* (London, 1840), passim.

committee to expose to public view the defects of the old tariff system. No
longer was this simply an economic issue; it was very much a political one
as well. The Whig ministers now recognized this and were willing to act
accordingly. On the other hand, the government's new stress on free-trade
measures solidified Tory opposition and caused some Whigs with agricultural interests to desert the ministry.[171]

Russell was aware that raising the free-trade issue might mean disaster
for the Whigs. He had decided that they could not go on much longer
anyway; nearly every division was a struggle. By establishing Whig
support for reduced sugar, timber, and corn duties, Russell believed that
the Whigs, if necessary, would be able to go to the electorate with a popular
cause. He was determined that Peel would not have the initiative. Should
the ministry's economic measures fail, Melbourne and Russell planned to
dissolve Parliament rather than permit Peel and the conservatives to form a
new government.[172]

Hume applauded the administration's emphasis on reduced tariffs; he
assumed it resulted from the evidence presented by his committee and also
from the ministry's desire to maintain the loyalty of the free-trade radicals.
He hoped that the liberal phalanx in the House of Commons would be
large enough to carry through the Whig proposals. Alas, it was not. On
May 18 the government's duties bill was defeated by thirty-six votes; nearly
forty Whigs failed to side with Russell. This defeat all but finished the
Melbourne ministry. It was obvious that the Whigs' only hope was to
appeal to the country, and that is what they planned to do in May 1841.
Hume thought this was the proper course. "We shall see how the Whigs
stand with the people," he wrote to Chadwick, "I think with proper
pledge[s] we may see our old friends [securely] in office again."[173]

[171]See Brown, *Board of Trade*, 220; Walpole, *Life of Lord John Russell*, 1: 368.
[172]Prest, *Lord John Russell*, 173–78.
[173]Hume to Chadwick 2, June 1841, Chadwick Papers, UCL.

CHAPTER VII.

"RUDDERLESS", 1841–1847

In June 1841 Sir Robert Peel, having seen the Whigs defeated on their tariff measures, moved a vote of "no confidence" in the government of Lord Melbourne. It passed 312 to 311. The Whigs bowed to the inevitable and announced their intention to take their case to the people. On 22 June, the queen dissolved Parliament as preparations for a general election were already under way. Based on the conviction that the electorate favored free-trade legislation, Whigs and radicals went into the campaign with high hopes. Their spirit was greater than anyone could have imagined a few months earlier.[1]

The 1841 election had special significance for Hume. He was invited by a large number of liberal electors to seek election for Leeds.[2] The city's two reform members, Edward Baines and Sir William Molesworth, had decided to give up their seats. The exact reason for Molesworth's surrendering his seat is unclear, but Baines's health had deteriorated to such a degree that he believed he could no longer withstand the rigors of political life. The liberals in Leeds were pleased with Baines's decision for they wanted to bring in someone more flamboyant in the cause of reform. Baines was a free-trader and he had no hesitation in giving his considerable support to Hume.[3] Like other liberals in Leeds he was impressed with Hume's national reputation as a man of high character and independence, who spoke for the interests of "the people." Leeds seemed ready for Hume, but Hume was not yet certain he was ready for Leeds.

There had been an attempt by some Edinburgh radicals to interest liberal electors in that city in a Hume candidacy. Hume had encouraged the effort, but he did not do a great deal to advance his cause. "Amidst the contest which seems to be going on in Edinbro," he wrote to a friend, "it is not for me, in any way, to mingle—the electors must decide."[4] He confessed that it would " be pleasing to me to represent the metropolis of my native country," but he suspected that the "Whig clique" in Edinburgh would undermine his chances. He was prepared to accept an invitation to campaign from the first constituency that made up its mind; providing it was in a district where he had "a chance to succeed."[5] Near the end of May, Hume convinced himself that Leeds offered a better opportunity than Edinburgh, and he asked that nothing further be done on his behalf in Scotland.[6]

Hume eagerly accepted the challenge in Leeds. He saw it as the perfect

---

[1] S. Maccoby, *English Radicalism 1832–1852* (London, 1935), 224.
[2] *Leeds Mercury,* 5 June 1841.
[3] *The Life of Edward Baines,* by his son Edward Baines (London, 1851), 271–73.
[4] Hume to J. Burton, 24 May 1841, Burton Papers, NLS, MS. 9392.
[5] Ibid.
[6] Hume to Burton, 28 May 1841, Burton Papers, NLS, MS. 9392. Later, Hume was requisitioned to stand for Newcastle, but he promptly refused. See *Leeds Times,* 19 June 1841.

setting in which to prove his popularity; his ego had been singed by the Middlesex result in 1837, and he had never found any satisfaction in sitting for Kilkenny. Hume did make one stipulation to his supporters in Leeds—he would not conduct a personal canvass. On 1 June, Hume made his first appearance before the electors and, according to the sympathetic *Leeds Mercury*, made a favorable impression. The *Mercury* was published and edited by Edward Baines. All of Hume's radical virtues were recounted, including his work on the committee investigating import duties. There was one difficult moment. Someone raised the familiar, if distasteful, matter of Hume's alleged atheism. The *Leeds Mercury* called this a "base" charge and insisted that Hume was a "better church goer" than most other members of Parliament.[7]

Despite the success of Hume's first appearance in Leeds, the campaign promised to be a tough one. There were four men, two Tories and two free-trade radicals, competing for Leeds's two parliamentary seats. The *Leeds Mercury* pushed Hume's campaign as much as possible. It also reprinted articles (obviously placed by Hume's supporters and probably Hume himself) from London's *Morning Chronicle*.[8] As the election drew near, Hume's campaign literature highlighted his votes against capital punishment and his desire to mitigate the criminal codes. He was presented as someone who would bring national attention to Leeds. Hume and the other free-trade candidate, William Aldam Jr., spent the last week before the election addressing electors in all sections of Leeds. Hume emphasized the need for continued reform and economy. He never failed to elicit a powerful response from the radicals and the reform-minded Whigs. Tories and conservative Whigs, on the other hand, were increasingly appalled by the "excessive" conviction Hume brought to the campaign.[9]

Throughout the month of June the Tories attacked Hume for his radical tendencies and called him "demagogue," "revolutionist," "anarchist," "infidel," and "Atheist." The *Leeds Times* defended Hume against these accusations that displayed the "grossest bigotry and intolerance." The residents of Leeds, wrote the *Times,* did not want a "father confessor," but a political representative. The paper was quick to see that the most serious charge against Hume remained the old bugbear about his atheism. The Tories had dredged it up out of desperation, yet it could not be taken lightly. Many Methodists, for example, were readily swayed by such arguments.

The *Leeds Times* tried to show that Hume had stood for civil and religious liberty throughout his life, and that dissenters in Edinburgh had urged him to campaign in that city. "Mr. Hume, having seized upon a principle," wrote the *Leeds Times,* "never abandons it." It was Hume, after all, who had labored for years, finally with victory, to end the Bible monopoly in Scotland. By making Scripture available at low prices had he not done more than any other man to advance the cause of religion?[10] It is

[7]*Leeds Mercury,* 5 June 1841.
[8]*Leeds Mercury,* 19 June 1841.
[9]*Leeds Mercury,* 25 June 1841.
[10]*Leeds Times,* 5 June 1841.

difficult to tell just how much the "Atheist issue" influenced the electors, but, in an area heavily populated with evangelicals, it cannot be discounted.

In the last week in June, the Scotsman's opponents added another, possibly more damaging, strategem. They spread a report that Hume was playing a double game in Leeds. Hume had responded indiscreetly to a proposal that he stand for election in Dundee (this was subsequent to the invitation from Edinburgh) by saying that he wished to wait for the result in Leeds before making up his mind. He also explained to his Dundee petitioners that he *preferred* to retire from the Leeds contest and only his concern for the cause of free trade prevented him from taking that step. The Tories had acquired a copy of Hume's remarks which they promptly distributed among the Leeds electors. The Scotsman's followers immediately charged forgery, but their candidate reluctantly admitted he had written the letter in question. Furthermore, he could see nothing untoward in his behavior.[11] The revelation of Hume's comments hurt the radical cause. In a close election, as this one seemed certain to be, such embarrassments were not easily overcome.

Hume's name was officially placed in nomination by Edward Baines on 1 July. He told the large gathering in Woodhouse Moor that they could do no better than to elect Hume. "No man has kept a more tight hand upon the public purse strings," said Baines about Hume, "and there is this merit about Mr. Hume . . . he has also taken care to keep his own hands free from all contamination."[12] Baines then went on to extol Hume's "independence" as well as his devotion to "civil and religious liberty" and to the "principles of Free Trade." He concluded by saying that men like Hume were needed in the House of Commons to balance the strength of the landed interest.[13] Baines's speech drew a loud reaction from the crowd; he was cheered by the reformers and hissed by the Tories.

The election developed into one of the most exciting in Leeds history. Flags were displayed for more than a week in violation of election laws. The reformers distributed orange flags with such phrases as "All for each," "Hume and Aldam the Poor Man's Friend," "Free Trade—Plenty and Prosperity," "Let Monopoly Perish." Hume and Aldam were active all week speaking at breakfast meetings and marching in parades. Naturally, the intensity of the campaign brought forth charges of bribery and coercion from both sides. Such accusations were always present when reformers and conservatives met in a close race.[14]

When the polling began on 2 July most of the attention focused on the progress of Hume's canvass. The Scotsman took an early lead and the free-traders were roseate; then the Tory votes began to mount. The final results showed Hume defeated by the Tory banker, William Beckett, and by his fellow reform candidate, William Aldam. Hume trailed Aldam by 10 votes and Beckett by 43. "Old Joe's" defeat was a huge disappointment

[11]*Leeds Intelligencer*, 3 July 1841.
[12]*Life of Edward Baines*, 275; *Northern Star*, 3 July 1841.
[13]*Life of Edward Baines*, 276.
[14]*Leeds Mercury*, 3 July 1841; *Leeds Intelligencer*, 3 July 1841.

for radical interests in Leeds. Baines's *Mercury* mourned that Leeds had missed "an honour" by not returning Hume. "That such a man as Hume should be out of Parliament, cannot for a moment be thought of," wrote the *Mercury*.[15]

There were many theories advanced to explain the election results. Most agreed that the radicals had not plumped for him the way conservatives and some Whigs had plumped for his opponents.[16] In addition, the *Leeds Times* thought many poor voters had been "intimidated" by anti-Hume forces. The Methodists received their share of blame for believing the stories about Hume's atheism.[17] No doubt a combination of these factors, plus the enormous influence wielded by a banker of Beckett's stature, brought down Hume.[18] Not all were saddened by the outcome. The *Leeds Intelligencer* thought it appropriate that such a "champion of ministry" should fall to a young man of no political experience. The *Intelligencer* attributed Hume's loss to public anger over his double-dealing and to hostility arising from his support for the new Poor Law.

After all the votes were counted, Hume addressed a crowd of disappointed, but cheering, followers. He told them he did not need cheers; he was accustomed to defeats. Hume blamed his setback on corrupt tactics by the conservatives and moderate Whigs. He cited the case of two men in Bromley who had promised him votes, but who had later been assured jobs if they stayed away until after the election. He charged that an appeal had been made to electors but not to "the people." Hume concluded by noting that 150,000 people lived in Leeds, yet there were only 4,000 registered voters. He hoped his defeat would lead to demands for political reform, and especially for the ballot. He seemed convinced that the lack of a ballot was the primary explanation for the Tories' gain of 79 members in the 1841 election.

Even before the disturbing results in Leeds, Hume had been a leader among the free-trade radicals in pushing for a new parliamentary reform bill. He generally supported the demands of the Chartists, but he knew that most of his friends would never accept the principle of universal suffrage. In February 1841 Hume tried to persuade William Lovett to accept the term "household suffrage," but Lovett and the London Chartists were no more likely to accept "household suffrage" than Hume's friends were to accept "universal suffrage."[19] Place also attempted to moderate Chartist demands. He was part of a "New Move" in Leeds to bring about a union of Chartists and free-trade reformers. Place had waited until January 1841 to undertake the effort on the theory that neither side would have accepted a cooperative venture before that time.[20] To his dismay, he discovered that the Chartists were still not ready to work with the free-traders. O'Connor used

[15]See also *Northern Star*, 3 and 10 July 1841.

[16]*Leeds Mercury*, 3 July 1841; *Leeds Times*, 3 July 1841.

[17]*Leeds Mercury*, 3 July 1841.

[18]*Leeds Mercury*, 3 July 1841.

[19]Hume to Place, 3 February 1841, BL, Add. MS. 35151; Place to Hume, 10 February 1841, BL, Add. MS. 35151.

[20]Homer Stansfield to Place, 13 January 1841, BL, Add. MS. 35151.

the *Northern Star* to encourage Chartists to turn their backs on the "New Move."[21] Place retaliated by telling the leaders of the London Chartists that "O'Connor and his *Northern Star* were the worst enemies the working people had."[22] Lovett and his colleagues were not impressed with Place's reasoning.

After the failure of the "New Move," Hume believed that the free-traders must go forward with their plan of reform "without referring to the Chartists in any way." He did suggest that they make their reform plan "as liberal as we can."[23] Hume also proposed to create an association "for the extension of the suffrage in the hopes of getting the working classes to join the middle class reformers." It was to be called the Metropolitan Registered Suffrage Association.[24] Hume wanted the working class to understand that political reform beyond the 1832 bill required cohesion among the reformers. This appeal for cooperation was consistent with similar efforts made by Hume when the Whigs were in power in the mid-1830s.

Hume did not dispute the propriety of the Chartists' demands; in early 1841 he seemed to endorse, with some minor qualifications, all of the People's Charter. His objection to the Chartists stemmed from two considerations: a majority of them were anti-free trade and their tactics provoked negative reactions from middle class liberals. Hume was still trying to reconcile the reform objectives of middle class reformers like himself to those of the working class when he was defeated in the July election.[25]

Following his defeat in Leeds, Hume remained out of Parliament for the next seven months. His activities during much of this hiatus cannot be traced. For the most part he was quiet. In December *The Times* noted his absence from the political scene with a brief poem:

Ye winds that rove onward from ocean to ocean,
O'er mountains and molehill in sunshine and gloom,
Say, bodiless vagabonds, have ye a notion
Where lingers the Joseph that mortals call Hume?
Oh no, let us hope that poor Joseph neglected,
His balderdash silenced, his hair growing grey,
By Middlesex spurned, and by Leeds, too, rejected
Is humoring conscience, and trying to pray.

Wherever Hume was in the autumn of 1841, he certainly regretted the collapse of the Whig ministry in September. Nearly everyone acknowledged that since 1837 the Melbourne government had been a severe disappointment, yet Hume still preferred Whigs to conservatives. The fact that the new prime minister, Sir Robert Peel, was a man he respected did not alter his opinion. It was always possible that Peel would consent to what Hume thought were "minor" reforms, but Corn Law repeal and political reform seemed remote possibilities.

[21]See Wallas, *Francis Place*, 387–88.
[22]Place to Hume, 10 February 1841, BL, Add. MS. 35151.
[23]Hume to Place, 11 February 1841, BL, Add. MS. 35151.
[24]Hume to Brougham, 15 February 1841, BL, Add. MS. 35113.
[25]Hume to Brougham, 17 July 1841, BL, Add. MS. 10034.

Hume tested Peel's liberalism late in 1841 and found it wanting. The Scotsman appealed to the prime minister to grant amnesty to all political offenders in the empire. His primary concern was to gain release for those who were being held in Canadian prisons. Peel consulted Lord Stanley (secretary for war and colonies) and was advised that amnesty in Canada "would be dangerous." Peel took Stanley's view of the situation and told Hume that he considered it "more natural to let the law pursue its even course than to interrupt it."[26]

Peel's government had much more to worry about in the autumn and winter of 1841–1842 than the plight of political dissenters. These were difficult months of high prices, low food supplies, and unemployment. In Birmingham, Manchester, Carlisle, and Glasgow troops had to be called out to quell rioting. The distress in the country served in one way or another to inflame all reformers. The Chartists gained followers where economic circumstances were most severe. The free-traders blamed the "disastrous economy" on the Corn Laws, and preached that all would prosper when the government accepted the political economy of Smith, Ricardo, and Bentham.

Since there was no chance of uniting the Chartists with the free-trade reformers, the free-traders, early in 1842, planned to take the ground from the working class leaders. Hume, Place, and several members of the Radical Club (a monthly dinner meeting of radicals) decided to organize the Metropolitan Parliamentary Reform Association that, among other things, would seek to enlighten the public on the question of franchise reform. The association would be distinct from the Radical Club and it would avoid such inflammatory terms as "Charter," "universal suffrage," and "annual Parliaments." The free-trade radicals hoped to use the association to convince moderate reformers that franchise reform was a reasonable goal. The Radical Club had come to the conclusion that the activities of the Chartists jeopardized all reform efforts. This would be one way to show that the "irresponsible" Chartists were not the only ones to favor the ballot, expanded voting rights, and shorter parliaments.

The Metropolitan Parliamentary Reform Association began its operation on 20 May 1842.[27] It lasted about one year; and, in truth, it did not prove to be very successful. Yet, it does have some importance for the biographer of Hume. The formation of this society marked the end of Hume's long friendship with Francis Place. Their falling out resulted from a misunderstanding over an address (to come from the Radical Club) announcing the creation of the Metropolitan Association. Initially, conflict arose when Hume thought there was unnecessary delay in printing the address. On 17 March, he wrote to Place, "I rather expected to have had the address in print ere this, as it is important our cause should be known as soon as possible."[28] This irritated Place for, although the address would be

[26]Hume to Peel, 13 November 1841, BL, Add. MS. 40494; Stanley to Peel, 11 November 1841, BL, Add. MS. 40494; Peel to Hume, 16 November 1841, BL, Add. MS. 40494.
[27]See BL, Add. MS. 27810. Also, Huch, "Promise and Disillusion," 497–512.
[28]Hume to Place, 17 March 1842, BL, Add. MS. 27810.

announced as coming from the Radical Club, he had assumed the responsibility for writing the statement.[29]

The worst was still to come. When Place had finished the address he sent it to Hume for examination before printing. Hume took it upon himself to revise the document without consulting Place. He then sent it directly to the printer. The next time Place saw his statement it was in proof copy. He reacted angrily to this slight. He charged that Hume had made "nonsense of some of it." Place told one and all of Hume's "unpardonable" conduct.[30] Others in the Radical Club agreed that Hume's action was "irregular and reprehensible" and something "no one else would have done."[31] Although Hume and Place had often quarreled in the past about similar matters, this time there was no reconciliation. Place always thought Hume a meddler. Had he not found Hume useful in Parliament he might well have broken the friendship earlier. He certainly had considered taking that step in the 1830s when Hume appeared to have softened his approach to the Whigs. Now in his seventies, and beset by chronic bronchitis, it may have been that Place's reservoir of patience for Hume had finally run dry. It had taken great effort on his part to finish the address in question, and to have Hume revise it in the space of a few hours and commit it to print behind his back proved to be more than he could tolerate. A full year after the incident, Place explained to Perronet Thompson that he had not had any kind of communication with Hume for eleven or twelve months and he did not "suppose there will be any future acquaintance between us."[32]

Apparently Hume made no attempt to set things right with Place. The Scotsman had his own reasons for being annoyed. It seemed to him that Place did not really think that further political reform was possible; Hume wondered whether he even thought it desirable. The Corn Laws dominated Place's thinking. He did not complain so much about the damage the Chartists were doing to the cause of parliamentary reform as he did about how they were undermining Corn Law repeal by "foolishly alarming the middle class."[33] Hume had long advocated repeal of the Corn Laws, and all other tariffs, but he thought political reform a far greater necessity at the moment. He sensed correctly that after 1840 Place considered eliminating the Corn Laws a much more likely prospect than franchise reform.[34]

There were other reasons that Hume did not seem to mind the end of his thirty-year association with Place. They never had been warm friends. There was mutual respect, but Place did not shy from giving the impression that Hume's "reputation" in Parliament had come mostly as a result of his (Place's) direction. That Place succeeded in establishing this opinion is obvious in the number of books and articles that claim the Scotsman

[29]Place to Samuel Harrison, 21 February 1842, BL, Add. MS. 27801.

[30]Place to the Committee of the Metropolitan Reform Association, 2 April 1842, BL, Add. MS. 27810.

[31]S. Harrison to Place, 4 April 1842, BL, Add. MS. 27810.

[32]Place to Colonel Thompson, 20 March 1843, BL, Add. MS. 35151.

[33]Place to S. Harrison, 15 February 1842, BL, Add. MS. 27810.

[34]See Wallas, *Francis Place,* 391.

provided the Radical Tailor's voice in the House of Commons.[35] This view prevails in historical literature despite their numerous disagreements over the years. Although all who knew Hume aver that he could never harbor resentment for anyone, it may have been that he did build up some in his dealings with Place. In his mind he was the superior politician, and he no longer saw any need to soothe Place's injured feelings.

In the midst of his dispute with Place, Hume was returned to Parliament once again for the Montrose district. He had refused to engage in a personal canvass in Scotland, but had declared himself a candidate when a majority of the electors signed a petition asking him to stand.[36] He was returned without opposition on 16 April. Seeing the Scotsman once more in the chamber gave a lift to the old radicals who had watched their numbers dwindle in 1841.[37]

Hume reentered Parliament at just the time the Chartists were presenting their national petition in the House of Commons. He urged the House to accept the petition. Hume regretted the violence of the Chartists, but said the men only wanted constitutional rights. They were called upon to defend their country, argued Hume, so it seemed just that they should be able to vote. He did not think all of the Chartist demands need be accepted at once. It was always wise to "give some now and more later." He thought the surest way to prevent revolution was "to listen to and redress the well-grounded complaint of the people." In addition to Hume, Bowring, Villiers, and Cobden, all leaders of the free-trade movement supported the petition, but the Commons rejected it by a vote of 287 to 49.[38]

The overwhelming defeat for the Chartists had a salutary affect on Hume. He saw that Place had been right about the bleak prospects for political reform. He lost interest in the Metropolitan Parliamentary Reform Association and did not even attend its first formal meeting in late May. Over the next few years he seemed to most observers to be "rudderless." He returned to the scatter-gun tactics he had used throughout his early parliamentary career.[39] He attacked the government for excessive spending, for failing to act in the face of economic distress, and for its evil policies in Canada and Ireland.

His efforts brought him the same kind of abuse he had suffered in the 1820s. *The Times* called him "mad" and *John Bull,* an old conservative nemesis, said in 1843 that Hume proved "men no longer die when their brains are gone."[40] Amid his constant railings about the need to reduce spending, Hume was primarily concerned between 1843 and 1847 with eliminating tariffs and with creating a system of national education. For any free-trader, these two causes were complementary. Abolishing all barriers to free trade would open the door to more competition, and more competition would lead to greater prosperity for every citizen in the long

[35]Ibid., 183.
[36]Hume to J. Burton, 30 March 1842, Burton Papers, NLS, MS. 9404.
[37]W. A. Munford, *William Ewart,* 110–11.
[38]*Hansard,* third series, 63: 63.
[39]See Norman McCord, *The Anti-Corn Law League, 1838–1846* (London, 1958), 79.
[40]*John Bull,* 17 June 1843.

run. A national system of education, with its emphasis on reading, writing, and arithmetic, would make Englishmen better prepared for success in a free-market economy. As was true with other Benthamites, Hume saw no contradiction to his laissez faire philosophy in the public support required to establish national education. The most important thing was to have schools that provided "secular and moral" training for all English children. Hume believed that learning required discipline and discipline strengthened moral fiber.

Neither free trade nor national education made fast enough progress to satisfy Hume in the early 1840s. He supported Cobden's Anti-Corn Law League and urged the repeal of all tariffs whenever he had the opportunity. He tried to show how English duties adversely affected international trade; he argued that the highly protective American tariff act of 1842 resulted from the policy followed by England. Hume also thought that questions over duties with France, Portugal, and Spain injured British merchants.[41] In May of 1843 he supported Charles Villiers's motion to abolish the Corn Laws. This effort failed 381 to 125.[42] One month later Lord John Russell attempted to revive the issue by moving for a committee of the whole House to consider the Corn Laws. Hume endorsed this suggestion, but the motion was easily defeated.[43]

After these two setbacks, Hume turned his attention to the issue of education. On 25 July, he introduced a bill to create a national system at the public expense

without wounding the feelings or injuring the rights of any sect or class of the community, but confining the business of the schoolmaster to the secular and moral training of the children, and leaving all religious instruction to religious teachers distinct from the school.[44]

This was a measure that Hume had talked about bringing forward for more than thirty years. He pointed out that Parliament in 1840–41 had set the precedent for public aid to education when it granted £25,000 to Church of England schools and £1,000 to the British and Foreign School Society. Hume's arguments were reasonable, and his bill had merit, but there were just forty members in the House when he began his speech. After he talked for nearly three hours fewer than fifteen were still in attendance. *John Bull* took pleasure in noting that when he had finished belaboring the "martyrs" who had remained in their seats, Hume had nothing to do but put his "smothered resolution" in his hat and head for his Bryanston Square home.[45]

The summer was never a good time to raise matters of substance in the House of Commons, and Hume knew this as well as anyone. In making his proposal he acknowledged that his timing was poor, but he thought the issue of sufficient importance that it could not be delayed. The dismal

[41]Hume to Aberdeen, 12 April 1843, BL, Add. MS. 43200.
[42]*Hansard,* third series, 69: 26ff.
[43]*Hansard,* third series, 69: 1445–70.
[44]*Hansard,* third series, 70: 1329–48.
[45]*John Bull,* 29 July 1843.

reception his plan received in the House of Commons, and the general lack of interest in any sort of reform, left Hume angry and feisty. In November, 1843, he wrote to George Grote, "I believe you are disgusted with the House of Commons, but not more than I am. . . ." He blamed the Whigs as much as the Tories for this attitude. "I had wished to take my leave," he told Grote, "as few of those I have to act with will go the length I would wish to go, seeing the Whigs deceived us, and injured the popular cause so much." He thought that "Lord Grey and the leaders of the Reform movement of 1830–2" had "betrayed the cause. They completely humbugged *me,* I must confess." But Hume was far from downhearted. He tried to rally Grote by telling him "the cause flourishes and every person capable should be willing to join the contest going on and *to* go on."[46]

There were two events that particularly cheered Hume in the autumn of 1843. His old radical ally, Henry Warburton, was reelected to the House of Commons after a two-year hiatus. Hume knew that Warburton would provide much needed help for the parliamentary radicals. The Scotsman also was impressed by the Anti-Corn Law League's exuberant claims of electoral influence in the late summer and autumn of 1843. Hume's optimism was short-lived. He could discern no change in attitude on the part of the ministers, and no improvement in the strategy of the reformers during the parliamentary sessions of 1844 and 1845. Although he remained the gadfly he had been in the past, Hume became, by his standard at least, somewhat subdued. He spoke hundreds of times in the 1844 session, but he spoke only about half as long as usual. This led to speculation that his health had deteriorated. Since there is no evidence that Hume had any debilitating illness, it is likely that his lack of enthusiasm (for him at least) reflected a temporary disenchantment with Parliament. At one point he attacked members for "lack of interest," and for refusing to listen attentively to those who wished to revise "bad legislation."[47]

The "bad legislation" that most concerned Hume in 1844 was the new Factories Bill introduced by Sir James Graham. The bill provided that children between eight and thirteen should work no longer than six and one-half hours per day; that females should not work longer than twelve hours: and that accidents should be promptly reported. As a free-trader, Hume had no use for any factory legislation, but he did seem sympathetic to the idea that children's work time should be reduced in order to give them some time to learn reading and writing. His biggest concern was that supporters of "ten hours" legislation would not succeed in amending the proposal to suit their interest. He need not have worried. Although the ten hours question had a full debate in 1844, it did not become part of the Factory Bill. In the end, Hume offered some minor criticisms of the bill's provisions and voted for it.[48] Apart from several speeches on the need to reduce the sugar duties, and occasional harassment of the government for

[46]Hume to Grote, 10 November 1843, in George Grote, *Posthumous Papers,* edited by Mrs. Grote (London, 1874), 79–80.
[47]*Hansard,* third series, 73: 165lff.
[48]Ibid., 1669ff.

allowing the post office to open certain correspondence,[49] Hume made little contribution to parliamentary business after the Factory Act gained approval. For one of the rare times, he was relieved when Parliament was prorogued on 5 September.

It was much the same story in 1845. Hume continued to attend Parliament as religiously as ever, but he displayed none of his customary verve. He acted as if he were convinced the Peel government could never achieve important reforms. Political reform obviously had no chance; and, while he knew the prime minister wanted to phase out the Corn Laws, Hume believed the landed interests in the conservative party would cause Peel to stop short. "The Duke of Richmond [the most prominent protectionist in the House of Lords] and his party are bullying him [Peel]," wrote Hume to an Edinburgh acquaintance, "and I fear Sir Robert is too much of a coward to go against them."[50]

Hume's assessment of the situation was reasonably accurate early in 1845, but by the end of the year things had changed. Two developments brought Peel to the brink of submitting a bill to repeal the Corn Laws. One was a natural disaster and the other a personal matter. The potato blight made it necessary to expand importation of foodstuffs; hence, reducing or eliminating agricultural tariffs was a logical step.[51] The personal matter was Peel's realization that he no longer cared about remaining in office. As Norman Gash eloquently describes in his biography of Peel, the prime minister had grown tired and frustrated in his effort to govern the country. The workload was enormous and the rewards slim. He was badgered in the House of Commons on just about every issue, and his cabinet was divided between those who wanted a greater measure of free trade and those who wanted less. The balance did seem to be shifting in favor of free trade, especially after the potato disaster became known. By December even such die-hard protectionists as Stanley and the duke of Buccleuch (lord privy seal) were ready to admit that the Corn Laws were doomed.

With his ministry in disarray, and with his will to carry on apparently broken, the whole of December 1845 was one long political crisis for Peel. He resigned in the first week and resumed command in the third. The queen had summoned Lord John Russell to form a government upon Peel's resignation, but soon found that the opposition leader could not put together a ministry. He lacked cooperation from several prominent Whigs. When Russell admitted his failure, Peel told Victoria that he would continue to lead the government. Moreover, he promised to return to the political wars with one new resolve. Soon after his meeting with the queen, he informed his cabinet that he intended to offer Corn Law reform. Peel made it clear that the Corn Law question could not be allowed to continue as the cause of political chaos. Within a short time the prime minister managed to bring stability to his government; he entered 1846 with more

[49]See Gash, *Sir Robert Peel*, 468–69.
[50]Hume to J. Burton, 28 January 1845, Burton Papers, NLS, MS. 9404.
[51]McCord, *The Anti-Corn Law League*, 196–97.

strength than any reasonable observer could have imagined in early December.[52]

Hume had every reason to be happy with the news that Peel had made up his mind to repeal the Corn Laws. The Scotsman had not regretted Russell's inability to form a ministry. He resented the fact that the Whigs had been so tardy in understanding the need for tariff reform. Despite political differences over more than twenty-five years, there was mutual respect between Peel and Hume; a respect coming from the fact that each gave maximum attention to parliamentary business. In January 1846, Hume prepared a public letter in which he praised the prime minister for having "adopted every one of my principles."[53] To show his good faith, Hume pledged not to oppose Peel's plan to increase appropriations for the army and navy. This, above all else, shows how much Hume appreciated Peel's interest in tariff repeal. Cobden also found the prime minister's position appealing, but he did not proclaim his regard for Peel the way Hume did.[54]

When Peel made his proposal for Corn Law reform on 22 January, he suggested something less than "total and immediate" repeal. He recommended that a small but diminishing tariff be retained for a few years.[55] This came as no surprise to Hume; the Tories had told him that Peel would offer a compromise.[56] Leaders of the Anti-Corn Law League, and free-traders in general, were not of one mind in their reaction to Peel's plan, but a majority supported it. The higher echelon of the League eventually decided not to offer opposition. Although he had expected Peel to propose "entire if not immediate" repeal, Lord John Russell did not hesitate to endorse the plan. Hume was in full agreement with Russell on this occasion.[57] He preferred immediate repeal, yet he thought Russell correct to ask all reformers to support the government.[58]

There were many prominent free-traders, however, who wanted to push hard for "total and immediate" repeal in 1846. One of them, the earl of Radnor, urged Peel to change his mind and eliminate the Corn Laws altogether. Peel replied that he was determined to recommend something that would "receive the sanction of both Houses" of Parliament. "I . . . still retain a firm conviction," wrote Peel to Radnor, "that had I proposed total and immediate repeal of the Corn Laws I should have had little chance for success." His decision was based strictly on political expediency. The prime minister gave every indication that he personally favored total and immediate repeal, and would not be disappointed with a strong vote in support of these objectives in the House of Commons.

With Peel's permission, Radnor passed this word to leaders in the

[52]Gash, *Sir Robert Peel*, 562–64.

[53]James Laverne Sturgis, "British Parliamentary Radicalism, 1846–1852" (Ph.D. dissertation, University of Toronto, 1972), 48.

[54]Ibid.

[55]Gash, *Sir Robert Peel*, 563–71; McCord, *The Anti-Corn Law League*, 196–97.

[56]Hume to Cobden, 5 January 1846, BL, Add. MS. 43667.

[57]Ibid.

[58]*Hansard*, third series, 84: 466–67.

Anti-Corn Law League.[59] It was this information that led Charles Villiers to move an amendment to Peel's bill calling for "total and immediate" repeal. During debate on Villiers's amendment, Hume rose to explain his position. He spent the first two-thirds of his speech criticizing the selfish interests of the landowners; then, to the surprise of his colleagues, he announced that he could not vote for the amendment. He used the old "half-a-loaf is better than none" argument which had been his most reliable phrase during the 1830s. He wanted it known that his position made him no less a free-trader, but he could see no reason to jeopardize a good bill.[60] Roebuck expressed amazement at Hume's patience, Villiers was confused, and Cobden called Hume "obtuse."[61] The amendment failed by a vote of 265 to 78; and Cobden was right to observe that Peel would have preferred a larger minority, something that Villiers and Cobden reckoned would have been achieved if Hume had given his support. They probably overestimated the Scotsman's influence on this issue. It is difficult to know who might have changed his vote because of Hume's stand. Ewart, Bright, Cobden, Ellice, and Warburton all voted for the amendment anyway, and these were the individuals most likely to have been swayed by Hume. After the defeat of Villiers's motion, Hume did not show much interest in the Corn Law question. He was quite willing to permit Peel's gradual repeal measure to advance without controversy.

If Peel experienced exaltation at the success of his repeal measure, it did not last very long. On the very day (25 June) that the Corn Bill passed its third reading in the upper House, the government conceded defeat in the House of Commons on the second reading of the Irish Crimes Bill. The prime minister had known for some time that his ministry could not carry the Irish bill, especially since many protectionists, piqued over the Corn Law legislation, planned to vote with the opposition. Several free-traders, including Cobden, advised Peel that he could remain in office by dissolving Parliament and holding elections under the slogan "Peel and Free Trade." The prime minister rejected these pleas. He did not think it possible to maintain a government based on a coalition of Peelite conservatives and free-traders; Peel did not want (nor did his followers) an alliance with the Whigs. More important than political realities, however, was the fact that Peel lacked the desire to continue. The past five years had given him his fill of running the government. Debates in the House of Commons now ran on for so long, and demanded so much time and energy that Peel found it increasingly difficult to summon the strength to attend each session. He sought a more peaceful life, and only the politically selfish in his party could deny that he had earned it.

In late June, Peel informed his cabinet that he intended to resign for the good of conservatism. He urged the rest of his cabinet to do the same. No one demurred. In a moving speech on 26 June, the prime minister

[59]See Ronald K. Huch, *The Radical Lord Radnor,* 160–61.
[60]*Hansard,* third series, 84: 551–78.
[61]See McCord, *The Anti-Corn Law League,* 202–5; Huch, *The Radical Lord Radnor,* 161; Sturgis, "British Parliamentary Radicalism," 59.

announced his resignation in the House of Commons. He spoke proudly of the repeal of the Corn Laws, but, with his usual fairness, gave most of the credit to Richard Cobden. Peel had chosen the right moment to step aside with honor and adulation. The cheers rang down from every corner of the chamber. No one applauded more loudly than Hume. The resignation opened the door for Russell to create a new government, while Peel, at least temporarily, gained the peace and quiet he desired.[62]

Hume seemed just as weary as Peel in the summer of 1846. Although known for his perseverance in attending almost every minute of debate, he agreed with Peel that discussions in the Commons had reached gargantuan proportions. It was, he said, a major chore to get over the easiest of hurdles. We can imagine how severe the problem must have been if Hume complained about lengthy sessions! As one journal had put it, Hume "could bore and endure to be bored to any extent."

On the night Peel resigned, Hume happily prepared to depart for Burnley Hall, his country residence near Yarmouth, Norfolk. Hume enjoyed walking the winding paths through the lush shrubbery, flowers, and trees that surrounded the estate house. Clumps of oak, chestnut, and fir were complemented by roses and jasmine planted nearby. The serenity of Norfolk provided Hume the rest he needed. His health had been unsteady for most of the year; he did not suffer any serious ailment, but he had frequent discomfort from recurring flu-like symptoms. In several instances he had been required to leave the chamber before the day's work was completed. This was a clear sign that he was under duress. From time to time he attributed his "not feeling well" to the increasing demands of parliamentary business and to the fact that the years might be catching up with him. Even at sixty-nine this was an unlikely prospect for Hume. When he was below par he still had more stamina than most of his colleagues—or so it seemed. It was certainly true that the longer he stayed away from Westminster the more he yearned to get back.

[62]See Gash, *Sir Robert Peel*, 594–604.

CHAPTER VIII.

THE LITTLE CHARTER, 1847–1855

Hume returned to his Bryanston Square residence in December 1846 ready to renew the reform campaign. The free-trade radicals appeared to have reason for optimism in the early days of the 1847 session. The starvation conditions in Ireland temporarily brought free-traders and protectionists into agreement that, at least until the next harvest, all tariffs on grain should be suspended. The potato failure had diminished the likelihood of a protectionist upswing. Hume drew some satisfaction from this apparent vindication (at least as he saw it) of his free-trade arguments; yet in the long run the session that had just begun would be one of his most disappointing.

The radicals seemed bereft of spirit and causes.[1] There was little pressure for reform from out of doors, and inside the House there seemed to be a reluctance to jeopardize Whig-radical cooperation before the upcoming summer elections.[2] Hume sensed early on that he had little chance to raise successfully issues of economic and parliamentary reform.[3] What surprised many of his friends was that Hume did not appear especially disturbed by this prospect. He had dealt with Whig governments in the past and he imagined that Russell would continue the maddeningly moderate approach practiced by Melbourne and Grey.

Despite his willingness to allow most matters to drift, there were several issues in 1847 that brought Hume to his feet in the House of Commons. One was the question of national education. He insisted that the government was not moving quickly enough to establish a comprehensive system of secular education. He was certain that crime and sloth would be greatly diminished when such a system came into existence.[4] The Ten Hours Bill also caused Hume some concern. Free-traders were not of one mind on this question, but Hume opposed all factory legislation as detrimental to the well-being of employers and workers. Such measures, according to his reasoning, weakened the position of English manufacturers in relation to foreign industries. To the dictums of free trade, as expressed by Ricardo, James Mill, and Bentham, the Scotsman remained loyal.

During the course of the 1847 session, Hume became a leading advocate of the Health of Towns Bill introduced by Lord John Russell. This legislation appealed to followers of James Mill and Bentham because it emphasized efficient administration of the proposed regulations. The responsibility for administering the terms of the bill was to rest in the hands of a national board similar to that established for the administration of the Poor Law. Edwin Chadwick, a leading proponent of the legislation from out of doors, solicited Hume's help in pushing the bill in the Commons and

---

[1]There is no foundation to Maccoby's contention that there was a revival of radical activity in 1847. See Maccoby, *English Radicalism, 1832–1852* (London, 1935), 271.

[2]Sturgis, "British Parliamentary Radicalism, 1846–1852," 58–59.

[3]*The Montrose, Arbroath and Brechin Review,* 19 February 1848.

[4]*Hansard,* third series, 91: 117ff.

also in making certain adjustments in some of the clauses. Hume eagerly cooperated with Chadwick. The biggest concerns for Chadwick were the potential for "local jobbing" and the opportunity for poorly qualified persons to receive posts under the Board of Health.[5] Hume promised that he would make every effort to see that the Health of Towns Bill provided protection against the abuses Chadwick feared. But Hume could not carry through on this pledge.

His attention was diverted from the sanitation legislation by the administration's reaction to a liberal rebellion in Portugal. The foreign secretary, Lord Palmerston, showed no inclination to help the Portuguese liberals against the monarchy. Encouraged by his radical colleagues, Hume announced that he would move a resolution condemning the Russell ministry for its "reactionary" stand on Portugal. The Whigs were concerned by Hume's position because it appeared that many protectionists would join with the free-trade radicals and vote against the government. The protectionists cared little about the situation in Portugal; they wanted to embarrass the administration.

Palmerston was so worried about the potential damage from Hume's motion that he tried to persuade the Scotsman to defer his resolution until all the "facts" were known. Hume did delay somewhat, but eventually introduced his motion on 11 June. Several days lapsed between the time Hume presented his resolution and debate on the matter. During that time an attempt was made by a group of Whigs and radicals to dissuade Hume from forcing a division. Hume refused to listen, but he offered little resistance when J. A. Roebuck submitted a new motion emphasizing British dedication to protecting Portuguese liberties. Roebuck pursued this course, so he said, in order to avoid friction between the Whig and radical camps on the eve of a general election. Most radicals in the Commons seemed to support Roebuck. In any event the debate disintegrated after Roebuck's initiative and the matter was dropped in late June.

Although the Portuguese question had not brought the feared humiliation to the government, Hume knew that the ministers were not pleased with his actions. Even when he was relatively quiet, as he had been throughout the 1847 session, he could never bring himself to sit through a whole session without causing some trouble. On 2 July, he explained to Chadwick that he would not be able to take any further part in the debate on the Health of Towns Bill because "they [the ministers] are in great anger at my proceedings on the Portuguese [question]. . . . My interference would be an injury instead of a benefit."[6] Subsequently, the government withdrew the Health of Towns Bill from consideration on 8 July. The members were impatient to get on with the impending general election, and the ministry sensed that few were willing to sit still for the many adjustments required in the legislation. The bill was reintroduced in 1848 in altered form and passed.

---

[5]Chadwick to Hume 15 June 1847 and Chadwick to Hume, 5 July 1847, Chadwick Papers, UCL.
[6]Hume to Chadwick, 2 July 1848, Chadwick Papers, UCL.

Following the dissolution of Parliament, Hume prepared to return to Scotland for his reelection campaign. On this occasion he had opposition. David Greenhill, a liberal with views similar to those of Hume, decided to enter the Montrose election. Greenhill argued that Hume had done nothing for the workingman in the Angus burghs, and tried to prove his contention by noting that "Old Joe" had voted against the Ten Hours Bill. He also made the point—*de rigueur* for all Hume's opponents by now—that Hume was an atheist who desecrated the Sabbath.[7]

Hume countered these attacks by reviewing his long parliamentary career for the electors in Montrose. He reminded them of his role in the elimination of the Combination Laws and his work over the years on behalf of economy and parliamentary reform. He maintained again that accusations he was an atheist should not be taken seriously. Although Greenhill appeared to have strong backing during his canvass of the electors, when the polling ended on 11 August, Hume held a substantial margin. Hume thanked the residents of the burghs for their support, but expressed his dismay that so few were eligible to vote in a population of some 58,000.[8]

The general election resulted in a slightly strengthened Whig government. The supporters of the ministry totalled about 315; the conservatives 325, but nearly 110 of these were Peelites who could be relied upon to help Russell on most occasions. On the other hand, the parliamentary radicals (counted among the supporters of Russell) had done exceeding well in the elections. This gave rise to speculation in the autumn of 1847 that the government might need to placate the radicals in order to maintain its majority.[9] But Russell was not the sort to move in the direction of the radicals. Norman Gash has quite rightly observed that Russell's ministry at the end of 1847 did not differ much from that of Lord Melbourne in 1841.[10] Russell revealed his true colors when he could not quite bring himself to add Cobden to his cabinet. The prime minister planned to rely on the Peelites to keep his ministry afloat, only to discover that a large number of Peelites would not cooperate. "In many respects," writes Gash, "the independent role of the Peelites between 1846 and 1852 paralysed the whigs."[11]

Russell's headlong plunge into moderation contrasted with a strong revival of radical hopes in 1848. For most radicals, indeed for nearly all politicians, 1847 had been a year of recovering from the excitement of 1846. The general election of 1847 attracted the lion's share of political attention in that year. The members seemed unable, or unwilling, to concentrate for very long on any issues raised in the House of Commons. The excitement returned in 1848, and Hume can be credited with creating a large measure of the new enthusiasm.

Even before Parliament reassembled in February, Hume gave indication that he would not be as reticent to make trouble for the prime minister as he

[7] *The Montrose, Arbroath and Brechin Review*, 6 August 1847.
[8] See Gash, *Reaction and Reconstruction*, 192.
[9] Gash, *Sir Robert Peel*, 625–27; Maccoby, *English Radicalism, 1832–1852*, 275–77.
[10] Gash, *Reaction and Reconstruction*, 195.
[11] Ibid. 193–94.

had been in 1847. The radical contingent was much stronger after the general election and Hume wanted to use this strength to push Russell. He had no desire to see the Whig government fail, yet he could see no good reason why the ministry should continue to avoid policies of retrenchment and parliamentary reform. On the matter of retrenchment, Hume told Cobden he would do what he thought necessary "whatever may be the consequences." He believed the ministers had "lost their senses." He hoped people would attend public meetings and demand relief, they must "enforce their views [on] their representatives or there is little that can be done."[12] Cobden, who placed a higher premium on retrenchment than Hume, had no reason to disagree. Both of them undertook such a vigorous attack against government spending in February that the conservative *Morning Herald* observed "to hear Hume [and] Cobden it seems as if national ruin will occur when the army and navy estimates are passed."[13]

The radicals, no matter how energetic and united, could not defeat the government on budget issues without assistance. In February they received support from protectionists when the cabinet tried to increase the income tax. The coalition of protectionists and radicals in the Commons forced the ministry to withdraw the proposed increase. This setback for Russell meant that the ministers were not strong enough to force their will in the House.[14]

This evidence of weakness coincided with a renewed wave of Chartist activity. Chartism gained strength from the agitation of radicals against the income tax and from news of the successful revolution in France. A Chartist meeting in London voted to send a delegation to Paris to congratulate the new republican regime; in Glasgow angry dissidents smashed shops and shouted "Bread or Revolution."[15] Plans were undertaken for a new National Petition and for another Chartist convention. The Chartist leaders, especially O'Connor, were ready to emulate the continental developments in Paris, Vienna, and Berlin. There was talk of Chartists allying with "Young Ireland," a nationalist movement spurred toward revolutionary activity by the famine.

Despite the obvious potential for violence, the huge Chartist gatherings in London were quite peaceful and drew only modest crowds. There had been considerable worry over the great meeting planned for Kennington Common on 10 April, but the event did not bear out the grim prophecies of conservatives and middle class liberals. Only about fifteen thousand people turned out to hear a subdued speech from Feargus O'Connor. Chartism had been born in the despair and depression of the late thirties and early forties, and already the improved economic conditions had siphoned away support. Still, the rising tenor of discontent, and the ministry's inability to respond to the clamor for extreme measures, caused many parliamentary radicals (particularly the doctrinaire free-traders) to seek some method of

[12]Hume to Cobden, 1 February 1848, BL, Add. MS. 43667.
[13]21 February 1848.
[14]Gash, *Reaction and Reconstruction*, 195.
[15]Maccoby, *English Radicalism, 1832–1852*, 279.

defusing the Chartists while simultaneously taking advantage of the government's discomfort to push for substantial reforms.

In this effort Hume had a major part. He had worried for more than a decade about the likelihood of an irreconcilable division between the working class reformers and the middle class reformers. In a letter to the men of West Riding, Hume warned that Chartist violence caused "so-called" liberals to turn against just demands for reform. He hoped the working class of Leeds would join with middle class reformers to achieve worthy goals. If they did this England could avoid the anxiety that France went through.[16]

At the time Hume appealed for this support, he led a newly organized radical reform faction in the House of Commons. On 11 April, one day after the Chartist rally at Kennington, a number of free-trade radicals met at the Free Trade Club to discuss the state of politics and the prospects for reform. Out of this gathering came a resolution to the effect that "more cordial understanding and cooperation" were urgently required among the members who were "favorable to the extension of the suffrage, an equitable arrangement of taxation, a reduction of expenditure, and the general advance of reform principles."[17] The resolution eventually obtained the signatures of fifty-one members. Hume was elected chairman of the group (those at the meeting called it "the committee") and Cobden was made deputy chairman.[18] Speculation immediately arose that Hume and Cobden would attempt to entice as many Chartists as possible to join forces with the more "reasonable" radicals.[19] This is precisely the step Hume and Cobden made in the spring of 1848. With the failure of the most recent wave of Chartism to gain support in the Commons, this objective did not seem unrealistic.

Hume threw himself into his new task with an enthusiasm he had not shown for several years. At sixty-nine his health was sound, and he gave every indication that he considered the situation to be very similar to what it had been in the early 1830s. The fact that a sizeable number of his radical colleagues had selected him to lead this new reform effort (the first time he had ever received official recognition as a leader of a parliamentary faction) no doubt made him feel personally responsible for its success or failure. The work undertaken by Hume, Cobden, and other radicals who endorsed the April resolution became known as the "New Reform Movement."[20]

From the very beginning Hume thought the first goal of the parliamentary radicals should be to win backing for reform of representation. He saw this as the surest way to bring working class and middle class together. He had taken the same position in 1831. Cobden placed a greater importance

---

[16]*The Times,* 25 April 1848. See Henry Weisser, *April 10: Challenge and Response in England in 1848* (Lanham, Maryland, 1983).

[17]*The Sun,* 14 April 1848; *The Morning Advertiser,* 17 April 1848.

[18]See *The Examiner,* 15 April 1848; Sturgis, "British Parliamentary Radicalism, 1848–1852," 112.

[19]*The Morning Advertiser,* 17 April 1848.

[20]*The Sun,* 2 June 1848; Hobhouse Diary, 6 May 1848, BL, Add. MS. 43752.

on retrenchment and taxation reform, but he also desired parliamentary reform. Cobden made no issue of this difference of emphasis in the spring of 1848 since he knew that Hume's commitment to economy at least equalled his own. On 17 April, Hume told the House of Commons that soon he would call the attention of the members to the representation of the people. The liberal *Morning Chronicle* contended that the Scotsman faced a difficult task for he needed to lay down a plan that would "pacify existing constituencies without swamping them."[21]

Hume planned to bring in his reform bill sometime late in May. He intended to use the intervening weeks to whip up interest for the cause and to put together a series of proposals that would meet radical approval. He wrote public letters appealing for support from workers in several northern cities and he appeared at various rallies in London. His theme was constant: the 1832 Reform Act left much to be desired and the best way to improve the representation was for working class and middle class radicals to cooperate. Hume had decided to present his reform motion to the House on 23 May. On that day he went to the Commons with his speech prepared, but at the last minute he hesitated. A delay was necessary, he said, because he had not had the opportunity to address the House until very late in the evening. He would have to reschedule his proposal for 20 June. It seems more likely, however, that the change was part of a strategy to provide more time to build public fervor for the reform motion.[22] Feargus O'Connor thought the postponement ill-advised. He called Hume "indifferent" to reform and accused him of collaborating with the conservatives. O'Connor's attack on Hume did not stem from his belief that the reform bill had a chance for success, but rather from his desire to get the Scotsman's scheme out of the way. He knew that Hume planned a national appeal, and he feared that "Old Joe" might just make some gains among the working class. Cobden defended Hume against O'Connor's attack, and then accused the Irishman of being the "great enemy of the working classes." Lord John Russell ended the discussion by saying that the people were not anxious for the reforms envisioned by either O'Connor or Hume, but rather for "peace and quiet" and for an opportunity to see "safe and gradual improvement in their institutions."[23]

Peace and quiet, desirable though it may have been for the prime minister, was not on Hume's agenda. By saying that he would bring forward his reform bill on 23 May, and then delaying it until 20 June, Hume guaranteed that his proposals would receive widespread public attention. The newspapers reported the basic objectives of Hume's scheme and one of them, *The Sun,* had an advance copy of the speech Hume intended to give on 23 May. What Hume planned to offer was a truncated, and slightly revised, version of the "People's Charter." It therefore became known as the "Little Charter." Hume's reform plan included four basic provisions: the extension of the franchise to include all householders who

[21]*Morning Chronicle,* 25 April 1848.
[22]*Hansard,* third series, 98:1307–12.
[23]Hobhouse Diary, 25 May 1848, BL, Add. MS. 53752.

were residents in the electoral district for twelve months; the ballot; triennial parliaments; more equitable apportionment of representation.[24]

Throughout the first three weeks of June, Hume organized numerous public meetings designed to secure petitions and resolutions in support of his Little Charter.[25] Whenever possible he attended these gatherings himself. He appeared in the workhouse yard in Marylebone where, amidst great cheering, he heard himself described as an "old, tried, staunch, and veteran reformer." Hume promised the working classes that if they accepted his plan they would receive all they desired. As an "old" reformer he asked to "get all they could now and then the rest as soon as possible." A motion to support Hume's reform legislation was approved by the crowd shortly thereafter.[26] Assemblies in Edinburgh, Doncaster, and Hereford followed suit.[27] The results were not always so favorable. In Sheffield the town council, influenced by the Chartists, voted overwhelmingly to disapprove Hume's plan. It was in Sheffield that O'Connor announced to the gathering that he and Thomas Duncombe were leaders of a separate radical faction in the House of Commons. They did not look to Hume and Cobden because they were not true radicals. He complained that the Humeites imagined themselves superior to the Irish members.[28]

O'Connor's opinion notwithstanding, public interest in the Little Charter increased dramatically during the month of June. Hume was pleased, even inspired, by the reception he had encountered in most communities. He did not like the Chartist hecklers, but he was confident the Chartists shortly would discover that his proposal provided their only hope. It is clear, however, that Hume did not expect the Commons to show strong support for his "Little Charter." Whenever he thought his cause would win or do well in Parliament (as in the Corn Law debate in 1846) Hume kept quiet. He resisted making a nuisance of himself. If he had anticipated a large minority for his reform measure he would not have forced his free-trade colleagues to endure another of his orations on the "poor" West Indian colonists the night before presenting his "Little Charter."

Every time Hume defended the West Indian planters he made his radical associates squirm. He tried to explain to free-traders that circumstances were different in the West Indies from other areas. He contended that West Indian colonists were not fairly compensated for loss of slave labor. The price of sugar rose in consequence of the need to pay wages. "Negro labourers," said Hume, "go to work with silk umbrellas . . . and, in fact, since the Emancipation Act, the servants [have] taken the place of masters, and the masters that of the servants." He thought the government should find a remedy for the planters—they needed protection and help to avoid ruin.

Hume's concern for the West Indian planters was as consistent as his desire for retrenchment and parliamentary reform. Whether it stemmed, as

[24]*The Sun*, 23 May 1848; *The Times*, 24 May 1848.
[25]*The Times*, 1 June 1848; *The Sun* 9 June 1848.
[26]*The Examiner*, 10 June 1848.
[27]*The Sun*, 15 June 1848.
[28]*The Morning Post*, 16 June 1848.

several alleged, from worry over financial interests he had in the West
Indies, or whether prompted by a misplaced sense of justice, Hume's
defense of the planters never failed to confuse and aggravate all categories
of reformers. Therefore, if he had given his reform scheme any chance for
success he would not have risked this speech on 19 June.[29] Hume's West
Indian remarks did disturb his followers, but most preferred to look
forward to the debate on reform.[30]

The atmosphere in the House of Commons was electric when, as
promised, Hume introduced his parliamentary reform bill on 20 June.
There were no surprises in what Hume proposed; the four provisions that
had been discussed since May were included. It was also no surprise that
Hume spoke for over two hours, or that his speech was laced with
population statistics. In the course of presenting his measure, the Scotsman
reiterated his view that the time had come to improve on the 1832
legislation. The need existed for "the people" to have better representation
in the House of Commons. Hume charged that Russell had so far ignored
all reasonable pleas for parliamentary reform and had bound himself to a
position of "finality." After Bowring seconded Hume's proposal, Cobden
spoke forcefully in behalf of Hume's opinions. He argued that the system of
representation in 1848 was a "sham." According to Cobden the preserva-
tion of peace in the country depended upon the Commons' acceptance of
Hume's plan. He hoped that England would not follow the path of France,
Austria, and Prussia.[31]

Lord John Russell answered the reformers in a conciliatory fashion. He
seemed impressed with the support Hume and Cobden had garnered for
the "Little Charter" outside of Parliament. Yet Russell gave no sign,
beyond some vague assurances about the future, that his government had
any intention of supporting political reform. The prime minister acknowledged that the electoral system had imperfections, but he did not think
either the Chartists or the Humeites offered solutions acceptable to the
majority.[32]

The most telling objections to Hume's scheme came from Henry
Drummond (a conservative banker who represented West Surrey) and
Benjamin Disraeli. Drummond said that Hume's phrase "the people" was
nothing more than an abstraction. What "people" did he mean when he
said "the people" were improperly represented? Did he mean workers,
shopkeepers, the unemployed? Disraeli attacked Hume in the traditional
manner; he pretended not to take the Scotsman seriously. Hume, said
Disraeli, must always be in search of "some great question even before
another has been put to port." He thought Hume had no interest in
laborers, but was concerned with becoming a middle class hero. Disraeli
also blamed the Anti-Corn Law League for being the source of the reform

---

[29] *The Post*, 20 June 1848.
[30] Debates now ran very long in the House of Commons. Both ministerialists and opposition
members (including Hume) complained that the debates were going on so long the work of the
House could not be completed.
[31] *Hansard*, third series, 99:879–906; Molesworth, *History of England*, 2:301.
[32] Maccoby, *English Radicalism, 1832–1852*, 289.

agitation in the spring of 1848. The old leaders—Cobden, Bright, George Wilson—seemed to have nothing better to do after the repeal of the Corn Laws.[33] There was just enough truth in Disraeli's comments to make Hume a bit uncomfortable.

The introduction of the "Little Charter" produced extensive commentary in the national press. Such conservative publications as *John Bull* and the *Morning Post* maintained a steady barrage against Hume's plan. "There is only a slight difference," opined *John Bull,* "between Mr. Hume and the enthusiastic gentleman, who, in Paris, at the latter end of February, shot the officer in command of the street door of the Foreign Minister." The paper concluded that "England will have nothing to do with [such] anarchists."[34] The *Post* argued that it was useless for Mr. Hume and his reforming friends to be "groping among the old rubbish of extended suffrage, and fantastical methods of election of members of Parliament. . . ." Englishmen could not live with government by "ordinary" persons. "We want relief, not certainly from aristocratic influence," wrote the *Post,* "but from the pressure of a multitude of small interests and small minds."[35]

The moderately conservative *Times* contended that Hume's "Little Charter" had nothing to recommend it over O'Connor's "Great" Charter. *The Times* described Hume's long address on the subject of reform as political "suicide." There was nothing significantly different in his proposals from what was in the "People's Charter, " except that Hume offered four points where the "People's Charter" had six. It appeared to *The Times* that "Mr. O'Connor's mountain gave birth to a mouse."[36]

The liberal reform papers generally applauded Hume's effort, but noted that he had little chance for success. There was some grumbling that he had asked for too much. The *Morning Chronicle* told its readers that Hume had performed superbly in explaining the situation in the House of Commons; yet, the *Chronicle* thought he should have offered only those reforms with which the "moderate reformers" could agree. Furthermore, the *Chronicle* believed that the Humeites erred in thinking of Russell as "Finality Jack."[37] In the north, Edward Baines's *Leeds Mercury* said that Hume's motion deserved respect, but thought it was "too close" to universal suffrage. The *Mercury* feared that the Scotsman's plan would "swamp" the national constituency with laborers who had never before voted.[38]

In the major radical newspapers, Hume's bill found mixed reception.[39] The *Sun* and the *Morning Advertiser* (London) supported his entire program. Both agreed that there was no "Reformed Parliament" under present circumstances.[40] The *Examiner* gave strong backing to parliamen-

[33]Grey Journal, 24 June 1848, Durham Record Office (U. of Durham), C 3/14; *Hansard,* third series, 99:944ff.
[34]*John Bull,* 24 June 1848.
[35]*The Morning Post,* 21 June 1848.
[36]*The Times,* 22 June 1848.
[37]*Morning Chronicle,* 21 June 1848.
[38]*Leeds Mercury,* 24 June 1848.
[39]*Morning Advertiser,* 21 June 1848.
[40]*The Sun,* 21 and 22 June 1848.

tary reform, but considered Hume's "Little Charter" ill-conceived. "If Mr. Hume had intended to frame a motion so as to unite the smallest number of reformers," wrote the *Examiner,* "he could not have proceeded more ingeniously than by connecting the proposals as to which there is the most agreement with those as to which there is the greatest difference of opinion."[41] The paper observed that reformers who supported the ballot did not all agree on triennial parliaments. Many who endorsed the ballot and triennial parliaments could not bring themselves to support household suffrage. The *Examiner* thought that Hume should have introduced the ballot alone. Hume understood the complaint that he tried to do too much, but the only alternative was to offer one reform at a time. He believed this to be unacceptable.

While discussion of the "Little Charter" continued unabated in the newspapers, the debate in the House of Commons was postponed until 6 July. The delay was necessary because it had become customary in the 1840s for decisions on the bulk of public business to be put off until late in the session. Hume objected to this tendency (though he often contributed to it), but he agreed with Russell that some matters of immediate concern should take precedence over the reform bill debate.[42] When consideration of the reform measure resumed the basic question on the minds of the reformers was what would be the size of the minority that supported the legislation. To the surprise of many, O'Connor announced, in the midst of an attack on Russell, that he would vote for Hume's plan even though he found it insufficient. The vote on the "Little Charter" came near midnight and it lost by a count of 351 to 84.[43]

There was much cheering by the proponents of the bill since the size of the minority had exceeded expectations.[44] Radical newspapers called the vote a moral victory for parliamentary reform; it showed that the "Little Charter" could not be "dropped into the bottomless pit of oblivion." There may well have been, at the time, some merit in this analysis, but the prevailing middle class mood in July 1848 was perhaps better explained by another journal. "Did it ever occur to Hume and Cobden," opined the liberal *Morning Chronicle,*

that political agitation is in itself a great evil? that it interrupts business and wastes time and property, unsettles the minds of the people, and leads to such meetings as those in which the Cuffays and Fussells indulge their diseased craving for notoriety.[45]

The size of Hume's minority momentarily invigorated the "New Reformers," and caused some distress among the majority. On reflection, however, both sides must have realized that the minority of eighty-four did not really represent a significant number in favor of electoral reform. Certainly there was no reason for Russell to concede anything at this stage.

[41] *The Examiner,* 24 June 1848.
[42] *The Times,* 30 June 1848; *Leeds Mercury,* 1 July 1848.
[43] *Hansard,* third series, 100:225-27.
[44] Hobhouse Diary, 6 July 1848, BL, Add. MS. 43752; *Morning Chronicle,* 8 July 1848.
[45] *Morning Chronicle,* 8 July 1848.

Whether the number of members who supported his "Little Charter" was significant or not, Hume had determined to make approval of his reform scheme his primary goal for the remainder of his career. In this he deviated somewhat from the course followed by Cobden. The latter continued to place a higher premium on economy, although both men believed that retrenchment and parliamentary reform were closely connected.[46]

Early in 1849 Cobden tried to persuade Hume to focus his parliamentary action on the question of government waste. He gave some specific suggestions in this regard:

I hope you will make a direct appeal to the county members to cooperate with you and the free traders in securing a reduction of taxation, by the only practicable way—viz, a diminution of expenditures—it rests with them to achieve cheap government, and it is by their votes that the government can alone maintain its extravagance—I hope you will make a strong appeal to the "farmer's friends."[47]

Cobden was certain that the county members would see that lowering taxes was the only way to improve the economy. Hume cooperated with Cobden's wishes as much as possible. He called for lower taxes, improved tax collection, reduced spending by the Admiralty and the Army, and for an end to the practice of government agencies spending more money than was appropriated by the legislature.[48] But more and more Hume came to realize that economy did not have much appeal as an issue in 1849.[49] There were few radicals willing to vote against the Whigs on budget matters.

Radical opinion was also divided on the Irish question early in 1849. Hume and the free-trade radicals joined the government members in supporting the suspension of habeas corpus in Ireland.[50] John O'Connell, the third son of Daniel O'Connell, accused Hume and other free-traders of forgetting their oft-stated principles of liberty. O'Connell referred to Hume in debate as the "former friend" of Ireland. It was difficult for Hume to endorse any restrictive bill, but he had supported such measures for Ireland since 1846. He reasoned that remedial efforts could only be successful in an atmosphere of "peace and quiet." Hume told the Commons that he had always defended Ireland and that he now hoped the government would initiate the necessary reforms to prevent further suspension of the constitution.[51] The Irish radicals in the lower house never understood, or forgave, what they saw as Hume's desertion of their cause. They did not find the Scotsman's explanation at all satisfactory.

Disagreement over issues and strategy left the radical reformers without momentum in the spring of 1849. Hume's mind wandered back to the excitement and optimism that had characterized the radical camp in April of 1848. He thought it still might be possible to rekindle that spirit by reintroducing his "Little Charter." He told friends that he would present

[46]See Sturgis, "British Parliamentary Radicalism, 1846–1852," 132–33, 146–47.

[47]Cobden to Hume, 27 January 1849, BL, Add. MS. 43668.

[48]The Morning Advertiser, 17, 31 March 1849; The Sun, 26 January 1849.

[49]Sturgis, "British Parliamentary Radicalism, 1846–1852," 158–62.

[50]The Morning Advertiser, 31 March 1849.

[51]See Hansard, third series, 102:532ff; The Sun, 10 February 1849; The Examiner, 24 February 1849; The Morning Advertiser, 20 February 1849.

his reform package sometime in the middle of May. These plans were interrupted by a sudden attack of influenza and rumors spread that "Old Joe" might not survive.[52] Hume did need to stay at home for over two weeks, but he returned to the Commons in good health during the first days of June.

On 5 June, Hume brought forward his motion for reform of Parliament. It did not differ in any significant way from his 1848 proposal. In making his presentation Hume asserted that it was unsafe to withhold power from the people. He knew that agreement on parliamentary reform, even among friends, posed a difficult problem.[53] It was nevertheless one that had to be addressed. Russell answered Hume's speech in a conciliatory tone. He paid tribute to Hume's moderation, fairness, and lack of bitterness. The prime minister thought that England had the government best suited to its people. He saw monarchy, aristocracy, and democracy acting together to produce liberty and happiness.[54]

No one, least of all Hume, expected the "Little Charter" to win approval in the Commons. The Scotsman's purpose in moving for reform was to keep the "Little Charter" alive, to provide a rallying point for the free-trade radicals, and to apply some pressure on Russell to recommend a reform bill of his own.[55] Hume's proposal went down to defeat by 268 to 82. Although the minority vote was only two fewer than in 1848, the reformers were angered and dispirited by the results. The vote itself did not weigh as heavily as did the reluctance of the Whig leadership to offer any hope for the future. The *Sun* pointed out that the reformers were strong outside of Parliament, but were "weak" inside. Whether the reformers were actually impressive outside of Parliament is a relative judgment; they were not threatening enough to worry Russell.[56]

For one of the rare times in his career, Hume seemed resentful over the setback for his reform scheme. He had never expected it to carry the House, yet it is easy to see why frustration took hold of him. He had come to think of his leadership in the new parliamentary reform movement as a capstone to his political career. He had believed that some reform—at least the ballot—would result from his efforts. It angered Hume when Russell spoke with such smug self-assurance, and without the slightest acknowledgment that any immediate need for reform existed. Hume was also disappointed that the radicals had not shown a greater sense of purpose and unity during the debate. His effort had revealed the weakness, and not the strength, of the radical reformers in the House of Commons. The "New Reform Movement" had collapsed.

The strain Hume felt came to the surface in July. He joined with Feargus O'Connor in condemning the Whig ministry. Furthermore, he was one of just thirteen members to vote for the "People's Charter" when

[52]*The Times,* 26 May 1849.

[53]*Hansard,* third series, 105:1156–71.

[54]Ibid., 1211–24; *The Sun,* 6 June 1849.

[55]Molesworth, *History of England,* 2:322.

[56]*The Sun,* 6 June 1849; *The Morning Post,* 7 June 1849; Sturgis, "British Parliamentary Radicalism, 1846–1852," 162–63.

O'Connor introduced it again on 3 July. In announcing his support for the Charter, Hume said he recalled a popular toast of the 1820s: "The People, the source of all legitimate power." He opposed the continuation of taxation and policies in which the people had no representation.[57] Hume's spiteful alliance with O'Connor did not impress other reformers in the Commons. Ralph Bernal Osborne (Whig M.P. for Middlesex) severely criticized Hume for his actions. This led Hume to announce that he would no longer support the ministry on any issue if every reform motion was going to be rejected.[58] But even if Hume meant what he said on this occasion, the radicals as a group had no wish to abandon the Russell government. They could not escape from the opinion that Whigs, inadequate though they may be, were still better than Tories.

The radicals faced a familiar problem in 1849; they could not agree on leadership or policy. The "New Reform Movement" of 1848 had not lasted very long. All attempts to bring about a concerted effort by the parliamentary radicals broke down in failure in 1849.[59] There was agreement among the free-trade radicals that retrenchment and parliamentary reform were closely connected, but their two most prominent leaders, Hume and Cobden, were at odds over which ought to have priority. This difference of opinion, kept under the surface in 1848 and 1849, became more of a problem in the early 1850s. The radicals were also hurt by the suspicions they had aroused among the Irish reformers. These Irishmen thought themselves betrayed by other ultra-radicals, like Hume, who voted in favor of suspending habeas corpus in Ireland.

From Hume's perspective, the reform movement had reached its lowest point in two years in the summer of 1849. He did not hold out hope that a resurgence of public opinion in support of reform might induce a more favorable reception in Westminster. There was little evidence of sustained public interest in the autumn months, but the National Reform Association planned to organize rallies in support of parliamentary reform early in 1850. The NRA came into existence in December 1849. It was an expansion of a local reform society founded by Sir Joshua Walmsley (radical M.P. for Bolton). Hume saw considerable promise in the NRA and became a member of its governing council.[60] He promised Walmsley and other supporters that he would bring in his reform proposal much earlier in the next session than he had in 1848 and 1849. Reform meetings were then planned for London and Manchester; Walmsley took charge of organizing the gatherings. The purpose was to show that the working class and the middle class could agree on the need for electoral reform. This was a strategy Hume had urged since the early 1840s. But the rallies had little success; whatever enthusiasm they generated fizzled before the end of February. O'Connor had predicted the failure of the meetings because employers were only concerned with lowering taxes and the workers were too well fed.

[57] *Hansard,* third series, 106:268–74.
[58] Sturgis, "British Parliamentary Radicalism, 1846–1852," 166.
[59] Gash, *Reaction and Reconstruction,* 195.
[60] See *The Sun,* 9 January 1850.

O'Connor's attitude did not enhance his popularity with Hume, Cobden, or Walmsley. Cobden wanted O'Connor excluded from all Association activities, but Walmsley feared that the time was not right to alienate O'Connor. He wanted to retain whatever chance remained for an impressive showing on the "Little Charter." In any event the position of the reformers was anything but encouraging.

As he had promised, Hume brought his reform bill before the House of Commons in February. *The Times* reported that this "annual debate" was a "great waste of time." His only purpose seemed to be to "provoke the less fortunate classes into a still fiercer warfare than that they now wage against wealth and order."[61] Hume could only wish that *The Times*'s warning had merit! He admitted that a great majority of the members were not interested in his plan, but he thought the question of parliamentary reform more important than ever before. He reminded his colleagues that his reforms represented a compromise with Chartism and with his own beliefs. He related how he had once agreed with Major Cartwright that annual parliaments were essential; now he would be content with a triennial arrangement. The only issue on which there could be no compromise was the ballot.

With O'Connor derisively cheering him on, Hume told the House that he wanted to make the constitution more popular. In the 1790s advocates of popular rights were commonly admonished: "If you don't like the country, leave it." He hoped the mood in 1850 would be more enlightened. At one point in his speech, Hume pointed out that in 1831 Lord John Russell had made similar warnings. It was Hume's opinion that when Whigs gained power they operated by Tory principles.[62]

Hume, much to the annoyance of his adversaries, often cited positions and votes of his colleagues from as far back as thirty years in some instances. The parliamentary library at his Bryanston Square residence was reputed to be a "perfect phenomenon" in extent. Every blue book, every stray leaf of every vote paper, and every scrap of a return was meticulously cataloged so that Hume could put his finger on it at once. Some of his contemporaries thought his excessive interest in arithmetic helped to make him a compulsive cataloger of information. Such collections were obviously a reservoir of security for Hume; they seemed to give him an advantage over other members. Hume compensated for what he lacked in imagination and spontaneity by being better prepared; at least that was his aim.

As the debate on Hume's Charter progressed, Sir George Grey (a moderate liberal from Northumberland) goaded Hume into admitting that he favored women's suffrage and an elected House of Lords! The Scotsman never would have proposed these reforms, but Grey's purpose was to make him appear as extreme as possible. Roebuck, who always managed to nettle Hume, said that he did not see his friend's connection between taxation and

---

[61]1 March 1850.
[62]*Speech of Joseph Hume on parliamentary reform* (London, 1850); *Hansard,* third series, 109:137ff.

representation. He referred to Hume's assertion that when the people were better represented they could expect taxes to be reduced. For his part, Roebuck supported the measure solely for the purpose of staving off discontent.[63]

Russell responded to Hume's presentation with considerably less reserve than he had shown nine months earlier. He angrily denied that Whigs acted like Tories when they took power. The prime minister intimated that Hume's main reason for renewing the debate on reform was to create tension in the country. Russell did concede that he thought a need for reform existed, but a more "considerate" one than that proposed by Hume. Although Hume frequently was said to be without rancour no matter what transpired in the House of Commons, he did not soon forget the prime minister's dismissal of his efforts on this occasion. Two years later he still complained of Russell's "sarcastic" remarks about him.

The vote against the "Little Charter" in February 1850 was 242 to 96. The minority total had increased by 12 over 1849; yet, there were few radicals who saw much hope in this. Even the optimistic *Daily News* admitted that progress did not seem "very marked or rapid."[64] In April, the reformers made another attempt to reestablish the momentum of 1848. Cobden, Bright, Walmsley, Hume, et al. attended "friends of reform" conferences, but no advance was made toward radical unity. O'Connor was not permitted to address the meetings and Hume once again began to refer to him as an enemy of reform.[65]

With the "Little Charter" a dead issue, and with the radicals in their usual disarray, Hume spent the remainder of the 1850 session debating matters much less exciting to him. His principal efforts were directed toward retrenchment, putting an end to pluralities, urging unlimited emigration of West African slaves to the West Indies, allowing Jews to sit in the House of Commons, and promoting the cause of national education.[66]

In early July the routine of parliamentary business was broken for Hume, and for all of his colleagues, by the unexpected death of Sir Robert Peel. The former prime minister fell from his horse on 29 June; three days later he died. On 3 July, in the absence of Lord John Russell, Hume moved the adjournment of the House. It remained in recess until the following night. Hume could hardly believe that his old friend was gone. More than any other government minister in the first half of the nineteenth century, Peel had held Hume's respect. In an attempt to show working class appreciation for Peel, Hume took charge of a committee for a Poor Man's Monument to the former prime minister, the contributions to which were limited to a penny.[67] The money was to be collected in a one day national

[63]Sturgis, "British Parliamentary Radicalism, 1846–1852," 227.

[64]*Hansard,* third series, 109:218; Sturgis, "British Parliamentary Radicalism, 1846–1852," 227.

[65]Sturgis, "British Parliamentary Radicalism, 1846–1852," 227–28.

[66]*The Times,* 3 August 1850; *Hansard,* third series, 110:1081–82; Hume to Burton, 9 February 1850, NLS, MS. 9394.

[67]Gash, *Sir Robert Peel,* 701–4; *The Times* 6 July 1850.

subscription, but the collection met with considerable opposition. The effort had to be extended over several weeks. Workingmen who had supported the People's Charter were not willing to contribute their pennies to what appeared to be a middle class memorial. The resistance to the Poor Man's Monument showed anew that a coalition of free-trade reformers and Chartists was an unlikely prospect.

There was some sentiment, particularly in conservative circles, that Peel's death would force Russell to accommodate some of the radical demands. This idea held that the conservatives, without Peel's moderation in the House of Commons, would now come together in a united opposition to Russell. The prime minister would then need to court favor from the radicals to sustain his ministry. While there is some evidence that Russell accepted this assessment of the political situation in the autumn of 1850, his government did not respond according to prediction. There was adamant opposition to any parliamentary reform in the Whig cabinet.[68]

For their part, the reformers were in no position to apply much pressure in the autumn and winter of 1850–51. Beset by fragmentation of purpose, organization, and strategy, there seemed little chance of providing comprehensive, effective leadership. The radicals were not helped by the apathy prevalent in most industrial towns in the early 1850s. Only the National Reform Association offered any possibility of marshalling public opinion in support of political reform. The Association planned a major rally in London, but some prominent members, John Bright among them, refused to attend. Bright also resigned from the Association's council in protest over the continuing effort to accommodate the Chartists. The presence of O'Connor at Association meetings proved to be more than some free-traders could tolerate. Bright, Cobden, and Hume as well, thought Walmsley had gone beyond the bounds of good sense in catering to O'Connor's wishes. They knew that O'Connor used their platform as an opportunity to keep his own movement alive. If all of this were not devastating enough to the radical cause, the anti-Roman Catholic mania of the early 1850s further siphoned interest away from political reform.[69]

Hume deplored the time lost on discussion of such a "minor matter" as papal influence in England. The ministry, he said, should put an end to the Catholic nonsense and focus on the important question of parliamentary reform.[70] But Russell's government had no inclination to heed the Scotsman's advice. In February Hume asked the prime minister whether he intended to bring in a reform bill "this year." Russell replied that he would consider presenting a reform plan at a "fit time."[71] The prime minister's response disappointed Hume, but he decided there was no point in pursuing the matter. Moreover, unlike the three previous years, he did not intend to introduce his "Little Charter." Discouraged by the slow progress

[68]Sturgis, "British Parliamentary Radicalism, 1846–1852," 262.

[69]Ibid., 262–64.

[70]*Hansard*, third series, 114:1051–53.

[71]*The Greville Diary Including Passages Hitherto Withheld From Publication*, edited by Philip Whitwell Wilson (New York, 1927), 2:268–69.

of the reform effort, Hume showed almost no interest in the session until after April.

The strength of the Whig government varied in the early weeks of 1851, and many radicals thought it might collapse. There were several close divisions, particularly on tax matters when radicals and protectionists were often in agreement. But the Russell government continued to hold on and even claimed to be increasing its strength. After the Easter recess, the opposition ("if only for the fun of it," wrote Disraeli) planned to harass the ministers as much as possible.[72] Hume had regained his fighting spirit by this time and he was ready to make a major contribution to the badgering of Russell.

It was not electoral reform that brought "Old Joe" back into action in April; it was the proposed extension of the income tax that captured his attention. Hume had advocated for a long time direct taxes over indirect taxes, yet he also believed that the income tax left something to be desired. He had supported it during the Peel administration, but he now argued the time had come to investigate the entire system by which the government collected revenue. He hoped to prove that the income tax, in its present form, was not fair to earned income. On 2 May, Hume moved to limit the extension of the income tax to one year and to create a select committee to study the whole tax situation in England.[73] Hume's motion, disparaged by Cobden (he did not agree with Hume that earned income should be eliminated from taxation), won immediate support from protectionists. The coalition of free-traders and protectionists enabled the opposition to carry Hume's resolution by 244 to 230. When someone asked Hume whether voting on the same side as the protectionists did not cause him alarm, he replied that he would take supporters wherever he could get them. He knew that many members would endorse his motion who were not political economists.

The victory over the government provided satisfaction but not much else. Hume's aim to improve the income tax was not realized. The protectionists who supported his motion cared neither a fig nor a feather about earned income. Moreover, the Select Committee on Income and Property Tax made no headway in the summer of 1851. With Hume as the chairman, the committee included such active free-traders as Thomas Baring, Cobden, James Wilson, and J. A. Roebuck. The group met nine times and interviewed seventeen witnesses before Hume recommended it cease its labors on 21 July. By this time it had become evident that the committee could come to no useful conclusions on what to do with the tax. Everyone acknowledged that it was needed and that it ought to be made more equitable. There was, however, no consensus on the adjustment to be made. In the end, the House had such slight interest in the work of the committee that Hume's motion to print the evidence collected failed on a vote of 62 to

---

[72]See William F. Monypenny and George E. Buckle, *The Life of Benjamin Disraeli* (New York, 1914), 3:300–03.

[73]*Hansard*, third series, 116:432–42, 495–96, 726–28.

50.[74] The success in May had not provided the impetus for reform that Hume had anticipated. Russell's government staggered on without much vision on any issue.

The income tax question was not the only reform at a standstill; nothing had happened to improve the prospects for parliamentary reform. Russell's "fit time" for introducing political reform was yet to arrive, and Hume seemed convinced that opposition to his "Little Charter" had intensified over the summer. Nevertheless, he helped to organize a September meeting of the National Reform Association in Manchester. In a show of unity the local Chartists were asked to join ranks with the free-trade radicals. George Wilson, a former leader of the Anti-Corn Law League, chaired the rally, but Bright and Cobden did not appear. Hume was furious. Their absence, he wrote, would have "the worst effect against the movement." Bright's failure to attend resulted from his long-standing disagreement with Walmsley over administration of the Association. Cobden, on the other hand, was simply tired of the struggle; he wanted to retreat for a time.[75]

Hume did not understand Cobden's reluctance to push parliamentary reform. On 4 October, he wrote to his old friend, "There is great objection to my reform movement at this time amongst the whig leaders and I have heard you and Bright named as objecting to the question being brought forward at this time."[76] He told Cobden that he would make his opinions known on reform no matter what other free-traders thought. A week later Hume appeared before a rally in Edinburgh called by the local Chamber of Commerce. Hume had asked the Chamber to arrange the meeting so that he could gauge the reaction of Edinburgh citizens to his reform plans. He explained to those gathered that tax reform and political reform were essential to the future security of the country. The crowd responded with lusty cheers and a "Vote of Thanks" for his concern for the people.[77]

At the very time Hume was in Edinburgh, Lord John Russell was, at last, working to prepare a reform bill. He planned to introduce the legislation when Parliament met again in February. In the first week of October Lord John established a committee to help him write a reform bill. Despite considerable opposition in his cabinet, the prime minister encouraged the committee to extend voting privileges to a sizeable segment of the working class. He made no mention of the ballot, but did insist on a redistribution of seats. By the time the committee finished its work in mid-December, the Russell reform bill contained neither an industrial franchise nor the ballot. Furthermore, the fear of complaints from certain members of the cabinet prevented the committee from effectively overhauling the voting districts.[78]

As word of Russell's reform measure spread, Hume, Walmsley, and other members of the Reform Association's council debated what approach

---

[74]See "Select Committee on Income and Property Tax," *British Sessional Papers,* 10:339–46; *Hansard,* third series, 118:1951–63.

[75]Sturgis, "British Parliamentary Radicalism, 1846–1852," 309–10.

[76]Hume to Cobden, 4 October 1851, BL, Add. MS. 43668.

[77]*The Times,* 15 October 1851.

[78]John Prest, *Lord John Russell* (Columbia, S.C., 1972), 331–36.

the free-traders should take toward the proposal. December meetings were held in Glasgow, Edinburgh, Manchester, and other cities to discuss the situation. While the radicals mulled over their plans, they learned that Palmerston (foreign secretary) had been dismissed from the government. This development had nothing to do with the reform issue, but as Palmerston had never favored parliamentary reform, his dismissal caused considerable glee in the radical camp. Hume's reaction was more subdued. He thought Palmerston an effective, but misplaced, cabinet officer.[79] Misplaced or not, Palmerston's absence meant the imminent collapse of the ministry. For more than a year the foreign secretary had been the strongest, most popular, member of Russell's cabinet.

The prime minister was determined to go on as long as possible; he did not want to resign before bringing in his reform legislation. On 9 February Russell introduced the measure in the House of Commons, knowing full well that it had no chance for success. There was stiff opposition to any reform in the Commons, and there was little enthusiasm for the bill in the countryside. After Russell presented his proposal Hume provided a lengthy commentary on the subject. He was impressed by the contents of the legislation, but he did not think the measure went far enough. He thought the people had a "right" to vote; it was not a privilege as Russell had suggested in his address. The Scotsman saw in Russell's plan nothing more than an attempt to "patch up" the 1832 bill. Hume considered the ballot to be essential as well as some reduction in the length of parliaments. Both of these issues were avoided by the prime minister. Hume admitted that there was not much public pressure for these reforms, but he hoped the government would not wait until there was.[80]

Russell's reform bill was still under consideration when, on 21 February, the Whig cabinet had no alternative to resignation. The government struggled on virtually every vote and finally Russell gave up the fight.[81] The Whigs were replaced with a minority administration led by Lord Derby, which included Benjamin Disraeli as Chancellor of the Exchequer. Having returned to opposition, Lord John withdrew his reform measure on 12 March. Hume expressed dismay at this action. It was not a good bill, he said, but it might have been improved in committee.[82] He had wished for a vote on a plan of political reform introduced by someone other than himself. Hume and Walmsley had tried very hard to keep the reform bill alive despite the change in government. Their failure to accomplish this left Hume "rather sulky," according to Cobden. It also did nothing to enhance Hume's opinion of Russell. He told Russell pointedly "we must not have the old party back again after we have turned out the Tories."[83]

When Derby took command in February, his ministry was not expected to last beyond three weeks. But the inability of the Whigs to reunite under

[79]Sturgis, "British Parliamentary Radicalism, 1846–1852," 310–16; Prest, *Lord John Russell*, 337.

[80]*Hansard*, third series, 119:268–70.

[81]Prest, *Lord John Russell*, 340–41.

[82]*Hansard*, third series, 119:971.

[83]Quoted in Sturgis, "British Parliamentary Radicalism, 1846–1852," 325.

Russell's leadership allowed Derby and Disraeli to remain in power until the summer. At that point Derby called for a dissolution. The ensuing election increased the number of conservatives in the Commons, but did not provide Derby with a working majority.

At the time the election was held, Hume's attitude toward the Tory government was quite ambivalent. He did not approve of its opposition to parliamentary reform, yet he did find promise in Disraeli's support for free trade. He would have been doubly pleased had he known that Derby now agreed with Disraeli on this issue. What Hume did not want was to replace Derby and Disraeli with another administration that offered no hope on either reform front.

Hume had the opportunity to stand for London in the July election, but he refused, choosing instead to continue to sit for the Montrose district. "A strong effort was made to get me to be a candidate for London," he wrote to his Scottish friend Mackenzie, "and free of expense and without trouble I believe I should have been elected. But the turning out of Rothschild[84] or Lord John would have done much ill to the liberal cause. . . ." It was in this letter to Mackenzie that Hume made clear his one remaining wish as a parliamentarian: "I hope yet to see my little charter of reform carried and then I am confident the abuses now so rank will speedily be removed."[85] Hume spent several weeks in Scotland during the summer in order to, as he said, "give a lift" to the reformers there.[86]

When Hume returned to Bryanston Square in September, he devoted most of his time to developing a strategy on political reform. He was no longer of the opinion that a Whig government was more likely to preside over parliamentary reform than a Tory one. He seemed willing to give the Tories a chance; this attitude stemmed in part from his highly favorable view of Disraeli. The chancellor's attention to budget cutbacks pleased Hume, especially as Disraeli frequently noted that the country was indebted to the Scotsman's good advice on retrenchment. Some of Hume's friends, particularly Bright and Cobden, thought he had acquired quite a "Whigphobia" perhaps brought on by Disraeli's flattery as much as by Whig mistakes.[87]

While it is true that "Old Joe" saw nothing very promising or new in Whig ideas, and that he harbored resentment for Russell, he did not delude himself into thinking the Tories were anxious for parliamentary reform. He wanted guarantees from whatever men were in power, or aspired to be in power, that they would earnestly pursue changes in electoral procedures. He thought reformers should remain aloof from all parties; they would thereby prove their sincerity and gain support from the people. All of these opinions Hume expressed in two letters to Cobden in early October. On

---

[84]Baron Lionel Nathan de Rothschild was first elected for London in 1847, but did not take his seat until 1858. A Jew, Rothschild waited until he was permitted to omit objectionable words in the oath before taking his seat.

[85]Hume to Mackenzie, 12 July 1852, Peter Mackenzie Papers, Kirkintilloch Town Council Library (Glasgow).

[86]Hume to Burton, 19 June 1852, Burton Papers, NLS, MS. 9404.

[87]See Sturgis, "British Parliamentary Radicalism, 1846–1852," 331.

8 October he wrote,

I have stated to Mr. [Edward] Ellice, who is you know the devoted partisan of the whigs ... that I will not agree to support Lord John or any other party in opposition until I am satisfied as to the course of the policy on which Lord John or any other party shall be prepared and pledged to act if they should come to power.

Hume did not hesitate to confirm his distaste for Russell. "Does he think," said Hume, "that his sarcastic remarks and imputation of motives to me when I brought forward my motion for the scheme of Parliamentary Reform two years ago ... are forgotten by us"?

Hume was most agitated by the fact that Russell in 1852 had proposed an extension of the franchise similar to what he [Hume] had offered in 1850. Russell's provisions for reform were virtually the same ones that he had once said would sweep away all existing institutions when Hume brought them before the House. It was the Scotsman's belief that reform would have been a reality if Russell had supported it in 1848, 1849, or 1850. That is why, he explained to Cobden, he would back no party that refused to "guaranty *acts* if they came to power."[88] On the following day, 9 October, Hume again wrote to Cobden about reform strategy. He emphasized his opinion that reformers needed to stand apart from all parties, even from the Irish members. He thought radicals should work through the National Reform Association to generate popular support for the ballot and other parts of the "Little Charter."[89]

There had been some disagreement between Hume and Cobden over the merits of the Reform Association. Cobden never fully approved of the emphasis Walmsley and Hume placed on the Association; nor had he been enthusiastic for all the points in Hume's "Little Charter." He endorsed the ballot, but thought Hume overly generous in his plans to expand voting privileges. Cobden had been far from conscientious in attending Reform Association meetings and he had quit going altogether in 1851. In the autumn of 1852 Hume tried to induce him to resume his participation in Association activities. Cobden indicated that he would return to the Association—as an advocate of the ballot alone.[90] Hume urged him to reconsider his position. He wanted Cobden to understand that the Reform Association had "resolved and re-resolved" for four years that the object of reform legislation was to give power to the "Democracy" (by which Hume meant the people) in the House of Commons. "Do you not know," wrote Hume, "that extension of the suffrage and protection of the voter are the two demands ... that the mass of the people—the mass of the skilled artisans are determined to have." Hume acknowledged that with "bellies full and comparative comfort there is a quiet and apathy in the grand mass of the working class," but he expected this to change because the workers were "daily acquiring additional knowledge about rights and the best mode of obtaining them."

The working class would soon realize that "good government" required

[88]BL, Add. MS. 43668.
[89]Ibid.
[90]Hume to Cobden, 28 September 1852, BL, Add. MS. 43668.

the ballot and the extension of the franchise. Hume told Cobden not to believe Tory and Whig leaders who said it was possible to carry the ballot without extension. He must be wary of the "weak" reformers who want to split up the "Little Charter" into separate points. They were only interested in deceiving the people in order to get elected. Hume thought Cobden was too readily persuaded to take a moderate course; as an example, he cited Cobden's opposition to his motion for limiting the income tax to one year. Russell had influenced Cobden to oppose Hume's effort even though the vast majority of free-traders had given their support.

Hume concluded his appeal to Cobden by admitting that the Reform Association had not achieved what he had hoped it would: i.e., a united radical reform movement. It had, however, "kept the question before the people." If Cobden and others could now see the necessity to coalesce behind the Association's goals (Little Charter) the opportunity for success still existed. It was Hume's opinion that the establishment of a democracy required the sacrifice of individual preferences for the greater good.[91]

Hume's attempt to marshal the radical forces under the banner of the Reform Association came just before the new parliament began its deliberations in November. From the time of the summer elections there had been much speculation on the future of the Derby-Disraeli administration. Russell had worked during September and October on creating an alliance with Lord Aberdeen, the leader of the Peelite faction in the House of Commons. But Aberdeen and the Peelites decided to wait until the strength and policies of the Derby government were clear. This was the customary "on the fence" position for the Peelites.

During the early weeks of what was to be a very short session, Hume showed his usual enthusiasm. He demanded to know when the government would propose representational reform; and he, to the amusement of everyone, gave strong support to an unsuccessful motion to place a time limit on members' speeches. The pace of "Old Joe's" activities in the Commons belied his disappointment over recent developments in the reform movement. Cobden had not come around to seeing things Hume's way, and the Scotsman now responded by refusing to attend free-trade meetings organized by Cobden.[92]

The radicals were not the only ones with difficulties at the end of 1852. The Derby government was about to collapse. Gladstone and Palmerston had successfully attacked the administration on budget matters; the opposition was poised to deliver the final blow in the middle of December. On 17 December, the government could no longer sustain a majority and the queen sent for Lord Aberdeen. After several days of delicate negotiations Aberdeen formed a coalition ministry with Lord John Russell agreeing to serve as foreign secretary and leader of the House of Commons.[93] The

---

[91]See Hume's long letter to Cobden, 27 October 1852, BL, Add. MS. 43668.

[92]Sturgis, "British Parliamentary Radicalism, 1846–1852," 332.

[93]In February 1853 Russell gave up his post at the Foreign Office, but remained in the cabinet as a minister without office. There had been strained relations between Russell and Aberdeen from the start. Aberdeen assumed he was head of a Peelite ministry, while Russell assumed that he and Aberdeen were co-leaders of a coalition government. Eventually the latter view prevailed.

cabinet also included Palmerston (home secretary), Gladstone (Chancellor of the Exchequer), and Sir James Graham (first lord of the Admiralty). Sir William Molesworth (first commissioner of Works) was the only radical in the ministry.[94]

Hume did not see much to recommend this new government. He doubted the depth of commitment to parliamentary reform by any administration that included Aberdeen, Palmerston, and Russell. Early in the 1853 session Lord John did insist that the government bring in a reform bill; he threatened to leave the cabinet if his demand were ignored by Aberdeen. But there was much opposition to this reform plan, particularly from Palmerston. Russell ultimately agreed to postpone the effort. He did receive assurances from Aberdeen that a reform bill would be introduced in 1854. Accustomed to such delays by now, and without much use for Russell's scheme anyway, Hume did little more than pout to some friends about the insincerity of Whigs, Tories, and Peelites. He did hope that the ministry would follow through on its pledge to introduce the reform question in the next session.

Hume was not quite so active in 1853 as he had been in previous sessions of Parliament. From what can be gathered, this does not appear to be a consequence of diminished vitality so much as a reflection of his unhappiness with the progress of reform. He did become involved in the continuing debate on the income tax, and he also spoke his mind in favor of a national police force. He thought such a system would reduce the power of the magistrates who too often conducted their offices in an arbitrary manner.[95]

Although he was convinced that coalition government would follow through on its pledge to bring in a parliamentary reform bill in 1854, Hume did not view events in 1853 as conducive to the passing of reform legislation. During the second half of 1853 a great deal of attention was directed toward the Middle East. The long-standing rift between Russia and Turkey had taken on more serious implications with the failure of a Russian peace mission in May. When negotiations between the Porte and St. Petersburg broke down, Tsar Nicholas I ordered Russian troops to move into the Turkish provinces at the mouth of the Danube. This action made the emperor an ogre in the eyes of most Englishmen; it also made Nicholas the target of much abuse in the British press. Thanks to Russian intervention in Hungary in 1849, and to the propaganda campaign of Louis Kossuth, the Magyar patriot, England was prepared to believe the worst about the tsar. Palmerston and Russell did nothing to restrain the growing anti-Russian sentiment.

Hume was alarmed by the reaction in England to the Turkish-Russian conflict. He saw it as a prelude to interference. He had never supported Palmerston's aggressive policies in the past, and now he thought they had helped to bring England to the doorstep of war. To Cobden he wrote on 2 October, "I am sorry to see the military spirit and tendency in the British public." It made him angry, he told Cobden, that Lord John and

[94]See Prest, *Lord John Russell*, 353–57; J. B. Conacher, *The Aberdeen Coalition, 1852–1855* (Cambridge, 1968), 3–36.

[95]*Hansard*, third series, 126:547.

Palmerston "glorify themselves" that England had always interfered to help the people struggling for better government, yet all the while they had both been afraid of "democracy" at home. Hume believed the emphasis on interference meant there would be "little hope for reform."[96]

Nearly everyone in the coalition cabinet agreed with Hume that war in the Middle East was, sooner or later, inevitable. Until that moment arrived, however, plans had to be made for the presentation of the major domestic legislation scheduled for 1854—the reform bill. As early as the first week in November 1853, Aberdeen appointed a committee to study Russell's reform scheme. Before the ministry finally approved the version of the bill to be introduced, there were two months of in-fighting and recriminations. Lord Palmerston had caused most of this by insisting that Russell's proposals went too far, especially with regard to extending the franchise to the working class. Others in the cabinet, Lord Lansdowne for one, wanted Russell to limit his effort to an adjustment of the 1832 bill, but none were as hostile as Palmerston. By the middle of December he was beyond control; no one seemed surprised when he resigned. As one newspaper put it, this was Palmerston's "December malady." While Aberdeen pondered what to do in this situation, Palmerston changed his mind and decided he wanted to remain a part of the coalition.[97] He returned after telling friends that his resignation had resulted from his opinion that Aberdeen and Russell would not compromise on reform; he now realized this had been a misunderstanding.[98] But when Palmerston returned Aberdeen refused to allow him to establish any conditions. There were some who saw, quite rightly, that Palmerston's return had nothing to do with any change in his thinking on the reform bill. He wanted to be back in the government because he believed England shortly would be at war in the Middle East and that this would mean a further postponement of political reform.[99] Palmerston did not wish to be "out" when his country went to war; he had looked forward to such an adventure for a long time.

With the home secretary again in the fold, the cabinet proceeded with its plan to introduce a reform measure early in the 1854 session. On 13 February, staving off a last minute attempt by Palmerston to change it, Russell brought in his bill to reform representation. It was not received with much enthusiasm. The thoughts of most members were on the situation in Turkey. The bill Russell introduced called for changes in electoral districts and extension of the franchise to £6 occupiers who had lived in the district for two and one-half years. This last provision was intended to qualify large numbers of laborers. Hume's reaction to Russell's proposal was moderate in tone, but he did argue that the franchise qualification should be lowered to £5 occupiers of one year's residence.[100]

---

[96]Hume to Cobden, October 2, 1853, BL, Add. MS. 43668; Conacher, *The Aberdeen Coalition*, 137–214, 261–87.

[97]Aberdeen asked Russell if he should step down and Russell said he should because of the "shabbiness of your colleagues."

[98]See Conacher, *The Aberdeen Coalition*, 215–32.

[99]Prest, *Lord John Russell*, 362.

[100]*Hansard*, third series, 130:520.

Whether or not Russell agreed to this alteration, Hume made it clear that he would vote in favor of the legislation.

Before the second reading of the bill, set for 13 March, Hume hoped to organize the radicals in support of Russell's plan. He undertook the task because he was "aware from long experience of the importance of union among the promoters of any measure," and because he was "anxious that due consideration should be given to the scheme of Reform which Lord [John] Russell has submitted to Parliament."[101] While Hume planned strategy, the ministry discussed yet another withdrawal of the reform legislation. Palmerston's December calculations proved to be correct; the House of Commons could not concentrate on parliamentary reform with attention focused on the Middle East. When England went to war in March it was just a matter of time until the decision was made to postpone the bill.[102]

Hume had opposed England's interference in the Russo-Turkish conflict from the start; the prospect of now sacrificing the reform bill to this intervention was more than he could accept. On 17 March, he moved to raise the income tax on property so that those who urged his government to get involved in the war would then be anxious to stop it.[103] But Hume knew there was no chance to prevent the war, just as he understood there was no way to save Russell's bill. When Russell moved to withdraw his legislation on 11 April, Hume commented that, under the circumstances, he agreed with the decision. He had hoped that members would see that this was a "conservative" bill, a compromise, and pass it quickly. As a "Radical Reformer" he had been willing to endorse such a half-way proposal; he was dismayed that his moderate and conservative colleagues were unable to do the same. The war had distracted their attention, but it seemed to him that the war was an excuse, not a reason, to postpone the reform measure.[104]

Hume finished out the 1854 session grumbling about the war, the income tax, the newspaper stamp duties, and, as ever, the need to retrench. As the session wound to a close, "Old Joe" admitted for the first time that his energy was on the wane. In July he wrote to Edward Ellice,

I know I have as much desire to see things right as I ever had, altho by no means the strength to carry them out. I am as ready and as willing to do as I have done . . . but I have not the power of . . . human strength as I formerly had.

He told Ellice that he still wished to see reform of Parliament become a reality.[105] On 12 August, the day on which Parliament was prorogued, Hume made what was to be his last speech in the House of Commons. There was nothing especially memorable in his remarks. He protested again England's intervention in the Middle East, pointing out that clearing Russian troops from the Danubian principalities seemed to be "frivolous

---

[101]Hume to G. H. Duthwood, 19 February 1854, Bodleian Library, MSS. Eng. Hist. C51, fol. 93.
[102]See Prest, *Lord John Russell*, 364–65.
[103]*Hansard,* third series, 131:987.
[104]*Hansard,* third series, 132:845.
[105]Hume to Edward Ellice, 22 July 1854, Ellice Papers, NLS.

grounds" for war.[106] Then, putting his papers in his hat for the final time, he sat down; thirty-seven years of toil had ended.

In the autumn of 1854 Hume left Burnley Hall for a visit to Scotland. He had been warned by his family not to make the strenuous trip, but he went anyway. During one stop in Aberdeen, Hume reminisced about his first appearance in that town thirty-six years earlier. He displayed a statement of his principles in the *Aberdeen Chronicle* of 1818 and spoke of his pride in not having wavered from those principles whether in "pitiful" minority or, as was seldom the case, "overwhelming" majority.[107] His visit to Scotland was filled with nostalgia, but not so much that he failed to mention the need for continued vigilance for parliamentary reform.

Not long after his return to Norfolk, Hume showed signs of irritability and extreme fatigue. By mid-January 1855 he was bedridden most of the time; his heart was failing. Hume's daughter, Mary, described his condition to Ellice:

I know you will be grieved to hear that since about a fortnight ago dear Papa's strength began to sink so rapidly that on Sunday last we had a physician down from town, who candidly told us that we must not hope to be able to remove him to town, but must content ourselves with doing our utmost to keep up his strength as much as possible by nourishment and stimulants.

It was clear to his family that "Old Joe" had little time left. His daughter seemed comforted that he had no pain, "but still we know," she wrote, "that his public life is over, and only trust to make his home as happy and peaceful as possible during the remaining space that may be alloted to him."[108] Two weeks later, at six o'clock in the evening on 20 February, he died.

---

[106]*Hansard,* third series, 135:1554.
[107]*Aberdeen Free Press,* 23 February 1855.
[108]Mary Hume to Edward Ellice, 7 February 1855, Ellice Papers, NLS.

EPILOGUE

When Hume's contemporaries attempted to describe his politics, they most frequently mentioned his consistency. The principles he brought with him when he began his thirty-seven consecutive years in the House of Commons were the same ones he took to the grave in 1855. Economy in administration, openness in government, Church reform, national education, and political reform were causes that he espoused at the beginning of his public career and at the end. These were reforms that were necessary to maintain the evolutionary development of the constitution. Except for an occasional instance when personal interest took hold, Hume never wavered from the tenets taught by James Mill, Bentham, and David Ricardo.

Hume was resolute in his philosophy, yet he knew when to make political compromises. Where politics was concerned, Hume followed the credo that "half-a-loaf is better than none." He was never moderate in his goals, but he was moderate in what he would accept. When there was nothing for the radicals to lose, usually the case in the 1820s, Hume proved himself as "ornery," tenacious, and obstreperous as any member who had ever set foot in the Commons. If he knew there was no chance to prevail on an issue, he would show his displeasure by giving marathon speeches on such exciting matters as the ordnance budget, reading lists of irrelevant statistics, forcing needless divisions, and irritating friends by suggesting they lacked his perseverance. As one conservative contemporary noted, Hume was "a teasing, biting flea" who would never permit any minister to sit "easy in his seat."[1] This aspect of his politics should not be underestimated; it is what made him so popular with England's malcontents. His assault on government malfeasance, calculated to spur the demand for economic and parliamentary reform, resulted in his becoming known as the "People's Member." Despite his poor speaking ability and lack of charm, he was regarded as an honest, steadfast, and exceedingly industrious public servant; qualities that were publicly praised in his early years in Parliament as well as in later years when he struggled for election in Leeds.

Hume's popularity was so great that he suffered very little in the eyes of the public for his part in the sorry business of the Greek loan. His mistake on that occasion came less from guile than from an overriding concern about money. Hume's free-trade philosophy and his personal parsimony tallied well together.

For all his obduracy in Parliament, Hume was transformed when he saw an opportunity to achieve a significant reform. We need only remember his behavior during the Combination Law crisis, the Reform Bill controversy, and Corn Law repeal to see that he could act with efficiency and with moderation. No one could manage a select committee any better than Hume.

During much of his parliamentary career, but particularly in the 1820s, Hume was thought to be little more than Francis Place's mouthpiece in the House of Commons. A final word ought to be said about their relationship.

[1]William L. Davidson, *Political Thought in England: The Utilitarians from Bentham to J. S. Mill* (New York, n.d.), 37.

It is true that Hume supplied Place with minutes of committee hearings and that he listened to, and sometimes followed, Place's advice on a variety of subjects. But he was just as likely to reject or modify Place's suggestions as he was to accept them. Hume frequently agreed with Place's general view of things, and he did not hesitate to consult with him on important matters right up to the time of their falling out. He retained, however, complete independence when he entered the House each day. Place was always more useful to him than he was to Place.

In the 1830s, much to the dismay of Place, Hume persisted in doing what he could to keep the Whigs in power. Although it would be an exaggeration to say that Hume's role was critical to the liberal alliance in those years, he made a major contribution to whatever success it had. Others were as steady as Hume in supporting the ministers; yet few in Parliament combined, as the Scotsman did, a commitment to the Whigs with an effort to keep in touch with such uncompromising radicals as Place and Roebuck.

Hume's support for the Whigs did not mean he was comfortable with them. He had imagined that after the Reform Bill there would be sweeping spin-off reforms relating to Church, economy, and Ireland. The Whigs, with help from the radicals, would surely be anxious to maintain the momentum for change. Some of the reforms did develop, but not in the form, or to the extent, that he had anticipated. As the promise of 1832 gave way to Whig apathy, Hume faced a dilemma. Should he continue to support the Whigs who, at best, were lukewarm toward continuing major reforms, or should he, as the "voice of the people" in Parliament try to force them out of office? Against the warnings of Place and Roebuck, he decided to stay with the Whigs. Their faults notwithstanding, the Whigs were more of a "reforming party" than were the Tories. Even Russell's "Finality" speech did not persuade Hume to give up hope. He was certain that as government numbers dwindled in the House of Commons, the Whigs would need to make concessions in order to maintain a majority. The concessions never came, at least not to the degree Hume expected.

With the accession of Peel and the Tories in 1841, Hume's role in the House of Commons became less significant. He devoted more of his time to stimulating reform demands outside of Parliament. Hume had always believed that protests from "the people" were the most useful element in bringing about reform. No amount of political maneuvering, no amount of parliamentary wizardry, could compensate for an apathetic populace. Like so many other reformers, Hume found himself having to wish for "bad times" so that the countryside would be more readily aroused. Hume understood that those in power, whether Whig or Tory, tended to protect the status quo unless they were convinced that "the people" were ready to do something dire, or that the electorate was ready to turn them out.

The need to encourage popular agitation was one reason Hume kept trying to work out some accommodation between the free-trade radicals and the Chartists. He agreed with the demands in the "People's Charter," but there was no way to throw a free-trade blanket over O'Connor. It indicates something about Hume's character that despite the abuse heaped upon him by O'Connor's *Northern Star* he continued to search for some basis of cooperation with the Chartists. Since the days of the Combination Laws, Hume had fancied himself a spokesman for the workingman; he never doubted that workers would achieve their greatest prosperity when free-trade principles were fully adhered to by men in power. It distressed him to think that the Chartists were detracting from the efforts of the Anti-Corn Law League. How could anyone, he wondered, castigate the League and its leaders as anti-working class?

After the Corn Laws were altered in 1846, and the Whigs were back in power, Hume emerged as an outspoken proponent of additional parliamentary reform. With help from Cobden and other former Anti-Corn Law Leaguers, he did all he could to advance the political reforms he outlined in the "Little Charter." But his proposals were too radical for the moderate reformers and too moderate for the Chartists. Hume thought the situation in the late 1840s and early 1850s was similar to that in the early 1830s, but he was wrong. There was very little support in the House of Commons for further electoral reform. More damaging to Hume's efforts was the lack of enthusiasm outside of Parliament. The "New Movement" never elicited the excitement necessary to frighten the government. People who were well fed and optimistic about the future did not make convincing revolutionaries. The failure to make any headway on political reform, and particularly on his favorite issue, the ballot, caused Hume much irritation. Only his fury over England's involvement in the Crimea distracted him from the struggle for franchise reform in his last years.

Right to the end Hume tried to carry out his political and parliamentary duties. Only a few weeks before his death he was still spending ten or more hours each day at his desk. The fact that Hume, in the words of Harriet Martineau, was "the center of influence, information, and energy" among the reformers in the House of Commons is reason enough for the historian to keep him in mind. But he is more important for the way he was viewed by "the people." He was not a selfless man, but that is the image he projected to those who saw him from a distance. He seemed incorruptible. He appeared determined to "keep the ruling few uneasy" even at the expense of his own reputation and advancement. Hume's very presence in the House of Commons provided a tonic for the disaffected. He was "proof" that middle class politicians were not always concerned with place and power and that the "system" could work. In England in the first half of the nineteenth century this was the ultimate utilitarian contribution. It is not difficult to understand why Bentham once wrote, with more than a little bias, that Hume was "the only true representative the people [of England] ever had, and one more than, under such a form of government, they have any right to expect to have."[2]

[2]Samuel C. Hall, *Retrospect of a Long Life: From 1815 to 1883* (London, 1883), i: 218.

BIBLIOGRAPHY

Manuscript Collections

Aberdeen University Library
    Hume Collection (eleven letters)
British Library Additional Manuscripts
    Aberdeen Papers
    Charles Babbage Papers
    Lord Broughton Papers
    Richard Cobden Papers
    Hobhouse Papers
    Holland House Papers
    Sir Robert Peel Papers
    Francis Place Papers
    Wellesley Papers
Kirkintilloch Town Council (Kirkintilloch, Scotland)
    Peter Mackenzie Papers
Lambton Estate Office, Fence Houses (Durham)
    Lambton Papers
National Library of Ireland (Dublin)
    Graham Papers (microfilm)
    O'Connell Papers
National Library of Scotland (Edinburgh)
    Ellice Papers
    John Burton Papers
    Miscellaneous
Public Record Office (London)
    Lord John Russell Papers
University College (London)
    Lord Brougham Papers
    Edwin Chadwick Papers
    Joseph Parkes Papers
University of Durham, Department of Paleography and Diplomatics
    Grey Papers
Worcester, Massachusetts (American Antiquarian Society)
    Joseph Lancaster Papers

Public Documents

Hansard Parliamentary Debates (first, second, third series)
Numerous reports from the Select Committees in *British Sessional Papers*

Newspapers

The Aberdeen Free Press
The Bury Post
Caledonian Mercury
The Constitutional
The Courier
Edinburgh Advertiser
Edinburgh Courant
The Examiner
John Bull

Kilkenny Journal
Leeds Intelligencer
Leeds Mercury
Leeds Times
Liverpool Mercury
London and Westminster Review
Montrose, Standard and Angus and Mearns Register
Montrose, Arbroath and Brechin Review
Morning Advertiser
Morning Chronicle
Morning Post
Northern Star
Pilot
The Scotsman
The Spectator
The Standard
The Sun
Tait's Edinburgh Magazine
The Times

Periodicals

The Annual Register
Blackwood's Edinburgh Magazine
The Edinburgh Review
The Gentlemen's Magazine
The Quarterly Review
The Westminster Review

Useful Books

Aspinall, Arthur. *Lord Brougham and the Whig Party*. Manchester, 1927.
———. *Politics and the Press*. London, 1949.
———, ed. *Three Early Nineteenth Century Diaries*. London, 1952.
Bain, Alexander. *James Mill: A Biography*. London, 1882.
Baines, Edward. *Life of Edward Baines*. London, 1851.
Barker, A. G. *Henry Hetherington, 1792–1840*. London, 1938.
Brougham, Henry Lord. *The Life and Times of Henry, Lord Brougham*. 3 vols. New York, 1872.
Broughton, Lord. *Recollections of a Long Life*. 5 vols. London, 1909.
Brown, Lucy. *The Board of Trade and the Free Trade Movement, 1830–1942*. Oxford, 1958.
Buckley, Jesse K. *Joseph Parkes of Birmingham*. London, 1926.
Cole, G. D. H. *Chartist Portraits*. London, 1941.
Cookson, J. E. *Lord Liverpool's Administration, 1815–1822*. Edinburgh, 1975.
Cooper, Leonard. *Radical Jack, the Life of the First Earl of Durham*. London, 1959.
Derry, John. *The Radical Tradition*. New York, 1967.
Erickson, Arvel. *The Public Career of Sir James Graham*. Cleveland, 1952.
Fagan, Louis. *The Reform Club: Its Founders and Architect*. London, 1887.
Fawcett, Millicent G. *The Life of Sir William Molesworth*. London, 1901.
Finer, Samuel. *The Life and Times of Sir Edwin Chadwick*. London, 1952.
Francis, John. *Chroniclers and Characters of the Stock Exchange*. London, 1849.
Gash, Norman. *Mr. Secretary Peel*. Cambridge, Mass., 1961.
———. *Politics in the Age of Peel*. London, 1953.
———. *Reaction and Reconstruction in English Politics, 1832–1852*. London, 1965.
———. *Sir Robert Peel after 1830*. London, 1972.
Goodway, David. *London Chartism, 1838–1848*. Cambridge, 1982.

Gordon, Barry. *Political Economy in Parliament, 1819–1823*. London, 1976.
———. *Economic Doctrine and Tory Liberalism*. London, 1979.
Grant, James. *Random Recollections of the House of Commons from the Year 1830 to the Close of 1835, including Personal Sketches of the Leading Members of All Parties*. Philadelphia, 1836.
Grote, Harriet. *The Personal Life of George Grote*. London, 1873.
———. *The Philosophical Radicals of 1832: Comprising the Life of Sir William Molesworth and some incidents Connected to the Reform Movement from 1832–1842*. London, 1886.
Hamburger, Joseph. *Intellectuals in Politics: John Stuart Mill and the Philosophical Radicals*. New Haven, 1965.
———. *James Mill and the Art of Revolution*. New Haven, 1963.
Hamer, D. A. *The Politics of Electoral Pressure: A Study in the History of Victorian Reform*. Brighton, 1977.
Harris, William. *The History of the Radical Party in Parliament*. London, 1885.
Hilton, Boyd. *Corn, Cash, Commerce: The Economic Policies of the Tory Governments, 1815–1830*. Oxford, 1977.
Hollis, Patricia. *The Pauper Press, A Study of Working Class Radicalism of the 1830's*. Oxford, 1970.
Huch, Ronald. *The Radical Lord Radnor: The Public Life of Viscount Folkestone, Third Earl of Radnor (1779–1869)*. Minneapolis, 1977.
Hume, Joseph. *The Provident Institution for Saving*. London, 1816.
———. *Short Account of A Plan for the New Silver Coinage*. London, 1816.
Johnson, L. G. *General T. Perronet Thompson*. London, 1957.
Journal of Mrs. Arbuthnot, 1820–1832. ed. Francis Bamford and Duke of Wellington. 2 vols. London, 1950.
Kinzer, Bruce L. *The Ballot Question in Nineteenth Century English Politics*. New York, 1982.
Kirby, R. G. and Musson, A. E. *The Voice of the People: John Doherty, 1798–1854*. Manchester, 1975.
Kitson Clark, George. *Peel and the Conservative Party*. London, 1964.
Le Marchant, Denis. *Memoir of John Charles Viscount Althorp, Third Earl Spencer*. London, 1876.
Leventhal, F. M. *Respectable Radical: George Howell and Victorian Working Class Politics*. Cambridge, Mass., 1971.
Maccoby, Simon. *English Radicalism, 1832–1852*. London, 1935.
McCaffrey, Lawrence. *Daniel O'Connell and the Repeal Year*. Lexington, Ky., 1966.
McCord, Norman. *The Anti-Corn Law League, 1838–1846*. New York, 1958.
McDowell, R. B. *Public Opinion and Government Policy in Ireland, 1801–1846*. London, 1952.
Machin, George I. T. *The Catholic Question in English Politics, 1820–1830*. New York, 1964.
Macintyre, Angus. *The Liberator: Daniel O'Connell and the Irish Party, 1830–1847*. London, 1965.
Martineau, Harriet. *Biographical Sketches, 1852–1868*. London, 1870.
Melbourne, William, Lord. *The Papers of William Lamb, Viscount Melbourne*. London, 1899.
Mitchell, Austin. *The Whigs in Opposition*. Oxford, 1967.
Molesworth, Sir William. *The History of England from the Year 1830–1870*. London, 1879.
Munford, W. A. *William Ewart, M.P., 1798–1869: Portrait of a Radical*. London, 1960.
Newbitt, G. L. *Benthamite Reviewing: The First Twelve Years of the Westminster Review, 1824–1836*. New York, 1934.
New, Chester. *Lord Durham: A Biography of John George Lambton, First Earl of Durham*. London, 1968.
Osborne, John W. *William Cobbett: His Thoughts and His Times*. New Brunswick, N. J., 1966.
Parker, C. S. *Life and Letters of Sir James Graham*. 3 vols. London, 1907.
Place, Francis. *The Autobiography of Francis Place (1771–1854)*. Ed. Mary Thale. New York, 1972.
Patterson, M. W. *Sir Francis Burdett and His Times*. London, 1931.

Poynter, J. R. *Society and Pauperism: English Ideas on Poor Relief, 1795–1834.* Toronto, 1969.

Prest, John. *Lord John Russell.* Columbia, S. C., 1972.

———. *Politics in the Age of Cobden.* London, 1977.

Read, Donald. *Feargus O'Connor: Irishman and Chartist.* London, 1961.

Reid, Stuart J. *Life and Letters of the First Earl of Durham 1792–1840.* London, 1906.

Roebuck, J. A. *The Life and Letters of J. A. Roebuck.* Ed. R. E. Leader. London, 1897.

———. *The Whig Ministry in 1830 to the Passing of the Reform Bill.* London, 1832.

Romilly, Sir Samuel. *Memoirs.* Ed. by his son. 3 vols. London, 1840.

Royal, Edward and Walvin, James. *English Radicals and Reformers, 1760–1848.* Lexington, Ky., 1982.

Rowe, D. J., ed. *London Radicalism, 1830–1843.* London, 1970.

Salmon, David. *Joseph Lancaster.* London, 1904.

Saunders' *Portraits and Memoirs of Prominent Living Political Reformers.* London, 1840.

Senior, Hereward. *Orangeism in Ireland and Britain, 1795–1836.* London, 1966.

Silver, Harold. *English Education and the Radicals, 1780–1823.* London, 1975.

Sraffa, Peter, ed. *The Works and Correspondence of David Ricardo.* Cambridge, 1952.

Thomas, W. E. S. *The Philosophical Radicals, 1817–1841.* Oxford, 1979.

Thompson, E. P. *The Making of the English Working Class.* New York, 1963.

Torrens, W. M. *Memoirs of the Right Hon. William, Second Viscount Melbourne.* 2nd edition. London, 1878.

Wakefield, C. M. *Life of Thomas Attwood.* London, 1885.

Wallas, Graham. *The Life of Francis Place, 1771–1854.* Revised edition. London, 1918.

Walpole, Spencer. *The Life of Lord John Russell.* 2 vols. London, 1891.

Weisser, Henry. *April 10: Challenge and Response in England in 1848.* Lanham, Maryland, 1983.

Wiener, Joel. *The War of the Unstamped: The Movement to Repeal the British Newspaper Tax.* Ithaca, 1969.

Zegger, Robert. *John Cam Hobhouse: A Political Biography, 1819–1852.* Columbia, Missouri, 1973.

Useful Articles

Aspinall, Arthur. "Le Marchant's Reports of the Debates in the House of Commons." *English Historical Review* 58 (1943): 78–105.

Burroughs, Peter. "Parliamentary Radicals and the Reduction of Imperial Expenditure in British North America." *Historical Journal* 11 (1968): 446–61.

Canaan, Edwin. "Ricardo in Parliament." *Economic Journal* 4 (1894): 249–61, 409–23.

Close, David. "The Formation of a Two Party Alignment in the House of Commons between 1832 and 1841." *English Historical Review* 84 (1969): 257–77.

Fetter, Frank. "The Rise and Decline of Ricardian Economics." *History of Political Economy* (1969): 67–84.

Finlayson, G. B. A. M. "Joseph Parkes of Birmingham, 1796–1865: A Study in Philosophical Radicalism." *Bulletin of the Institute of Historical Research* 46 (1973): 186–201.

Flick, Carlos. "Thomas Attwood, Francis Place and the Agitation for British Parliamentary Reform." *Huntington Library Quarterly* 34 (1971): 355–66.

George, M. Dorothy. "The Combination Laws." *Economic History Review* 6 (1936): 172–78.

———. "The Combination Laws Reconsidered." *Supplement to Economic Journal* (May, 1924): 214–28.

Graham, A. H. "The Lichfield House Compact, 1835." *Irish Historical Studies* 12 (1960–61): 209–25.

Huch, R. K. "Francis Place and the Chartists: Promise and Disillusion," *The Historian,* 45 (August, 1983), 497–512.

Hyde, Francis E. "Utility and Radicalism, 1825–1827: A Note on the Mill-Roebuck Friendship." *Economic History Review* 16 (1946): 38–44.

Kriegel, Abraham. "The Politics of the Whigs in Opposition, 1834–1835." *The Journal of British Studies* 7 (1968), 65–91.

Newbould, I. D. C. "William IV and the Dismissal of the Whigs, 1834." *Canadian Journal of History* 2 (1976): 311–30.
Osborne, John W. "Recent Writings and Work to be Done on British Radicalism." *The British Studies Monitor* 4 (1974): 23–29.
Parsinnen, T. M. "Association, Convention, and Anti-Parliament in British Radical Politics, 1771–1848." *English Historical Review* 88 (1973): 504–33.
Rowe, D. J. "Class and Political Radicalism in London, 1831–1846." *The Historical Journal* 13 (1970): 31–47.
———. "Francis Place and the Historians." *The Historical Journal* 16 (1973): 45–63.
Thomas, W. E. S. "Francis Place and Working Class History." *The Historical Journal* 5 (1962): 61–70.
Ward, W. R. "The Tithe Question in England in the Early Nineteenth Century." *Journal of Ecclesiastical History* 16 (1965): 67–81.
Whyte, J. H. "Daniel O'Connell and the Repeal Party." *Irish Historical Studies* 11 (1959): 297–316.
Wooley, S. R. "The Personnel of the Parliament of 1833." *English Historical Review* 53 (1938): 240–61.

Dissertations

Amundson, John Carroll. "Joseph Hume and Financial Reform in England, 1819–1822." Ph.D. dissertation, University of Pittsburgh, 1933.
Close, D. H. "The Elections of 1835 and 1837 in England and Wales." Ph.D. dissertation, Oxford University, 1966.
Hilton, A. J. B. "The Economic Policy of the Tory Governments, 1815–1830." Ph.D. dissertation, Oxford University, 1973.
McGarry, Kevin. "Joseph Lancaster 1778–1838: A Bibliographical Account of his Life and System of Teaching." Ph.D. dissertation, University of London, 1966.
Platt, Franklin. "The English Parliamentary Radicals—Their Collective Character, Their Failure to Find a Leader: A Study in the Psycho-Sociological Sources of Radical Behavior, 1833–1841." Ph.D. dissertation, Washington University, St. Louis, 1969.
Rapp, Dean Reginald. "Samuel Whitbread (1764–1815): A Social and Political Study." Ph.D. dissertation, The Johns Hopkins University, 1971.
Sturgis, James Laverne. "British Parliamentary Radicalism, 1846–1852." Ph.D. dissertation, University of Toronto, 1972.
Wasson, Ellis. "The Young Whigs: Lords Althorp, Milton and Tavistock and the Whig Party, 1809–1830." Ph.D. dissertation, Cambridge University, 1975.

INDEX